SAVING CHILDREN
FROM A LIFE OF CRIME

David P. Farrington
and Brandon C. Welsh

SAVING CHILDREN
FROM A LIFE OF CRIME

**Early Risk Factors
and Effective Interventions**

OXFORD
UNIVERSITY PRESS

2007

OXFORD
UNIVERSITY PRESS

Oxford University Press, Inc., publishes works that further
Oxford University's objective of excellence
in research, scholarship, and education.

Oxford   New York
Auckland   Cape Town   Dar es Salaam   Hong Kong   Karachi
Kuala Lumpur   Madrid   Melbourne   Mexico City   Nairobi
New Delhi   Shanghai   Taipei   Toronto

With offices in
Argentina   Austria   Brazil   Chile   Czech Republic   France   Greece
Guatemala   Hungary   Italy   Japan   Poland   Portugal   Singapore
South Korea   Switzerland   Thailand   Turkey   Ukraine   Vietnam

Copyright © 2007 by Oxford University Press, Inc.

Published by Oxford University Press, Inc.
198 Madison Avenue, New York, New York 10016

www.oup.com

Oxford is a registered trademark of Oxford University Press

Library of Congress Cataloging-in-Publication Data
Farrington, David P.
Saving children from a life of crime: early risk factors and effective interventions /
by David P. Farrington and Brandon C. Welsh.
p. cm.—(Studies in crime and public policy)
Includes bibliographical references.
ISBN-13 978-0-19-530409-1
ISBN 0-19-530409-8
1. Juvenile delinquency—United States—Prevention.
I. Welsh, Brandon, 1969–   II. Title.   III. Series.
HV9104.F37 2007
362.74'70973—dc22   2006015868

9 8 7 6 5 4 3 2 1

Printed in the United States of America
on acid-free paper

FOREWORD

Many people think that preventing crime is easy and should be our main goal; many others think it is impossible and should be ignored in favor of deterrence. Both groups are wrong. As David Farrington and Brandon Welsh make clear in this book, preventing crime is possible but not easy.

People who want to prevent crime often suppose that the root causes of crime are things that can be easily fixed, such as high unemployment rates or bad schools. In fact, reducing unemployment and improving schools, though eminently worthwhile things to do, are very hard tasks. But what is more important is that most of the root causes of crime are not these social issues but deeply ingrained features of the human personality and its early experiences.

Low intelligence, an impulsive personality, and a lack of empathy for other people are among the leading individual characteristics of people at risk for becoming offenders. And if these youngsters are raised in weak or abusive families, or broken and discordant ones, the risk of becoming an offender goes up. And if these families have very low incomes, live in a socially deprived area, and send their children to schools where many delinquents are found, the risks rise even higher.

Given these problems, it would be easy to abandon any hope of preventing crime. We have no way of increasing intelligence, can only with great difficulty modify personality, confront great difficulties in teaching parents how to stay together and raise children effectively, and know that putting children into good schools is not easily done.

The authors' optimism, and mine, about crime prevention rests on what scholars have learned about improving the lives of children despite these constraints on change. By a variety of ingenious interventions that have been thoroughly tested by careful experiments, we have learned how to make a difference. Conducting a careful experiment is not an easy or inexpensive task: one must randomly assign at-risk youth to either a planned intervention or to the status quo, measure the effects of the intervention on crime rates, and then estimate whether the benefits of the intervention exceed its costs.

Many programs that have captured the public's support, such as boot camps that expose delinquents to military discipline or certain drug-abuse resistance programs taught in public schools, turn out not to make much difference at all. The programs that do work are often ones that are totally unknown to most people. Farrington and Welsh list all of these programs and summarize the evidence that measures their effects. The lives of children are improved by certain kinds of daycare programs (but not all), ingenious methods of teaching parents how best to raise their children, home visitation programs run by professional nurses, and particular school programs that teach students how to achieve greater self-control.

Farrington and Welsh argue that programs that work ought to be part of a national strategy so that every at-risk child has access to them. In the United States and other countries where daycare and schooling are locally controlled programs and where parenting is thought to be a personal rather than governmental matter, installing a national program is not an easy matter.

Moreover, programs that work on a few hundred people served by skilled professionals operating in a carefully monitored experimental environment may not work as well as the same programs run by ordinary employees trying to help tens of thousands of youngsters, parents, and schools. The authors recognize this problem and know that programs must take root in local community efforts. The role of a national strategy should be to tell people what works and supply them with guidance about how research findings can best be turned into larger and lasting efforts. A national effort would supply communities with "best practice" manuals.

Criminology is now at a point that medicine reached several decades ago: the former must grasp what the latter has already learned, namely, the need for evidence-based interventions. People who wish to prevent crime must operate on the basis of careful knowledge about what works and not on the basis of speculations about what *ought* to work or ideological convictions about what *must* work. Farrington and Welsh skillfully set forth what we have learned about what *does* work.

James Q. Wilson

ACKNOWLEDGMENTS

This book focuses on saving children from a life of crime. The research described in this book is new and up-to-date. It covers the full range of the most important early crime risk and protective factors and effective early prevention strategies to reduce offending. Importantly, the book does not end with research conclusions. We outline a policy strategy that uses this current research knowledge to bring into sharper focus where our national crime fighting priorities ought to be. We recommend prevention efforts targeted on the childhood years.

The research described in this book has its roots in the important but relatively new evidence-based paradigm that has been embraced by criminology and other social and behavioral sciences. This involves the use of the highest quality scientific research available to encourage more efficacious and just public policy. That governments will cast aside political rhetoric and the need to satisfy the "mythical" punitive public in favor of research evidence is a tall order for sure, but we believe that this should be a top priority in striving for a safer, more sustainable society.

We are grateful to a number of individuals who helped make this book what it is. First and foremost, we thank Michael Tonry. It was his initial pitch that got us started, and his characteristically insightful comments improved the book along the way. Dedi Felman, our brilliant editor at Oxford University Press, is also much deserving of our appreciation. She was tremendously supportive of our work from the outset and provided valuable guidance as the writing came to a close. We also benefited from excellent research assistance from Gregory Amato and Elyse Karin at the University of Massachusetts Lowell, and first-class secretarial support from Maureen Brown and Joanne Garner at Cambridge University.

CONTENTS

SAVING CHILDREN

FROM A LIFE OF CRIME

Introduction

The Need for Early Prevention

I

In medicine and public health, it is widely accepted that prevention is better than cure. The same is true of offending. Public health prevention is often based on identifying and tackling key risk factors. For example, smoking, lack of exercise, and a fatty diet are important risk factors for heart attacks, and these risk factors can be tackled by media campaigns encouraging people to smoke less, exercise more, and eat more healthily. This book aims to summarize what is known about early risk factors for offending and about effective interventions that can be used to tackle these risk factors. Our immodest aim is to change national policies to focus on early childhood prevention rather than on locking up offenders.

Two separate but interrelated developments inform this book's focus on the importance of early intervention policy and programs to improve children's life chances and prevent them from embarking on a life of crime. First, after decades of rigorous study in the United States and across the Western world—using prospective longitudinal studies—a great deal is now known about early risk factors for delinquency and later criminal offending. Disappointingly, less is known about protective factors against offending, but recent empirical research provides some important insights. Early risk factors that are most strongly associated with delinquency and later criminal offending can be found at the individual, family, and environmental levels.

Among the most important individual factors that predict offending are low intelligence and attainment, personality and temperament, empathy, and impulsiveness. The strongest family factor that predicts offending is usually criminal or antisocial parents. Other quite strong and replicable family factors that predict offending are large family size, poor parental supervision, parental conflict, and disrupted families. At the environmental level, the strongest factors that predict offending are growing up in a low socioeconomic status household, associating with delinquent friends, attending high-delinquency-rate schools, and living in deprived areas.

The second development is the growing body of high-quality scientific evidence on the effectiveness of early intervention programs designed to tackle these risk factors and from which evidence-based conclusions can be drawn. Many early intervention trials have reached the point at which delinquency can be measured, and others have carried out long follow-ups. In addition, recent systematic literature reviews and meta-analyses of early intervention programs provide scientific evidence that a wide range of programs in different domains (individual, family, school, and community) can be effective and others promising in preventing delinquency and later offending.

For example, at the individual level, preschool intellectual enrichment and child skills training programs are effective in preventing delinquency and later offending. Results are also highly favorable and robust for these programs' impacts on other important life-course outcomes, such as education, government assistance (e.g., welfare), employment, income, substance abuse, and family stability. At the family level, parent education plus daycare services and parent management training programs are particularly effective in preventing delinquency and later offending. Among environmental approaches, a number of school-based interventions are effective in preventing delinquency among youths in middle school and high school, while after-school and community-based mentoring programs hold promise as efficacious approaches.

A National Strategy for Early Prevention

Recent U.S. national scientific commissions on early childhood development and juvenile offending that have examined some of this evidence have also identified the many benefits of early intervention programs, and called for concrete action to make early prevention a top government priority. These commissions include the National Research Council and Institute of Medicine's Committee on Integrating the Science of Early Childhood Development (Shonkoff and Phillips, 2000) and Panel on Juvenile Crime (McCord, Widom, and Crowell, 2001) and the Surgeon General's report on youth violence (U.S. Department of Health and Human Services, 2001).

But despite these promising developments, not to mention the important efforts of national not-for-profit organizations, such as the Children's Defense Fund, the Child Welfare League of America, and Fight Crime—Invest in Kids, federal government's interest in putting early intervention on the map in the nation's fight against crime has largely languished. The Clinton administration's Ounce of Prevention Council, headed by Vice President Al Gore, is one notable example of failure (Gest, 2001). Unlike other Western democracies, such as Canada, Sweden, the Netherlands, and Australia, the United States has no national strategy to harness this research and put into practice efficacious early intervention programs to reduce delinquency and later offending.

This is not to suggest that the federal government is the sole purveyor of early intervention policy and programs. Success stories abound at the local and state levels, and, as California criminologist Peter Greenwood (2006) reminds us in his new book, *Changing Lives: Delinquency Prevention as Crime-Control Policy*, "service delivery for prevention programs is primarily a local matter" (p. 155). But what the federal government does bring to the table, like the federal or central governments of

these other countries, is the ability to mobilize a diverse array of partners, governmental and nongovernmental, offer a vision for the nation
over the short and long term, and contribute sizable technical and financial resources to state and local governments.

The stakes are high. In the United States, crime rates are lower than
they have been in more than a generation. An opportunity exists to keep
crime rates in check, or perhaps lower them even still. Early intervention is by no means a panacea. But it does represent an integral part of
any plan to reduce the nation's crime rate and contribute to a safer, more
sustainable society. The time is right to move beyond past rhetoric and
implement a national risk-focused, evidence-based strategy for early
prevention.

What Do We Know?

The main aim of this book is to set out a national strategy for the prevention of delinquency and later offending that is focused on intervening early to save children from a life of crime and is grounded in the
leading scientific evidence on the causes of crime and what works best to
prevent crime.

In our reviews of risk and protective factors and prevention programs, we describe the highest quality research studies (prospective longitudinal studies and randomized experiments), as well as the most
rigorous literature reviews (systematic and meta-analytic) that include
only high-quality projects. This goes a long way toward ensuring that our
conclusions are based on sound evidence. Our reviews should not, however, be considered systematic in the true sense. Systematic reviews use
rigorous methods for locating, appraising, and synthesizing evidence
from evaluation studies. They have explicit objectives, explicit criteria for
inclusion or exclusion of studies, and wide-ranging methods of search-
ing for studies that are designed to reduce bias (e.g., including not only
published studies), and they are reported with the same level of detail
that characterizes high-quality reports of original research (Welsh and
Farrington, 2001). Our strategy is to describe the best studies, which are

rather few in number, in some detail. We believe that a great deal can be learned from these case studies.

Early Prevention

Early prevention, as the term is used throughout this book, has three defining features. First, it involves measures implemented in the early years of the life course, specifically, from or sometimes prior to birth through to early adolescence. Second, and closely tied to this feature, is the book's focus on intervening in the lives of children and youths before they engage in delinquency in the first place—that is, before the first delinquent act. In this respect, early prevention includes interventions applied to the whole community to prevent the onset of delinquency, and interventions targeted at children and youths who are at risk for becoming offenders because of the presence of one or more risk factors. (Throughout this book, we examine only the most important "changeable" risk factors. Gender, age, race, and biological factors are not discussed.) Third, early prevention involves measures that are largely of a developmental or social nature—preventing the development of criminal potential in individuals or improving the social conditions and institutions (e.g., families, peers, social norms) that influence offending. We do not review pharmacological or medication interventions (see Wasserman and Miller, 1998). Nor do we examine interventions designed to modify the physical environment to reduce opportunities for crime, commonly known as situational crime prevention (see Clarke, 1997).

This book is concerned with delinquency and later criminal offending. We distinguish between these two terms inasmuch as delinquency takes place during the juvenile years and criminal offending during the adult years. This distinction is particularly relevant to our coverage of early prevention programs because of our interest in reducing antisocial behavior over different stages of the life-course. In our reviews of early prevention programs, special interest is also paid to other important life-course outcomes, such as education, health, and employment.

This book's focus on early risk and protective factors and prevention programs is informed in part by the longstanding research one of us (Farrington) has done on the early causes of criminal offending over the life-course and research both of us have done on the effectiveness of early intervention programs to prevent delinquency and later offending. This book's early focus is based on our belief that early intervention is more effective than later treatment in promoting human capital and desirable law-abiding behavior.

Developmental theory postulates that the early years of life are most influential in shaping later experiences. Greg Duncan and Katherine Magnuson (2004, p. 101) note: "Principles of developmental science suggest that although beneficial changes are possible at any point in life, interventions early on may be more effective at promoting well being and competencies compared with interventions undertaken later in life." They further say: "early childhood may provide an unusual window of opportunity for interventions because young children are uniquely receptive to enriching and supportive environments. . . . As individuals age, they gain the independence and ability to shape their environments, rendering intervention efforts more complicated and costly" (pp. 102–103).

The Evidence

In our effort to identify and assess the most important early risk factors and effective early interventions, this book reviews only the highest quality research studies. For risk factors (and protective factors), these are prospective longitudinal studies. For interventions, these are experimental and high-quality quasi-experimental evaluations.

Longitudinal Studies

Prospective longitudinal surveys repeatedly measure and follow up the same people over time. The word "prospective" implies that risk and protective factors are measured before outcomes such as offending.

Therefore, there cannot be what is called "retrospective bias," where knowledge about an outcome (e.g., delinquency) biases a person's recollections of childhood. We focus on the best studies—those involving repeated personal interviews with hundreds of people and spanning a period of at least five years (see Farrington, 1979b).

Some projects combine both an experimental intervention and a longitudinal survey. (For a review of longitudinal-experimental studies, see Farrington, 2006.) One of the most famous is the Cambridge-Somerville Youth Study, carried out in two areas of Boston, Massachusetts. Schools, welfare agencies, churches, and police recommended both "difficult" and "average" boys to the program. Each boy was rated on his likelihood of becoming delinquent, and 325 pairs of boys were matched on this and on age, intelligence, family background, and home environment. By the toss of a coin, one member of each pair was randomly assigned to receive special counseling treatment, and the other was randomly assigned to the control group. Boys in both groups were followed up for at least 30 years after the ending of the treatment, which lasted, on average, from age 10 to 15 (McCord, 1978). This project evaluated the effects of the treatment, using the experimental design, and the effects of risk and protective factors on offending, using the longitudinal follow-up.

Evaluating the Effects of Programs

According to the experimental psychologist Donald Campbell and his colleagues (Campbell and Stanley, 1966; Cook and Campbell, 1979; Shadish, Cook, and Campbell, 2002), the methodological quality of evaluation studies depends on four criteria: statistical conclusion validity, internal validity, construct validity, and external validity.[1] "Validity refers to the correctness of inferences about cause and effect" (Shadish, Cook, and Campbell., 2002, p. 34).

Statistical conclusion validity is concerned with whether the presumed cause (the intervention) and the presumed effect (the outcome) are related. The main threats to this form of validity are insufficient statistical power[2] to detect the effect (e.g., because of small sample size) and the use of inappropriate statistical techniques.

Internal validity refers to how well the study unambiguously demonstrates that an intervention (e.g., parent training) had an effect on an outcome (e.g., delinquency). Here, some kind of control condition is necessary to estimate what would have happened to the experimental units (e.g., people or areas) if the intervention had not been applied to them—termed the "counterfactual inference." The main threats to internal validity are as follows (Shadish et al., 2002, p. 55).

- Selection: the effect reflects preexisting differences between experimental and control conditions.
- History: the effect is caused by some event occurring at the same time as the intervention.
- Maturation: the effect reflects a continuation of preexisting trends, for example, in normal human development.
- Instrumentation: the effect is caused by a change in the method of measuring the outcome.
- Testing: the pretest measurement causes a change in the posttest measure.
- Regression to the mean: where an intervention is implemented on units with unusually high scores (e.g., people or areas with high crime rates), natural fluctuation will cause a decrease in these scores on the posttest, which may be mistakenly interpreted as an effect of the intervention. The opposite (an increase) happens when the interventions are applied to low-crime areas or low-scoring people.
- Differential attrition: the effect is caused by differential loss of units (e.g., people) from experimental compared to control conditions.
- Causal order: it is unclear whether the intervention preceded the outcome.

Construct validity refers to the adequacy of the operational definition and measurement of the theoretical constructs that underlie the intervention and the outcome. For example, if a program aims to investigate the effect of interpersonal skills training on offending, did the training program really target and change interpersonal skills, and were arrests a valid measure of offending? The main threats to this form of validity rest on the extent to which the intervention succeeded in changing what it was intended to change (e.g., how far there was treatment fidelity or implementation failure) and on the validity and reliability of outcome measures (e.g., how adequately police-recorded crime rates reflect true crime rates).

External validity refers to how well the effect of an intervention on an outcome is generalizable or replicable in different conditions: different operational definitions of the intervention and various outcomes, different persons, different environments, and so on. It is difficult to investigate this within one evaluation study. External validity can be established more convincingly in systematic reviews and meta-analyses of a number of evaluation studies. (More details are provided in chapter 6.)

An evaluation of a prevention program is considered to be high quality if it possesses a high degree of internal, construct, and statistical conclusion validity. Put another way, we can have a great deal of confidence in the observed effects of an intervention if it has been evaluated using a design that controls for the major threats to these three forms of validity. Experimental (randomized and nonrandomized) and quasi-experimental research designs are the types of evaluation designs that can best achieve this aim.

The randomized controlled experiment is considered the "gold standard" in evaluation research designs. It is the most convincing method of evaluating crime prevention programs (Farrington, 1983; Farrington and Welsh, 2005, in press). The key feature of randomized experiments is that the random assignment equates the experimental and control groups before the experimental intervention on all possible extraneous variables. Hence any subsequent differences between the groups must be attributable to the intervention. Randomization is the only method of assignment that controls for unknown and unmeasured confounders as well as those that are known and measured. However, the randomized experiment is only the most convincing method of evaluation if it is implemented with full integrity. To the extent that there are implementation problems (e.g., problems of maintaining random assignment, differential attrition, crossover between control and experimental conditions), internal validity could be reduced.

Another important feature of the randomized experiment is that a sufficiently large number of units (e.g., people or areas) need to be randomly assigned to ensure that the treatment group is equivalent to the comparison group on all extraneous variables (within the limits of statistical fluctuation). As a rule of thumb, at least 50 units in each category are needed (Farrington, 1997a). This number is relatively easy to achieve with individuals but very difficult to achieve with larger units such as communities, schools, and classrooms.

An evaluation design in which experimental and control units are matched or statistically equated (e.g., using a prediction score) prior to intervention—what is called a nonrandomized experiment—has lower internal validity than a randomized experiment. It is important to note that statistical conclusion validity and construct validity may be just as high for a nonrandomized experiment as for a randomized experiment.

In area-based studies, the best and most feasible design usually involves before and after measures in experimental and comparable control conditions, together with statistical control of extraneous variables. This is an example of a quasi-experimental evaluation design. Even better, the effect of an intervention on crime can be investigated after controlling (e.g., in a regression equation) not only for prior crime but also for other factors that influence crime. Another possibility is to match two areas and then to choose one at random to be the experimental area. Of course, several pairs of areas would be better than only one pair. These are the best ways of dealing with threats to internal validity when random assignment of a large number of units to experimental and control conditions cannot be achieved. Here again, statistical conclusion validity and construct validity may not be any lower than in a randomized experiment.

Organization of the Book

This book has 10 chapters. Part I (chapters 2–5) focuses on early risk factors for and protective factors against delinquency and later offending. Chapter 2 sets out the definitions of risk and protective factors; it also discusses some key issues arising in risk factor research, particularly regarding the meaning of mediators and moderators and the problem of establishing causes. Chapter 2 also reviews the key longitudinal surveys on which chapters 3, 4, and 5 are based, and describes two surveys that will be given special attention: the Cambridge Study in Delinquent Development and the Pittsburgh Youth Study. Chapters 3, 4, and 5 review, respectively, the leading empirical research on individual, family, and environmental (socioeconomic, peer, school, and community) risk and protective factors.

Part II (chapters 6–9) focuses on early intervention programs to prevent delinquency and later offending. Chapter 6 reviews the classification of prevention programs. It also describes the risk-focused approach to prevention, and discusses two key issues in the "what works" debate over early prevention programs: the assessment of research evidence and value for money. Chapters 7, 8, and 9 review, respectively, the scientific evidence on what works to prevent delinquency and later offending through individual, family, and environmental (peer, school, and community) interventions that are delivered in the early years of life. Each of these three chapters draws upon results of state-of-the-science reviews. They also profile the highest quality programs that have demonstrated effectiveness in preventing delinquency and later offending.

Part III (chapter 10) sets out a comprehensive national early prevention strategy that has the expressed aim of saving children from a life of crime and is grounded in the leading scientific evidence on what causes and what works best to prevent crime. This strategy particularly targets the United States, but we believe it could and should be implemented in the United Kingdom and other countries. Despite recent declines, crime is still a very important social problem with devastating effects on people's lives. It is important to put a long-term prevention strategy in place now. It is surely better to teach children not to play with matches than to try to put out the fire when the house has started burning!

PART I

EARLY RISK AND PROTECTIVE FACTORS

Understanding Risk and Protective Factors   **2**

Risk Factors

By definition, a risk factor is a variable that predicts an increased probability of later offending (Kazdin, Kramer, Kessler, Kupfer, and Offord, 1997). For example, children who experience poor parental supervision have an increased risk of committing criminal acts later on. In the Cambridge Study in Delinquent Development, which is a prospective longitudinal survey of 400 London males beginning at age 8, 55% of those experiencing poor parental supervision at age 8 were convicted (up to age 32), compared with 32% of the remainder, a significant difference (Farrington, 1990). Since risk factors are defined by their ability to predict later offending, it follows that longitudinal studies are needed to discover them.

    The term "risk factor" is not used consistently. Often, a risk factor refers to an extreme category of an explanatory variable. Thus, the risk factor of poor parental supervision may be an extreme category of the explanatory variable of parental supervision. On other occasions, a risk factor refers to a dichotomous variable contrasting, for example, poor parental supervision with good or average parental supervision. For example, Dan Offord and Helena Kraemer (2000, p. 70) argued that risk factors "can be used to divide a population into high and low risk groups." On still other occasions, a risk factor refers to a continuous explanatory variable, such as a scale of parental supervision. For ease of exposition, we will use the term "risk factor" to refer to an explanatory variable, usually categorical or dichotomous (e.g., parental supervision), and "risk category" to refer to the extreme category (e.g., poor parental supervision).

Following a medical analogy, it would be desirable to map out a dose-response curve relating different levels of a risk factor or explanatory variable to different levels of offending. For example, it may be that the probability of delinquency does not vary much over most values of a risk factor but dramatically increases at certain extremely high values. In the Pittsburgh Youth Study, which is a prospective longitudinal survey of 1,500 Pittsburgh males beginning at ages 7, 10, and 13, this was true of the mother's age at the birth of her first child. Mothers who were very young (17 or less) at the time of their first child were disproportionately likely to have delinquent children, but otherwise there was little relationship between the mother's age when her first child was born and the delinquency of her children (Loeber, Farrington, Stouthamer-Loeber, and van Kammen, 1998a). The relationship was not linear over the whole range of values of the mother's age.

In the risk factor literature, it is common to dichotomize both the risk factor and the outcome and to measure the strength of the relationship using the "odds ratio" statistic. An odds ratio of 2 or greater, roughly indicating a doubling of the risk of offending, indicates a relatively strong effect (Cohen, 1996). Thus, we might say that poor parental supervision more than doubles the odds (risk) of offending, since its odds ratio versus convictions in the Cambridge Study was 2.6.

Prior to the 1990s, the odds ratio and associated statistical techniques (e.g., logistic regression) were rarely used in criminology. In tandem with the increasing focus on risk factors, these measures are now becoming more familiar to criminologists. The use of the odds ratio encourages a more optimistic view about the prediction, explanation, and prevention of offending (Farrington and Loeber, 2000), and certainly optimism about these issues increased greatly in the 1990s.

Most studies of risk factors for offending have been carried out by researchers using long-term longitudinal studies. Traditionally, the emphasis has been on investigating the extent to which individual, family, peer, school, and socioeconomic factors measured in childhood or adolescence predict the development of later offending. Only in the 1990s have longitudinal researchers begun to pay attention to neighborhood and community factors, and there is still a great need for them to investigate immediate situational influences on offending (Farrington, Sampson, and Wikström, 1993; Wikström, Clarke, and McCord, 1995). Existing research tells us more about the development of criminal potential than about how that potential becomes the actuality of offending in any given situation.

Problems of Risk Factors

A major problem is to determine which risk factors are causes and which are merely "markers" or correlated with causes. The three criteria for establishing a causal risk factor are that the risk factor (1) is associated with the outcome (e.g., offending), (2) precedes the outcome, and (3) predicts the outcome after controlling for (or independently of) all other variables. The third criterion (hence causality) can be established most securely by carrying out an experiment in which persons are randomly assigned to different values of the risk factor. As mentioned in chapter 1, the random assignment ensures that persons in one category are equivalent to persons in another category (within the limits of statistical fluctuation) on all measured and unmeasured extraneous variables that might influence the outcome. Unfortunately, few of the possible causes of offending (such as parental supervision) could be experimentally manipulated, other than situational factors (Farrington, 1979a). However, Stacy Najaka, Denise Gottfredson, and David Wilson (2001) attempted to draw conclusions about causality by analyzing relationships between risk factors and antisocial behavior in school-based intervention experiments.

After an experiment, the next most convincing method of establishing causes is through quasi-experimental, within-individual analyses in which each person is followed up before and after particular life events

(Farrington, 1988). Because the same individuals are investigated, many extraneous variables are held constant. For example, in the Cambridge Study, the effects of getting married and getting divorced were established by comparing a person's offending before and after these life events (Farrington and West, 1995). Offending decreased after getting married and increased after getting divorced. In addition, the effects of unemployment on offending were established by comparing a person's offending during unemployment periods with the same person's offending during employment periods (Farrington, Gallagher, Morley, St. Ledger, and West, 1986). Crimes of dishonesty were more frequent during periods of unemployment.

It is important to investigate whether risk factors established in within-individual analyses are similar to or different from risk factors established in between-individual analyses. Since prevention experiments require within-individual change, risk factors established in between-individual analyses may not necessarily be relevant to causes or prevention. Helena Kraemer and her colleagues (1997) argued that only risk factors that can change within individuals can have causal effects.

In the Pittsburgh Youth Study, risk factors for delinquency were compared both between individuals and within individuals (Farrington, Loeber, Yin, and Anderson, 2002a). Peer delinquency was the strongest correlate of delinquency in between-individual correlations but did not predict delinquency within individuals. In contrast, poor parental supervision, low parental reinforcement, and low involvement of the boy in family activities predicted delinquency both between and within individuals. It was concluded that these three family variables were the most likely to be causes, whereas having delinquent peers was most likely to be a correlate of the boy's offending.

Key Issues in Risk Factor Research

A key question is: Risk factors for what? Research is needed to establish to what extent risk factors are the same for different criminal career features such as onset, persistence, frequency, escalation, or desistance of offending (Piquero, Farrington, and Blumstein, in press), for the general population as opposed to the population of offenders, or for different outcomes such as juvenile versus adult offending, violent offending versus drug use, and so on. The key issue is whether the magnitudes of relationships between risk factors and outcomes are similar in all these cases. A single risk factor may predict or cause multiple outcomes, just as a single outcome may be predicted or caused by multiple risk factors. These alternatives were termed "multifinality" and "equifinality," respectively, by John Richters (1997). There may also be multiple causal pathways between risk factors and outcomes.

It is important to investigate mediators and moderators of relationships between risk factors and outcomes. Mediators are causal mechanisms that intervene between the risk factor and the outcome and that explain how the risk factor influences the outcome (Baron and Kenny, 1986; Kazdin et al., 1997). If mediating processes or developmental pathways could be established between risk factors and outcomes, this would help to bridge the gap between risk factor research and more complex explanatory theories, and would assist in devising prevention techniques.

Moderators are variables that affect the direction or the strength of the relationship between risk factors and outcomes or both (Baron and Kenny, 1986). The effects of risk factors may vary for different categories of persons (e.g., males versus females, African Americans versus Caucasians), although David Rowe, Alexander Vazsonyi, and Daniel Flannery (1994) concluded that there were racial differences in levels of risk factors but not in the strength of relationships between risk factors and outcomes. Risk factors may also differ for different types of offenders (e.g., adolescent-limited versus life-course-persistent offenders: Moffitt, 1993), for different criminal pathways, or in different types of contexts or neighborhoods. There has been increasing interest in the 1990s in both types of offenders and types of neighborhoods (Sampson, Raudenbush, and Earls, 1997). It is important to try to establish what are the most influential risk factors (in terms of both level of risk and strength of effect) for different types of people and neighborhoods (Wikström, 1998).

Risk factors tend to co-occur, making them difficult to disentangle. Independent, additive, interactive, and sequential effects of risk factors need to be studied, to establish how many different underlying theoretical constructs are important. Ideally, interventions should be targeted on risk factors that are causes; interventions targeted on risk factors that are merely markers will not necessarily lead to any decrease in offending. Unfortunately, when risk factors are highly intercorrelated, it is difficult to establish which are causes using statistical modeling. For example, the particular ones that appear to be independently important as predictors may be greatly affected by essentially random variations between samples. This is an argument in favor of targeting multiple risk factors in interventions.

To a considerable extent, risk-focused prevention is a variable-based approach, documenting relationships between particular risk factors and particular outcomes. Some researchers, especially Swedish psychologists David Magnusson and Lars Bergman (1988), have advocated a person-based approach, in which persons characterized by particular combinations of risk factors are studied. It is certainly true that persons with multiple risk factors tend to display multiple types of problem behavior, as David Fergusson, John Harwood, and Michael Lynskey (1994) found in the Christchurch (New Zealand) Health and Development Study (discussed later).

A key question is whether all relationships between risk factors and offending are essentially generated by the minority of multiple-risk-factor, multiple-problem people. In the Pittsburgh Youth Study, Rolf Loeber and his colleagues (1998b) found that relationships between risk factors and problem outcomes were attenuated but not eliminated by excluding multiple-problem boys. To a large extent, relationships between single risk factors and single types of problems (e.g., delinquency, substance abuse, physical aggression, etc.) were similar for multiple-problem boys and for boys with fewer problems.

In investigating the causal impact of risk factors, London psychiatrist Michael Rutter (2003) argued that it is important to distinguish between "social selection" and "social causation." Risk factors may predict outcomes either because risk factors cause outcomes (social causation) or because certain types of people (e.g., high-risk ones) are differentially exposed to certain risk factors (social selection). For example, coming from a broken home (disrupted family) may predict offending because children from broken homes disproportionately have criminal parents, and criminal parents predict delinquent children.

Protective Factors

In preventing offending, ideally, risk and protective factors should be identified and then risk factors should be reduced while protective factors are enhanced. However, both the definition and existence of protective factors are controversial. On one definition, a protective factor is merely the opposite end of the scale to a risk factor. Just as a risk factor predicts an increased probability of offending, a protective factor predicts a decreased probability. However, to the extent that explanatory variables are linearly related to offending, researchers may then object that risk and protective factors are merely different names for the same underlying construct.

On other definitions, protective factors may not be just the opposite of risk factors. For example, a variable with a nonlinear relationship to offending could be regarded as a protective factor but not a risk factor. This would be true if the risk of offending decreased from medium to high levels of the variable but did not change from medium to low levels. For example, if high income predicted a low risk of delinquency, while medium and low income predicted a fairly constant average risk, income could be regarded as a protective factor but not a risk factor. However, the reverse finding is more common (Farrington and Hawkins, 1991). For example, in the Cambridge Study, the risk of conviction was high for males from large families but fairly constant for smaller families.

It is important to investigate risk and protective effects in a way that allows them to be independent. For example, Magda Stouthamer-Loeber and her colleagues (1993) in the Pittsburgh Youth Study divided each explanatory variable into the "best" quarter, the middle half, and the "worst" quarter of boys. Risk effects were investigated by comparing the "worst" quarter with the middle half, while protective effects were investigated by comparing the "best" quarter with the middle half. They found many risk effects with counterpart protective effects, and many risk effects with no counterpart protective effects, but did not find protective effects with no counterpart risk effects. A later analysis showed that the efficiency of prediction of serious delinquency was improved by including protective factors as well as risk factors (Stouthamer-Loeber et al., 2002).

Another possible definition of a protective factor is a (moderator) variable that interacts with a risk factor to minimize the risk factor's effects (Rutter, 1985). If poor parental supervision predicted a high risk of offending only for males from low-income families, and not for males from high-income families, then high income might be regarded as a protective factor counteracting the effects of the risk factor of poor parental supervision. Problems of the meaning of protective factors may be alleviated by focusing on resilience or psychosocial skills and competencies or by focusing on protective processes. More research is needed to identify protective factors, linked to the use of interventions targeted on protective factors. Research is especially needed to identify protective factors with no corresponding risk factors, and protective factors that interact with risk factors.

Perhaps the most common method of studying protective factors is to identify a subsample at risk (with some combination of risk factors) and then to search for factors that predict successful members of this subsample (those who do not have the antisocial outcome). For example, in Hawaii, Emmy Werner and Ruth Smith (1982) studied children who possessed four or more risk factors for delinquency before age 2 but who nevertheless did not develop behavioral difficulties during childhood or adolescence. They found that the major protective factors included being the first-born, being an active and affectionate infant, small family size, and receiving a large amount of attention from caretakers.

The study of protective factors encourages optimism about ways of reducing crime and promoting a better society. There is a tendency for some interventions to focus mainly on enhancing protective factors rather than reducing risk factors, because a more positive program (e.g., promoting health and strengthening skills and competence) is likely to be more attractive to the people and neighborhoods involved. Reducing risk factors might imply criticism (focusing on inadequacies) and hence have negative connotations. However, in light of the relative lack of knowledge about protective factors, focusing only on them may not be an optimal strategy. In order to reduce delinquency outcomes, protective factors need to be enhanced for high-risk individuals (Pollard, Hawkins, and Arthur, 1999). Reducing risk factors may be more effective than enhancing protective factors, or it may be essential to include both approaches in an intervention program.

Prospective Longitudinal Surveys

As mentioned, prospective longitudinal surveys are needed to establish relationships between risk factors and offending. In this book, we focus especially on surveys of community samples of several hundred people with repeated personal interviews spanning a period of at least five years. These are the most relevant types of prospective longitudinal surveys for our purposes (Farrington, 1979b). In criminology, the main advantage of such surveys is that they provide information about the development of offending over time, about the effects of life events, and about the effects of risk and protective factors at different ages on offending at different ages (Farrington, 2003a). We focus on longitudinal surveys in Western industrialized countries, although there have been similar surveys in other countries (e.g., China; see Taylor, Friday, Ren, Weitekamp, and Kerner, 2004).

Findings in the next three chapters on different types of risk and protective factors are based on many different prospective longitudinal surveys. In order to facilitate understanding of these three chapters, the appendix at the end of this chapter summarizes key features of the most important prospective longitudinal surveys of offending, whose results are reviewed. It specifies the principal investigator(s), the sample initially studied, the length of the follow-up period, and the most important types of data collected. This appendix should be consulted when surveys are mentioned in the next three chapters.

The Cambridge Study

This book will especially focus on results obtained in the Cambridge Study in Delinquent Development, which is a prospective longitudinal survey of 400 London males from age 8 to 48 (see Farrington, 1995, 2003b). The males were originally assessed in 1961–62, when they were attending six state primary schools and were aged 8–9 (West, 1969). Therefore, the most common year of birth of the males is 1953. The males are not a sample drawn systematically from a population, but rather the complete population of boys of that age in those schools at that time. The vast majority of boys were living in two-parent families, had fathers in manual jobs, and were Caucasian and of British origin.

The Cambridge Study males have been interviewed and assessed nine times between age 8 and age 48. Attrition has been very low; for example, 95% of those still alive were interviewed at age 18, 94% at age 32, and 93% at age 48 (for information about how the subjects were traced, see Farrington, Gallagher, Morley, St. Ledger, and West, 1990). The assessments in schools measured such factors as intelligence, personality, and impulsiveness, while information was collected in the interviews about such topics as living circumstances, employment histories, relationships with females, leisure activities such as drinking, drug use, and fighting, and of course offending behavior.

The boys' parents were also interviewed about once a year, from when the boys were aged 8 until when they were aged 15. The parents provided details about such matters as family income, family composition, their employment histories, their child-rearing practices (including discipline and supervision), and the boy's temporary or permanent separations from them. In addition, the boys' teachers completed questionnaires when the boys were aged about 8, 10, 12, and 14. These furnished information about such topics as their restlessness or poor concentration, truancy, school attainment, and disruptive behavior in class. Searches of the criminal records of the subjects, of their biological relatives (fathers, mothers, brothers, and sisters), of their wives and cohabitees, and of any potential co-offenders were also carried out.

The data collected at age 48 have not yet been fully analyzed. However, the follow-up from age 32 (the previous interview) to age 48 made it possible to assess changes with age in criminal career features and measures of life success (based on accommodation, relationships, employment, violence, drinking, drug use, mental health, and offending). Between ages 32 and 48—the average length of criminal careers—the number of late-onset offenders (starting after age 21) increased considerably, life success generally increased, and violence decreased. The desisters (who stopped offending before age 21) were similar to unconvicted men in measures of life success at age 48, whereas they had been deviant (in fighting, drinking, drug use, and offending) at age 32 (Nagin, Farrington, and Moffitt, 1995).

About one in five of the subjects was convicted as a juvenile (under age 17 at the time), while 40% were convicted up to age 40. Most convictions were for theft, taking vehicles, burglary, deception, or violence; minor offenses, such as traffic infractions, drunkenness, or common assault, are excluded from these figures. In the next three chapters, we will describe many findings from this survey about risk factors (especially those measured at age 8–10) for offending.

The Pittsburgh Youth Study

We will also give special attention to results obtained in the Pittsburgh Youth Study (see Loeber et al., 2003). In this survey, about 1,500 Pittsburgh boys were followed up. Initially, 500 were in first grade (aged about 7), 500 were in fourth grade (aged about 10), and 500 were in seventh grade (aged about 13). The youngest and oldest samples were assessed at least once a year for 12 years, from age 7 to age 19 (youngest) and from age 13 to age 25 (oldest). The middle sample was assessed every 6 months until age 13, and then finally at age 22. Information was collected from the boys, their mothers, and their teachers.

The Pittsburgh Youth Study has measured many types of problem behaviors in addition to offending, including attention deficit, conduct problems, depression, and substance abuse. In general, all these problem behaviors tended to be interrelated, and a category of multiple-problem boys was identified. Many types of risk and protective factors have been measured, including child, family, peer, and neighborhood factors. In the next three chapters, we will set out conclusions we have drawn about the importance of these factors. It was often true that findings about Pittsburgh boys growing up in the 1990s were similar to findings about London boys growing up in the 1960s, increasing our confidence about the generalizability of conclusions about key risk factors (Farrington and Loeber, 1999).

Conclusions

Risk factors predict an increased probability of later offending. Protective factors either predict a decreased probability of later offending or tend to nullify the effects of risk factors in interaction with them. It is important to try to establish which risk factors have causal effects, using either experimental or quasi-experimental analyses. Risk factors often predict many other outcomes in addition to offending. Prospective longitudinal surveys are needed to advance knowledge about risk and protective factors, and in the next three chapters we will review findings from large-scale community surveys. We will pay particular attention to the findings of the Cambridge Study in Delinquent Development and the Pittsburgh Youth Study.

Because of our focus on early prevention, most of the results we discuss in the next three chapters focus on predictors of early onset rather than, for example, adult onset or persistence of offending (see Eggleston and Laub, 2002). We do not review the effects of later life events such as marriage or employment (see Blokland and Nieuwbeerta, 2005). Similarly, we focus on the prevention of offending in general, rather than on types of offenders, for example, "life-course-persistent" offenders (see Piquero and White, 2003). Most research has focused on males, but we report results obtained with females when they are available.

Appendix: Major Prospective Longitudinal Surveys of Offending

Bor, Najman

Mater University Study of Pregnancy: 7,661 women who gave birth, all single births, in Brisbane, Australia, in 1981. Mothers interviewed 3–5 days after birth, and when children were 6 months and 5 and 14 years. Children assessed at 5 and 14. Delinquency assessed at age 14 (Bor, McGee, and Fagan, 2004).

Cohen, Brook

New York State Longitudinal Study: 976 randomly sampled mothers in two upstate New York counties, with a child age 1–10, interviewed in 1975. Mothers interviewed three times up to 1991; children interviewed at an average age of 30. Focus on drug use. Children searched in criminal records in 2000 (Johnson, Smailes, Cohen, Kasen, and Brook, 2004).

Denno, Piquero, Buka

National Collaborative Perinatal Project: National U.S. multisite follow-up of pregnancies in 1959–66, focusing on perinatal factors. (1) 987 African American children born in Philadelphia in 1959–62, followed up in police records to age 22 (Denno, 1990); (2) 3,828 children born in Providence, Rhode Island, in 1960–66, followed up in police records to age 33 (Piquero and Buka, 2002).

Elliott, Huizinga

National Youth Survey: Nationally representative U.S. sample of 1,725 adolescents aged 11–17 in 1976. Interviewed in 5 successive years (1977–81) and subsequently at 3-year intervals up to 1993, and in 2002–3. Focus on self-reported delinquency, but arrest records collected (Elliott, 1994).

Eron, Huesmann, Dubow

Columbia County Study: All 856 third-grade children (aged 8) in Columbia County in New York state first assessed in 1960. Focus on aggressive behavior. Interviewed 10, 22, and 40 years later. Criminal records searched up to age 48 (Eron, Huesmann, and Zelli, 1991).

Farrington, West

Cambridge Study in Delinquent Development: 411 boys aged 8–9 in 1961–62 (included all male students of that age in six London schools). Boys interviewed nine times up to age 48. Information also from parents, teachers, and peers. Boys and all biological relatives searched in criminal records up to 1994 (Farrington, 2003b).

Fergusson, Horwood

Christchurch Health and Development Study: All 1,365 children born in Christchurch, New Zealand, in mid-1977. Studied at birth, 4 months, 1 year, annually to age 16, and at ages 18, 21, and 25. Data collected in parental interviews, self-reports, psychometric tests, teacher reports, and official records (Fergusson and Horwood, 1998).

Hawkins, Catalano

Seattle Social Development Project: 808 grade 5 students (age 10) in 18 elementary schools in Seattle in 1985. Also intervention study. Followed up annually to age 16 and then every 2–3 years at least to age 27, with interviews and criminal records (Hawkins et al., 2003).

Huizinga, Esbensen

Denver Youth Survey: 1,528 children aged 7, 9, 11, 13, or 15 in high-risk neighborhoods of Denver, Colorado, in 1988. Children and parents assessed at yearly intervals up to 1998. Youngest two cohorts assessed in

2002. Focus on self-reported delinquency; criminal record data collected up to 1992 (Huizinga, Weiher, Espiritu, and Esbensen, 2003).

Janson, Wikström

Stockholm Project Metropolitan: All 15,117 children born in Stockholm in 1953, and living there in 1963. Tested in schools in 1966. Subsample of mothers interviewed in 1968. Followed up in police records to 1983 (Wikström, 1990).

Kellam, Ensminger, McCord

Woodlawn Project: Information from teachers and mothers of 1,242 children in first grade (age 6) in African American Chicago neighborhood in 1966. Children and mothers interviewed in 1975. Focus on shy and aggressive behaviors and substance use. Follow-up interviews at age 32 (McCord and Ensminger, 1997).

Klinteberg

Young Lawbreakers as Adults: 192 delinquent and 95 control boys age 11–14 in Stockholm first examined in 1959–63 and followed up in criminal records to age 38–46 (Lang, Klinteberg, and Alm, 2002).

Kolvin, Miller

Newcastle Thousand Family Study: 1,142 children born in Newcastle-upon-Tyne, England, in mid-1947. Studied between birth and age 5 and followed up to age 15. Criminal records searched at age 33, and subsamples interviewed (Kolvin, Miller, Fleeting, and Kolvin, 1990).

Laub, Sampson

Glueck Longitudinal Study: 500 male delinquents in correctional schools in 1939–44 and 500 male nondelinquents matched on age, ethnicity, IQ, and neighborhood of residence in Boston, Massachusetts. Assessed by Sheldon and Eleanor Glueck at average ages of 14, 25, and 32. Delinquents followed up by Laub and Sampson; 52 interviewed up to age 70 (Laub and Sampson, 2003).

LeBlanc

Montreal Two-Samples Longitudinal Studies: (1) Representative sample of 3,070 French-speaking Montreal adolescents. Completed self-report questionnaires in 1974 at age 12–16 and again in 1976. (2) 470 male delinquents seen at age 15 in 1974 and again at ages 17 and 22. Followed in criminal records to age 40. Males interviewed at ages 30 and 40 (LeBlanc, 1996).

Loeber, Stouthamer-Loeber, Farrington

Pittsburgh Youth Study: 1,517 boys in first, fourth, or seventh grades of Pittsburgh public schools in 1987–88 (ages 7, 10, 13). Information from boys, parents, and teachers every 6 months for 3 years, and then every year up to age 19 (youngest) and 25 (oldest). Focus on delinquency, substance use, and mental health problems (Loeber et al., 2003).

Magnusson, Stattin, Klinteberg

Orebro Project: 1,027 children age 10 (all those in third grade) in Orebro, Sweden, in 1965. School follow-up data between ages 13 and 15. Questionnaire and record data up to age 43–45 (Klinteberg, Andersson, Magnusson, and Stattin, 1993).

McCord

Cambridge-Somerville Youth Study: 650 boys (average age 10) nominated as difficult or average by Cambridge and Somerville, Massachusetts, public schools in 1937–39. Randomly assigned to treated or control groups. Treated group visited by counselors for an average of 5 years, and all followed up in 1975–80 by interviews, mail questionnaires, and criminal records (McCord, 1991).

Mednick, Moffitt, Brennan, Hodgins

Danish Birth Cohort Studies: (1) All 358,180 persons born in Denmark in 1944–47. Followed in police records to age 44 (Brennan, Mednick, and Hodgins, 2000). (2) 4,169 males born in Copenhagen in 1959–61, with extensive perinatal data. Followed up in criminal records to age 34 (Brennan, Grekin, and Mednick, 1999).

Moffitt, Caspi, Poulton

Dunedin Multidisciplinary Health and Development Study: 1,037 children born in 1972–73 in Dunedin, New Zealand, and first assessed at age 3. Assessed every 2–3 years on health, psychological, education, and family factors up to age 32. Self-reported delinquency measured from age 13. Convictions collected up to age 32 (Moffitt, Caspi, Rutter, and Silva, 2001).

Patterson, Dishion, Capaldi

Oregon Youth Study: 206 fourth-grade boys (age 10) in Eugene and Springfield, Oregon, in 1983–85. Assessed at yearly intervals, with data from boys, parents, teachers, and peers, at least to age 30. Followed up in criminal records at least to age 30 (Capaldi and Patterson, 1996).

Pulkkinen

Jyvaskyla Longitudinal Study of Personality and Social Development: 369 children aged 8–9 in Jyvaskyla, Finland, in 1968. Peer, teacher, and self-ratings collected. Followed up five times to age 42 with interviews and questionnaires and in criminal records (Pulkkinen and Pitkanen, 1993).

Raine, Venables, Mednick

Mauritius Joint Child Health Project: 1,795 children age 3 recruited in 1972–73 from two towns in Mauritius. Focus on psychophysiological measures. Followed up at least to age 31 by interviews and up to age 23 in court records (Raine, Reynolds, Venables, Mednick, and Farrington, 1998).

Rasanen

Northern Finland Birth Cohort Study: 5,636 males born in 1966 and living in Finland at age 16. Followed up in criminal records to age 28 (Rasanen et al., 1999).

Thornberry, Lizotte, Krohn

Rochester Youth Development Study: 1,000 seventh- and eighth-graders (age 13–14) in Rochester, New York, public schools, first assessed in 1988, disproportionally sampled from high-crime neighborhoods. Followed up initially every 6 months, then every year, then at intervals to age 32. Self-reports and criminal records collected (Thornberry, Krohn, Lizotte, Smith, and Tobin, 2003).

Tolan, Gorman-Smith, Henry

Chicago Youth Development Study: 362 African American and Latino boys in fifth or seventh grades (age 11–13) of Chicago public schools in 1991. Followed up with data from boys, mothers, and teachers to age 25–28 (Tolan, Gorman-Smith, and Henry, 2003).

Tremblay

Montreal Longitudinal-Experimental Study: 1,037 French-speaking kindergarten boys (age 6) from poor areas of Montreal assessed by teachers in 1984. Disruptive boys randomly allocated to treatment (parent training plus individual skills training) or control groups. All boys followed up each year from age 10 to age 26, including self-reported delinquency and aggression (Tremblay, Vitaro, Nagin, Pagani, and Séguin, 2003).

Wadsworth, Douglas

National Survey of Health and Development: 5,362 children selected from all legitimate single births in England, Scotland, and Wales during one week of March 1946. Followed in criminal records to age 21. Mainly medical and school data collected, but samples were interviewed at ages 26, 36, 43, and 50 (Wadsworth, 1991).

Werner, Smith

Kauai Longitudinal Study: 698 children born in 1955 in Kauai, Hawaii, assessed at birth and ages 2, 10, 18, 30, and 40. Criminal records up to age 40. Focus on resilience (Werner and Smith, 2001).

Widom, Maxfield

Longitudinal Study of Abused Children: 908 children abused under age 11 identified in Indianapolis court records in 1967–71 and 667 matched control children. Followed up in arrest records to 1994 (Maxfield and Widom, 1996).

Wolf, Hogh

Copenhagen Project Metropolitan: All 12,270 boys born in 1953 in Copenhagen and tested in schools in 1965–66. Sample of mothers interviewed in 1968. Followed in police records to 1976 (Hogh and Wolf, 1983).

Wolfgang, Figlio, Thornberry, Tracy

Philadelphia Birth Cohort Studies: (1) 9,945 boys born in Philadelphia in 1945 and living there at least from age 10 to 17. Sample interviewed at age 26 and followed up in police records to age 30 (Wolfgang, Thornberry, and Figlio, 1987). (2) 27,160 children born in Philadelphia in 1958 and living there at least from age 10 to 17. Followed up in police records to age 26 (Tracy and Kempf-Leonard, 1996).

Individual Factors

3

I t is plausible to assume that offending, like all other types of behavior, arises from the interaction between the individual and the environment. This chapter focuses on the individual side of the equation (see also Farrington, 1998a). Explanations of the development of criminal persons (i.e., persons with a relatively high likelihood of committing criminal acts in different situations) are not at all incompatible with explanations of the occurrence of criminal acts. On the contrary, a comprehensive theory of crime should aim to explain both (see Farrington, 2005).

It is clear that individuals differ in their potential to commit criminal and related types of antisocial acts, given a particular opportunity, situation, or victim. Since "crime" is a socially and legally defined type of behavior, any potential to commit crimes is probably part of a broader potential to commit antisocial acts, but this book focuses particularly on crimes. We use the word "potential" (equivalent to "tendency") in preference to "propensity" or "predisposition" to describe the key theoretical construct underlying regularities in behavior, in order to avoid possible connotations of biological determinism.

An important assumption is that individual differences in criminal potential (or, more precisely, the rank orderings of individuals on criminal potential) are relatively stable over time and in different environments. A great deal of criminal career research (Farrington, 1997b) shows continuity and relative stability in offending over time; even though the absolute level of offending, and different types of offending, vary with age, the "worst" people at one age still tend to be the "worst" at a later age. Similarly, criminal career research shows a great deal of versatility and not much specialization in offending (Farrington, 1991); it is almost as though the most antisocial people commit different types of offenses at random, depending, presumably, on situational factors.

Criminal potential may be disaggregated into many different dimensions, some of which are probably different names for the same underlying construct. Terms such as antisocial, aggressive, or hostile seem essentially to refer to people with high criminal potential. Constructs such as low guilt, weak conscience, low self-control, high impulsivity, emotional coldness, callousness, low empathy, fearlessness, egocentricity (self-centeredness), poor conditionability, a poor ability to delay gratification, and a poor ability to manipulate abstract concepts seem more likely to be causes of high criminal potential. Obviously, it is important to establish the key underlying constructs that are linked to individual differences in offending behavior. For ease of exposition, this chapter focuses on criminal potential.

Long-term between-individual differences in criminal potential (intended to explain why some people are more likely to commit offenses than others in a particular situation) can be distinguished from short-term within-individual variations in criminal potential (intended to explain why people are more likely to commit crimes at some times and in some situations than other times and situations). Long-term criminal potential is likely to be influenced by biological, individual, family, peer, school, community, and societal factors. Short-term criminal potential is likely to be influenced by situational events such as getting insulted or frustrated, getting drunk, or seeing a tempting criminal opportunity. While both topics are important, the focus in this book is on explaining long-term differences in criminal potential.

Among the most important individual factors that predict offending are low intelligence and attainment, personality and temperament, empathy, and impulsiveness, as the meta-analysis by Mark Lipsey and James Derzon (1998) showed. All of these will be reviewed in this chapter, which concludes by discussing social cognitive skills and cognitive theories.

Low Intelligence and Attainment

Intelligence is usually measured according to scores on IQ tests. The IQ (Intelligence Quotient) indicates the relationship between a child's "mental age" (based on the test) and chronological age. For example, if a child of 8 achieved a score that was typical of a 10-year-old, that child's IQ would be 125 (IQ = 100 x 10 / 8). IQ scores are arranged to have an average of 100 and a standard deviation of about 15, so that two-thirds of the population would score between 85 and 115. Many of the tests measure the ability to manipulate abstract concepts and are designed to predict later school success. Some tests have separate "verbal" and "performance" IQ measures. The performance tests involve the manipulation of concrete objects, for example in picture arrangement, block design, or object assembly.

Low intelligence is an important predictor of offending, and it can be measured very early in life. For example, in a prospective longitudinal survey of about 120 Stockholm males, Hakan Stattin and Ingrid Klackenberg-Larsson (1993) reported that low intelligence measured at age 3 significantly predicted officially recorded offending up to age 30. Frequent offenders (with four or more offenses) had an average IQ of 88 at age 3, whereas nonoffenders had an average IQ of 101. All of these results held up after controlling for social class. In the Perry Preschool project in Michigan, Lawrence Schweinhart, Helen Barnes, and David Weikart (1993) found that low intelligence at age 4 significantly predicted the number of arrests up to age 27. In addition, in the Providence (Rhode Island) site of the National Collaborative Perinatal Project, Paul Lipsitt, Stephen Buka, and Lewis Lipsitt (1990) showed that low IQ at age 4 predicted later juvenile delinquency.

Similar results have been obtained in other countries. In the Philadelphia cohort of the National Collaborative Perinatal Project, Deborah Denno (1990) reported that low verbal and performance IQ at ages 4 and

7, and low scores on the California Achievement test at age 13–14 (vocabulary, comprehension, math, language, spelling) all predicted arrests for violence up to age 22. In the Woodlawn project in Chicago, Joan McCord and Margaret Ensminger (1997) discovered that low IQ at age 6 predicted arrests for violent crimes up to age 32. In Project Metropolitan in Copenhagen, Erik Hogh and Preben Wolf (1983) found that low IQ at age 12 significantly predicted police-recorded violence between ages 15 and 22. The link between low IQ and violence was strongest among lower class boys.

In the Cambridge Study, one-third of the boys scoring 90 or less on a nonverbal intelligence test (Raven's Progressive Matrices) at age 8–10 were convicted as juveniles, twice as many as among the remainder (Farrington, 1992c). Low nonverbal intelligence was highly correlated with low verbal intelligence (vocabulary, word comprehension, verbal reasoning) and with low school attainment at age 11, and all of these measures predicted juvenile convictions to much the same extent. In addition to their poor school performance, delinquents tended to be frequent truants, to leave school at the earliest possible age (15), and to take no secondary school examinations.

Low intelligence and attainment predicted both juvenile and adult convictions (Farrington, 1992b). Low intelligence at age 8–10 was also an important independent predictor of spouse assault at age 32 (Farrington, 1994a). In addition, low intelligence and attainment predicted aggression and bullying at age 14 (Farrington, 1989, 1993b), and low school attainment predicted chronic offenders (Farrington and West, 1993). Low nonverbal intelligence was especially characteristic of the juvenile recidivists (who had an average IQ of 89) and those first convicted at the earliest ages (10–13). Furthermore, low intelligence and attainment predicted self-reported delinquency almost as well as convictions (Farrington, 1992a), suggesting that the link between low intelligence and delinquency was not caused by the less intelligent boys having a greater probability of being caught.

Low nonverbal intelligence was about as strong a predictor of juvenile convictions as other important early risk factors (low family income, large family size, poor parental child-rearing behavior, poor parental supervision, and poor concentration or restlessness), but it was a weaker predictor than having a convicted parent or a daring (risk-taking) personality. Measures of intelligence and attainment predicted measures of offending independently of other risk factors such as family income and family size (Farrington, 1990).

Similar results have been obtained in other projects (Lynam, Moffitt, and Stouthamer-Loeber 1993; Moffitt and Silva, 1988a; Wilson and Herrnstein, 1985). Delinquents often do better on nonverbal performance tests, such as object assembly and block design, than on verbal tests (Walsh, Petee, and Beyer, 1987), suggesting that they find it easier to deal with concrete objects than abstract concepts. While most of the research has focused on low IQ, there have also been studies of offending by people with high IQ scores (e.g., Oleson, 2002).

The key explanatory factor underlying the link between intelligence and delinquency may be the ability to manipulate abstract concepts. People who are poor at this tend to do badly in intelligence tests such as Raven's Progressive Matrices and in school achievement, and they also tend to commit offenses, probably because of their poor ability to foresee the consequences of their offending and to appreciate the feelings of victims (i.e., their low empathy). Certain family backgrounds are less conducive than others to the development of abstract reasoning. For example, lower class, economically deprived parents tend to talk in terms of the concrete rather than the abstract and tend to live for the present, with little thought for the future, as the sociologist Albert Cohen (1955, p. 96) pointed out many years ago. In some ways, it is difficult to distinguish a lack of concern for future consequences from the concept of impulsiveness (discussed later).

There has been a great deal of recent interest in the concept of "emotional intelligence," which measures empathy, self-awareness, emotional control, and the ability to delay gratification. This is typically measured by items such as "I easily recognize my emotions as I experience them" and "I have control of my emotions" (Schutte et al., 1998). Emotional intelligence seems to reflect empathy and impulsiveness, which will be discussed later.

Low intelligence may be one element of a pattern of cognitive and neuropsychological deficits. For example, in the Dunedin (New Zealand) longitudinal study, Terrie Moffitt and Phil Silva (1988b) found that self-reported delinquency was related to verbal, memory, and visual-motor integration deficits, independently of low social class and family adversity. Neuropsychological research might lead to important advances in knowledge about the link between brain functioning and offending. For example, the "executive functions" of the brain, located in the frontal lobes, include sustaining attention and concentration, abstract reasoning and concept formation, anticipation and planning, self-monitoring of behavior, and inhibition of inappropriate or impulsive behaviors (Moffitt and Henry, 1991; Morgan and Lilienfeld, 2000). In the Montreal longitudinal-experimental study, Jean Séguin and his colleagues (1995) found that a measure of executive functioning based on cognitive-neuropsychological tests at age 14 was the strongest neuropsychological discriminator of violent and nonviolent boys. This relationship held independently of a measure of family adversity (based on parental age at first birth, parental education level, coming from a broken family, and low socioeconomic status). In the Pittsburgh Youth Study, the life-course-persistent offenders had marked neurocognitive impairments (Raine et al., 2005).

Alternatively, it might be argued that IQ tests are designed to measure ability to succeed in school (which may be a different construct from "intelligence"). Hence, low IQ predicts school failure, and there are many criminological theories suggesting that school failure leads to delinquency (e.g., through the intervening construct of status deprivation; see Cohen, 1955). Donald Lynam, Terrie Moffitt, and Magda Stouthamer-Loeber (1993) completed one of the most important attempts to test these and other possible explanations, using data collected in the Pittsburgh Youth Study. Their conclusions vary according to the ethnicity of the boys. For African American boys, they found that low verbal intelligence led to school failure and subsequently to self-reported delinquency, but for Caucasian boys the relationship between low verbal intelligence and self-reported delinquency held after controlling for school failure and all other variables. It may be that poor executive functioning and school failure are both plausible explanations of the link between low intelligence and offending.

Just as low intelligence is a risk factor for offending, it has been suggested that high intelligence might be a protective factor. This was tested by Hakan Stattin, Anders Romelsjo, and Marlene Stenbacka (1997) in a survey of over 7,500 Stockholm males conscripted for military service. They identified males with behavioral risk factors, including police contact, poor school conduct, truancy, running away from home, and drug and alcohol abuse. They also measured family risk factors, including low income, single-parent family, paternal alcohol use, and psychological problems. Stattin and his colleagues found that, among those with behavioral or family risk factors, high intelligence and emotional control predicted a low prevalence of adult convictions.

Personality

Antisocial behavior is remarkably consistent over time; or, to be more precise, the relative ordering of individuals is remarkably consistent over time (Roberts and del Vecchio, 2000). Psychologists assume that behavioral consistency depends primarily on the persistence of underlying tendencies to behave in particular ways in particular situations. These tendencies, such as impulsiveness, excitement-seeking, assertiveness, modesty, and dutifulness, are termed personality traits. Larger personality dimensions, such as extraversion, refer to clusters of personality traits.

Before 1990, the best known research on personality and crime was probably that inspired by the British psychologist Hans Eysenck in his theory and personality questionnaires (1996). He viewed offending as natural and even rational, on the assumption that human beings are hedonistic, seek pleasure, and avoid pain. He assumed that delinquent acts such as theft, violence, and vandalism were essentially pleasurable or beneficial to the offender. In order to explain why everyone was not a criminal, Eysenck suggested that the hedonistic tendency to commit crimes is opposed by the conscience, which he viewed as a fear response built up from childhood in a conditioning process.

On the Eysenck theory, the people who commit offenses are those who have not built up strong consciences, mainly because they have inherently poor conditionability. Poor conditionability is linked to Eysenck's three dimensions of personality: extraversion (E), neuroticism (N), and psychoticism (P). Examples of E items on the questionnaires are "Do you often make decisions on the spur of the moment?" (Yes) and "Do you prefer reading to meeting people?" (No). The E items seem to measure either sociability or impulsiveness. Examples of N and P items are "Do you worry about awful things that might happen?" (Yes; an N item) and "Would it upset you a lot to see a child or animal suffer?" (No; a P item).

According to Eysenck, people who have a high level of the E dimension build up conditioned responses less well, because they have low levels of cortical arousal. People who are high on the N dimension also condition less well, because their high resting level of anxiety interferes with their conditioning. In addition, since the N dimension acts as a drive, reinforcing existing behavioral tendencies, neurotic extraverts should be particularly criminal. Eysenck also predicted that people who are high on the P dimension would tend to be offenders, because the traits included in his definition of psychoticism (emotional coldness, low empathy, high hostility, and inhumanity) were typical of criminals. However, the meaning of the P scale is unclear, and it might perhaps be more accurately labeled psychopathy. Marvin Zuckerman (1989) suggested that it should be termed "impulsive unsocialized sensation-seeking."

A review of studies relating Eysenck's personality dimensions to official and self-reported offending concluded that high N (but not E) was related to official offending, while high E (but not N) was related to self-reported offending (Farrington, Biron, and LeBlanc, 1982). High P was related to both, but this could have been a tautological result, since many of the items on the P scale reflected antisocial behavior or were selected in light of their ability to discriminate between prisoners and non-prisoners. In the Cambridge Study, those high on both E and N tended to be juvenile self-reported offenders, adult official offenders, and adult self-reported offenders but not juvenile offenders, according to official records. These relationships held independently of other criminogenic risk factors such as low family income, low intelligence, and poor parental child-rearing behavior. However, when individual items of the questionnaire were studied, it was clear that the items measuring impulsiveness caused the significant relationships (e.g., doing things quickly without stopping to think). Hence it seems likely that research inspired by the Eysenck theory mainly identifies the link between impulsiveness and offending (discussed later).

Since 1990, the most widely accepted personality system has been the "Big Five" or five-factor model, developed by Robert McCrae and Paul Costa (1997, 2003). This model suggests that there are five key dimensions of personality: neuroticism (N), extraversion (E), openness (O), agreeableness (A), and conscientiousness (C). Openness means originality and openness to new ideas, agreeableness includes nurturance and altruism, and conscientiousness includes planning and the will to achieve. Openness and conscientiousness seem to be related to intelligence, or at least to social or emotional intelligence. These dimensions are measured using a personality inventory called the Neuroticism–Extraversion–Openness Personality Inventory (NEO-PI). Controversially, Robert McCrae and his colleagues (2000) argued that these personality dimensions are biologically based tendencies that follow intrinsic developmental pathways independently of environmental influences.

Because of its newness, the "Big Five" personality model has rarely been related to offending. In Canada, Stephen Hart and Robert Hare (1994) found that psychopathy was most strongly (negatively) correlated with agreeableness and conscientiousness. Similarly, in an Australian study Patrick Heaven (1996) showed that agreeableness and conscientiousness were most strongly (negatively) correlated with self-reported delinquency. Much the same results were obtained in the Pittsburgh Youth Study when the five dimensions were measured using mothers' ratings (John, Caspi, Robins, Moffitt, and Stouthamer-Loeber, 1994), and the relevance of agreeableness and conscientiousness was confirmed in a detailed review (Miller and Lynam, 2001). It is informative to measure elements ("facets") of the larger dimensions. Joshua Miller, Donald Lynam, and Carl Leukefeld (2003) did this and concluded that low straightforwardness, low compliance, and low deliberation were particularly related to aggression and conduct problems in a Lexington (Kentucky) longitudinal study.

Temperament

Temperament is basically the childhood equivalent of personality, although there is more emphasis in the study of temperament on constitutional predisposition and on biological factors (Robinson, Kagan, Reznick, and Corley, 1992). Modern research on child temperament began with the New York Longitudinal Study of Stella Chess and Alexander Thomas (1984). Children in their first 5 years of life were rated on temperamental dimensions by their parents, and these dimensions were combined into three broad categories of easy, difficult, and "slow to warm up" temperament. Having a difficult temperament at age 3–4 (frequent irritability, low amenability and adaptability, irregular habits) predicted poor adult psychiatric adjustment at age 17–24.

Remarkably, John Bates (1989) found that mothers' ratings of difficult temperament as early as age 6 months (defined primarily as frequent, intense expressions of negative emotions) predicted mothers' ratings of child conduct problems between ages 3 and 6 years. Similar results were obtained by Ann Sanson and her colleagues (1993) in the Australian Temperament Project, finding that children who were rated as irritable, not amenable, or showing behavior problems at age 4–8 months tended to be rated as aggressive at age 7–8. However, when information at each age comes from the same source, it is possible that the continuity lies in the rater rather than the child. Fortunately, other studies (e.g., Guerin, Gottfried, and Thomas, 1997) show that difficult temperament in infancy, rated by mothers, also predicts antisocial behavior in childhood rated by teachers.

Because it was not very clear exactly what a "difficult" temperament means in practice, other researchers have used more specific dimensions of temperament. For example, the Harvard psychologist Jerome Kagan (1989) classified children as inhibited (shy or fearful) or uninhibited at age 21 months, and found that they remained significantly stable on this classification up to age 7 years. Furthermore, the uninhibited children at age 21 months significantly tended to be identified as aggressive at age 13 years, according to self-report and parent reports (Schwartz, Snidman, and Kagan, 1996).

The Dunedin longitudinal study in New Zealand has obtained the most important results on the link between childhood temperament and later offending. Temperament at age 3 years was rated by observing the child's behavior during a testing session. Avshalom Caspi (2000), a psychologist at London University, reported that the most important dimension of child temperament was being undercontrolled (restless, impulsive, with poor attention) and that this predicted aggression, self-reported delinquency, and convictions at age 18–21.

Empathy

There is a widespread belief that low empathy is an important personality trait that is related to offending, on the assumption that people who can appreciate or experience a victim's feelings (or both) are less likely to victimize someone. This belief also underlies cognitive-behavioral skills training programs that aim to increase empathy (see chapter 7). However, its empirical basis is not very impressive. Therefore, because of inconsistent results, measures of empathy are not well validated or widely accepted, and there are no prospective longitudinal surveys relating early empathy to later offending.

A distinction has often been made between cognitive empathy (understanding or appreciating other people's feelings) and emotional empathy (actually experiencing other people's feelings). Darrick Jolliffe and David Farrington (2004) carried out a systematic review of 35 studies comparing questionnaire measures of empathy with official record measures of delinquent or criminal behavior. They found that low cognitive empathy was strongly related to offending, but low affective empathy was only weakly related. Most important, the relationship between low empathy and offending was greatly reduced after controlling for intelligence or socioeconomic status, suggesting that they might be more important risk factors or that low empathy might mediate the relationship between these risk factors and offending.

The best studies of the 1990s that have related empathy to offending in relatively large samples are as follows. In Australia, Anita Mak (1991) found that delinquent females had lower emotional empathy than non-delinquent females but that there were no significant differences for males. In Finland, Kaukiainen and colleagues (1999) reported that empathy (cognitive and emotional combined) was negatively correlated with aggression (both measured by peer ratings). In Spain, Maria Luengo and her colleagues (1994) carried out the first project that related cognitive and emotional empathy separately to (self-reported) offending, and found that both were negatively correlated.

Darrick Jolliffe and David Farrington (in press-a) developed a new measure of empathy called the Basic Empathy Scale. An example of a cognitive item is "It is hard for me to understand when my friends are sad," and an example of an emotional item is "I usually feel calm when other people are scared." In a study of 720 British adolescents aged about 15, they found that low affective empathy was related to self-reported offending and violence for both males and females, and to an official record for offending by females (Jolliffe and Farrington, in press-b). Low cognitive empathy was related to self-reported serious theft (including burglary and car theft) for males. Low affective and cognitive empathy were related to fighting and vandalism for males and to theft from a person for females. Therefore, low empathy may be an important risk factor for delinquency.

Impulsiveness

Impulsiveness is the most crucial personality dimension that predicts offending. Unfortunately, there are a bewildering number of constructs referring to a poor ability to control behavior. These include impulsiveness, hyperactivity, restlessness, clumsiness, not considering consequences before acting, a poor ability to plan ahead, short time horizons, low self-control, sensation-seeking, risk-taking, and a poor ability to delay gratification. Virtually all these constructs, measured in different ways, are consistently related to measures of offending (see, e.g., Blackburn, 1993, pp. 191–196; Pratt, Cullen, Blevins, Daigle, and Unnever, 2002).

Many studies show that hyperactivity predicts later offending. In the Copenhagen Perinatal project, psychologists Patricia Brennan, Birgitte Mednick, and Sarnoff Mednick (1993) discovered that hyperactivity (restlessness and poor concentration) at age 11–13 significantly predicted arrests for violence up to age 22, especially among boys who had experienced delivery complications. More than half of those with both hyperactivity and high delivery complications were arrested for violence, compared to less than 10% of the remainder. In the Mater University Study of Pregnancy in Brisbane, Australia, William Bor, Tara McGee, and Abigail Fagan (2004) found that problems of attention and restlessness at age 5 more than doubled the risk of delinquency at age 14.

In the Orebro longitudinal study, the Swedish psychologist Britt af Klinteberg and her colleagues (1993) reported that hyperactivity at age 13 predicted police-recorded violence up to age 26. The highest rate of violence was among males with both motor restlessness and concentration difficulties (15%), compared to 3% of the remainder. In another Swedish longitudinal study, Jenny Eklund and Britt af Klinteberg (2003) concluded that attention problems were the most important components of hyperactivity that predicted later violent offending.

In the Cambridge Study, boys identified by teachers as lacking in concentration or restless, those identified by parents, peers, or teachers as the most daring or risk-taking, and those who were the most impulsive on psychomotor tests at age 8–10 all tended to become offenders later in life. Later self-report measures of impulsiveness were also related to offending. Daring, poor concentration, and restlessness all predicted both official convictions and self-reported delinquency, and daring was consistently one of the best independent predictors (Farrington, 1992b). A combined measure of "hyperactivity-impulsivity-attention deficit" (HIA) significantly predicted juvenile convictions independently of conduct problems at age 8–10 (Farrington, Gallagher, et al., 1990). Donald Lynam (1996) argued that children with both HIA and conduct problems were at greatest risk of later chronic offending.

The most extensive research on different measures of impulsiveness was carried out in the Pittsburgh Youth Study by Jennifer White and her colleagues (1994). The measures that were most strongly related to self-reported delinquency at ages 10 and 13 were teacher-rated impulsiveness (e.g., "acts without thinking"), self-reported impulsiveness, self-reported undercontrol (e.g., "unable to delay gratification"), motor restlessness (from videotaped observations), and psychomotor impulsiveness (on the Trail Making Test). Generally, the verbal behavior rating tests produced stronger relationships with offending than the psychomotor performance tests, suggesting that cognitive impulsiveness (based on thinking processes) was more relevant to delinquency than behavioral impulsiveness (based on test performance). Future time perception and delay of gratification tests were only weakly related to self-reported delinquency.

The most recent questionnaire to measure impulsiveness—the UPPS—was developed by Stephen Whiteside and Donald Lynam (2001). This has four scales of urgency (e.g., "I have trouble controlling my impulses"), premeditation (e.g., "I have a reserved and cautious attitude toward life"), perseverance (e.g., "I generally like to see things through to the end"), and sensation-seeking (e.g., "I'll try anything once"). Miller, Flory, Lyman, and Leukefeld (2003) showed how these four scales were related to aggression, alcohol use, drug use, and antisocial personality disorder.

Theories of Impulsiveness

Many theories have been put forward to explain the link between impulsiveness and offending. One of the most popular suggests that impulsiveness reflects deficits in the executive functions of the brain, located in the frontal lobes (Moffitt, 1990). Persons with these neuropsychological deficits will tend to commit offenses because they have poor control over their behavior, a poor ability to consider the possible consequences of their actions, and a tendency to focus on immediate gratification. There may also be an indirect link between neuropsychological deficits and offending, which is mediated by hyperactivity and inattention in school and the resulting school failure. In discussing links between executive functions and offending, impulsiveness may be difficult to disentangle from intelligence, although Donald Lynam and Terrie Moffitt (1995) argued that they were different constructs.

A related theory suggests that low cortical arousal produces impulsive and sensation-seeking behavior. Offenders have a low level of arousal as shown by their low alpha (brain) waves on the electroencephalogram (EEG) or by autonomic nervous system indicators such as heart rate, blood pressure, or skin conductance, or they show low autonomic reactivity (Raine, 1993). In the Cambridge Study, a low heart rate was significantly related to convictions for violence, self-reported violence, and teacher-reported violence, independently of all other explanatory variables (Farrington, 1997b). In several regression analyses, the most important independent risk factors for violence were daring, poor concentration, and a low heart rate. Other researchers (Raine, Venables, and Williams, 1990; Wadsworth, 1976) have also identified a low heart rate as a replicable predictor and correlate of offending.

The Harvard scholars James Q. Wilson and Richard Herrnstein (1985) propounded an important criminological theory focusing on impulsiveness and offending. This theory suggested that people differ in their underlying criminal tendencies, and that whether a person chooses to commit a crime in any situation depends on whether the perceived benefits of offending are considered to outweigh the perceived costs. Hence Wilson and Herrnstein focus on cognitive (thinking and decision-making) processes.

The benefits of offending, including material gain, peer approval, and sexual gratification, tend to be contemporaneous with it. In contrast, many of the costs of offending, such as the risk of being caught and punished, and the possible loss of reputation or employment, are uncertain and long delayed. Other costs, such as pangs of conscience (or guilt), disapproval by onlookers, and retaliation by the victim, are more immediate. As many others have done, Wilson and Herrnstein emphasized the importance of the conscience as an internal inhibitor of offending, and suggested that it was built up in a social learning process according to whether parents reinforced or punished childhood transgressions.

The key individual difference factor in the Wilson-Herrnstein theory is the extent to which people's behavior is influenced by immediate as opposed to delayed consequences. They suggested that individuals vary in their ability to think about or plan for the future, and that this ability is linked to intelligence. The major determinant of offending is a person's impulsiveness. More impulsive people are less influenced by the likelihood of future consequences and hence are more likely to commit crimes.

In many respects, Michael Gottfredson and Travis Hirschi's (1990) theory is similar to the Wilson-Herrnstein theory. Gottfredson and Hirschi castigated criminological theorists for ignoring the fact that people differed in underlying criminal propensities and that these differences appeared early in life and remained stable over much of the life-course. They called the key individual difference factor in their theory "low self-control," which referred to the extent to which individuals were vulnerable to the temptations of the moment. People with low self-control were impulsive, took risks, had low cognitive and academic skills, were self-centered, had low empathy, and had short time horizons. Hence they found it hard to defer gratification, and their decisions to offend were insufficiently influenced by the possible future painful consequences of offending. Gottfredson and Hirschi also argued that between-individual differences in self-control were present early in life (by age 6–8), were remarkably stable over time, and were essentially caused by differences in parental child-rearing practices.

Social Cognitive Skills

Many researchers have argued that offenders use poor techniques of thinking and problem-solving in interpersonal situations (Blackburn, 1993, pp. 204–209). Offenders are often said to be self-centered and callous, with low empathy. They are relatively poor at role-taking and perspective-taking, and may misinterpret other people's intentions. Their lack of awareness or sensitivity to other people's thoughts and feelings impairs their ability to form relationships and to appreciate the effects of their behavior on other people. They show poor social skills in inter-personal interactions, fidgeting and avoiding eye contact rather than lis-tening and paying attention.

It is further argued that offenders tend to believe that what happens to them depends on fate, chance, or luck rather than on their own actions. Such thinking makes them feel that they are controlled by other people and by circumstances beyond their control. Hence they think that there is no point in trying to succeed, so they lack persistence in aiming to achieve goals. Arguably, offenders often externalize the blame for their acts to other people rather than taking responsibility themselves, and expect people to believe far-fetched stories. Furthermore, they fail to stop and think before acting and fail to learn from experience. These social cognitive deficits are linked to offenders' concrete, as opposed to abstract, thinking and their poor ability to manipulate abstract concepts (Ross and Ross, 1995). While this constellation of features fits in with many previously cited character-istics of offenders, it has to be said that the evidence in favor of some of them (e.g., the poor social skills of delinquents) is not convincing.

Perhaps the most elaborated theory to explain the development of social cognitive skills in relation to aggressive behavior is the social in-formation processing model of the Duke University psychologist Kenneth Dodge (1991). According to this, children respond to an environmental stimulus by (1) encoding relevant cues, (2) interpreting those cues, (3) retrieving possible behavioral responses from long-term memory, (4) considering the possible consequences of alternative responses, and (5) selecting and performing a behavior. According to Dodge, aggressive children are more likely to interpret cues as hostile, to retrieve aggres-sive alternative responses, and to evaluate the consequences of aggres-sion as beneficial.

University of Illinois psychologists Rowell Huesmann and Leonard Eron (1984) put forward a cognitive script model, in which aggressive behavior depends on stored behavioral repertoires (cognitive scripts) that have been learned during early development. In response to environmental cues, possible cognitive scripts are retrieved and evaluated. The choice of aggressive scripts, which prescribe aggressive behavior, depends on the past history of rewards and punishments, and on the extent to which children are influenced by immediate gratification, as opposed to long-term consequences. According to Huesmann and Eron, the persisting trait of aggressiveness includes a collection of well-learned aggressive scripts that are resistant to change.

There are other theories focusing on the thinking processes of offenders. The most popular "rational choice" theory of crime events suggests that they occur in response to specific opportunities, when their subjectively perceived benefits (e.g., stolen property, peer approval) outweigh their subjectively perceived costs (e.g., legal punishment, parental disapproval). For example, the British psychologists Ronald Clarke and Derek Cornish (1985) outlined a theory of residential burglary that included such influencing factors as whether a house was occupied, whether it looked affluent, whether there were bushes to hide behind, whether there were nosy neighbors, whether the house had a burglar alarm, and whether it contained a dog. This rational choice theory has inspired situational methods of crime prevention, which are not reviewed in this book (see Clarke, 1997).

Conclusions

Low intelligence and attainment, and low empathy and impulsiveness, are important risk factors for offending. All of these factors may reflect executive functioning deficits in the brain. The fact that low attainment predicts offending has inspired programs (especially in preschool) designed to improve school attainment. Similarly, the idea that offenders have high impulsiveness and poor social skills has inspired cognitive-behavioral programs, such as "reasoning and rehabilitation"," designed to reduce impulsiveness and improve social skills. We discuss programs targeting individual risk factors in chapter 7.

In the next chapter, we review family risk and protective factors.

Family Factors   **4**

When people are asked what they think are the main causes of
crime, they often nominate poor parental child-rearing methods, and especially poor discipline or control of children. For example, in
1988, the British newspaper the *Mail on Sunday* reported the results of a
survey of a quota sample of over 1,000 adults, who were asked what they
thought were the main causes of violent crime. The most popular cause
(nominated by 53%) was lack of parental discipline, followed by poverty
(20%), television violence (19%), lack of school discipline (15%), broken
homes (13%), and alcohol or drugs (13%). This chapter reviews the importance of family factors as predictors of offending (see also Farrington, 2002).

Academic research confirms the importance of family factors as predictors of offending. The American psychologists Rolf Loeber and Tom
Dishion (1983) extensively reviewed the predictors of male offending.
They concluded that the most important predictors were (in order) poor
parental child management techniques, childhood antisocial behavior,
offending by parents and siblings, low intelligence and educational attainment, and separation from a parent. Later, Rolf Loeber and Magda
Stouthamer-Loeber (1986) completed an exhaustive review of family
factors as predictors of offending. They found that the best predictors
were (in order) poor parental supervision, parental rejection of children,
large family size, low parental involvement with children, parental conflict, and antisocial parents.

More recent reviews confirm the importance of family factors. Carolyn Smith and Susan Stern (1997, pp. 383–384) concluded that:

> We know that children who grow up in homes characterized by lack of warmth and support, whose parents lack behavior management skills, and whose lives are characterized by conflict or maltreatment will more likely be delinquent, whereas a supportive family can protect children even in a very hostile and damaging external environment. . . . Parental monitoring or supervision is the aspect of family management that is most consistently related to delinquency.

Mark Lipsey and James Derzon (1998) reviewed the predictors at age 6–11 of serious or violent offending at age 15–25. The best explanatory predictors (i.e., predictors not measuring some aspect of the child's antisocial behavior) were antisocial parents, male gender, low socioeconomic status of the family, and psychological factors (daring, impulsiveness, poor concentration, etc.). Other moderately strong predictors were minority race, poor parent–child relations (poor supervision, discipline, low parental involvement, low parental warmth), other family characteristics (parent stress, family size, parental discord), antisocial peers, low intelligence, and low school achievement. In contrast, abusive parents and broken homes were relatively weak predictors. It is clear that some family factors are at least as important in the prediction of offending as are gender and race.

Reviewing these kinds of results reveals the bewildering variety of family constructs that have been studied, as well as the variety of methods used to classify them into categories. In this chapter, we group family factors into six categories: (1) criminal and antisocial parents and siblings; (2) large family size; (3) child-rearing methods (poor supervision, poor discipline, coldness and rejection, low parental involvement with the child); (4) abuse (physical or sexual) or neglect; (5) parental conflict and disrupted families; and (6) other parental features (young age, substance abuse, stress or depression, working mothers). These groupings are somewhat arbitrary and reflect the organization of topics of investigation within the field. For example, harsh discipline is usually studied along with poor supervision, but, at the extreme, it could shade into physical abuse. Physical neglect is usually grouped with physical abuse, but of course it usually coincides with emotional neglect (cold and rejecting parents).

Crime Runs in Families

Criminal and antisocial parents tend to have delinquent and antisocial children, as shown in the classic longitudinal surveys by Joan McCord (1977) in Boston and Lee Robins (1979) in St. Louis. The most extensive research on the concentration of offending in families was carried out in the Cambridge Study. Having a convicted father, mother, brother, or sister predicted a boy's own convictions, and all four relatives were independently important as predictors (Farrington, Barnes, and Lambert, 1996). For example, 63% of boys with convicted fathers were themselves convicted, compared with 30% of the remainder. Same-sex relationships were stronger than opposite-sex relationships, and older siblings were stronger predictors than younger siblings. Only 6% of the families accounted for half of all the convictions of all family members.

Similar results were obtained in the Pittsburgh Youth Study. Arrests of fathers, mothers, brothers, sisters, uncles, aunts, grandfathers, and grandmothers all predicted the boy's own delinquency (Farrington, Jolliffe, Loeber, Stouthamer-Loeber, and Kalb, 2001). The most important relative was the father; arrests of the father predicted the boy's delinquency independently of all other arrested relatives. Only 8% of families accounted for 43% of arrested family members.

In the Cambridge Study, having a convicted parent or a delinquent older sibling by the tenth birthday were consistently among the best age 8–10 predictors of the boy's later offending and antisocial behavior. Apart from behavioral measures such as troublesomeness and daring, these were the strongest predictors of juvenile convictions (Farrington, 1992b). Having a convicted parent or a delinquent older sibling were also the best predictors, after poor parental supervision, of juvenile self-reported delinquency.

There are six possible explanations (which are not mutually exclusive) for why offending tends to be concentrated in certain families and transmitted from one generation to the next (Farrington et al., 2001). First, there may be intergenerational continuities in exposure to multiple risk factors. For example, each successive generation may be entrapped in poverty, may have disrupted family lives, may have single and teenage parenting, and may live in the most deprived neighborhoods. Parents who use physical punishment may produce children who use similar punitive methods when they grow up, as indeed Leonard Eron, Rowell Huesmann, and Armando Zelli (1991) found in New York state. One of the main conclusions of the Cambridge Study is that a constellation of family background features (including poverty, large family size, parental disharmony, poor child-rearing, and parental criminality) leads to a constellation of antisocial features when children grow up, among which criminality is one element (West and Farrington, 1977). According to this explanation, the intergenerational transmission of offending is part of a larger cycle of deprivation and antisocial behavior.

A second explanation focuses on assortative mating; female offenders tend to cohabit with or marry male offenders. Children with two criminal parents are disproportionally antisocial (West and Farrington, 1977). There are two main classes of reasons why similar people tend to get married, cohabit, or become sexual partners (Rowe and Farrington, 1997). The first is called "social homogamy." Convicted people tend to choose each other as mates because of physical and social proximity; they meet each other in the same schools, neighborhoods, clubs, pubs, and so on. The second process is called "phenotypic assortment." People examine each other's personality and behavior and choose partners who are similar to themselves. In the Dunedin study in New Zealand, Robert Krueger and his colleagues (1998) found that sexual partners tended to be similar in their self-reported antisocial behavior.

The third explanation focuses on direct and mutual influences of family members on each other. For example, perhaps younger male siblings tend to imitate the antisocial behavior of older male siblings, or perhaps older siblings encourage younger ones to be antisocial. There is considerable sibling resemblance in delinquency (Lauritsen, 1993). In the Cambridge Study, co-offending by brothers was surprisingly common; about 20% of boys who had brothers close to them in age were convicted for a crime committed with their brother (Reiss and Farrington, 1991, p. 386). However, intergenerational mutual influences on offending seem less plausible, since co-offending by parents with their children was very uncommon in the Cambridge Study. There was no evidence that parents directly encouraged their children to commit crimes or taught them criminal techniques; on the contrary, a criminal father usually disapproved of his son's offending (West and Farrington, 1977).

A fourth explanation suggests that the effect of a criminal parent on a child's offending is mediated by environmental mechanisms. In the Pittsburgh Youth Study, it was suggested that arrested fathers tended to have delinquent sons because they tended to impregnate young women, to live in bad neighborhoods, and to use child-rearing methods that did not develop a strong conscience in their children (Farrington et al., 2001). In the Cambridge Study, Donald West and David Farrington (1977) suggested that poor parental supervision was one link in the chain between criminal fathers and delinquent sons, and Carolyn Smith and David Farrington (2004) showed that authoritarian parenting and parental conflict were mediating variables between parental antisocial behavior and child conduct problems. In the Glueck study in Boston, Robert Sampson and John Laub (1993) found that maternal and paternal deviance (criminality or alcoholism) did not predict a boy's delinquency after controlling for family factors such as poor supervision, harsh or erratic discipline, parental rejection, low attachment, and large family size.

A fifth explanation suggests that the effect of a criminal parent on a child's offending is mediated by genetic mechanisms. In agreement with this, twin studies show that identical twins are more concordant in their offending than are fraternal twins (Raine, 1993). However, an objection to these kinds of twin studies is that the greater behavioral similarity of the identical twins could reflect their greater environmental similarity.

Also in agreement with genetic mechanisms, adoption studies show that the offending of adopted children is significantly related to the offending of their biological parents (Brennan Mednick, and Mednick, 1993). However, an objection to adoption studies is that some children may have had contact with their biological parents, so again it is difficult to dismiss an environmental explanation of this finding. In a more convincing design comparing the concordance of identical twins reared together and identical twins reared apart, Minnesota psychologist William Grove and his colleagues (1990) found that heritability was 41% for childhood conduct disorder and 28% for adult antisocial personality disorder. This design shows that the intergenerational transmission of offending is partly attributable to genetic factors. An important question is how the genetic potential (genotype) interacts with the environment to produce the offending behavior (phenotype).

A sixth explanation suggests that criminal parents tend to have delinquent children because of official (police and court) bias against known criminal families, who also tend to be known to official agencies because of other social problems. At all levels of self-reported delinquency in the Cambridge Study, boys with convicted fathers were more likely to be convicted themselves than were boys with unconvicted fathers (West and Farrington, 1977). However, this was not the only explanation for the link between criminal fathers and delinquent sons, because boys with criminal fathers had higher self-reported delinquency scores and higher teacher and peer ratings of bad behavior. It is not clear which of these six explanations is the most important.

Large Family Size

Large family size (a large number of children in the family) is a relatively strong and highly replicable predictor of delinquency (Ellis, 1988; Fischer, 1984). It was similarly important in the Cambridge and Pittsburgh studies, even though families were on average smaller in Pittsburgh in the 1990s than in London in the 1960s (Farrington and Loeber, 1999). In the Cambridge Study, if a boy had four or more siblings by his tenth birthday, this doubled his risk of being convicted as a juvenile (West and Farrington, 1973). Large family size predicted self-reported delinquency as well as convictions (Farrington, 1992b). It was the most important independent predictor of convictions up to age 32 in a logistic regression analysis; 58% of boys from large families were convicted up to this age (Farrington, 1993a).

There are many possible reasons why a large number of siblings might increase the risk of a child's delinquency. Generally, as the number of children in a family increases, the amount of parental attention that can be given to each child decreases. In addition, as the number of children increases, the household tends to become more overcrowded, possibly leading to increases in frustration, irritation, and conflict. In the Cambridge Study, large family size did not predict delinquency for boys living in the least crowded conditions, with two or more rooms than there were children (West and Farrington, 1973). This suggests that household overcrowding might be an important intervening factor between large family size and delinquency.

David Brownfield and Ann Sorenson (1994) reviewed several possible explanations for the link between large families and delinquency, including those focusing on features of the parents (e.g., criminal parents, teenage parents), those focusing on parenting (e.g., poor supervision, disrupted families), and those focusing on economic deprivation or family stress. Another interesting theory suggested that the key factor was birth order: large families include more later-born children who tend to be more delinquent. On the basis of an analysis of self-reported delinquency in a Seattle survey, they concluded that the most plausible intervening causal mechanism was exposure to delinquent siblings. Consistent with social learning theory, large families contained more antisocial models.

Child-Rearing Methods

Many different types of child-rearing methods predict a child's delinquency. The most important dimensions of child-rearing are supervision or monitoring of children, discipline or parental reinforcement, warmth or coldness of emotional relationships, and parental involvement with children. Unlike family size, these constructs are difficult to measure, and there is some evidence that results differ according to methods of measurement. In their extensive review of parenting methods in relation to childhood antisocial behavior, Fred Rothbaum and John Weisz (1994) concluded that the strength of associations between parent and child measures was greater when parenting was measured by observation or interview than when it was measured using questionnaires.

Parental supervision refers to the degree of monitoring by parents of the child's activities, and their degree of watchfulness or vigilance. Of all these child-rearing methods, poor parental supervision is usually the strongest and most replicable predictor of offending (Farrington and Loeber, 1999; Smith and Stern, 1997). It typically predicts a doubled risk of delinquency. Many studies show that parents who do not know where their children are when they are out and parents who let their children roam the streets unsupervised from an early age tend to have delinquent children. For example, in the classic Cambridge-Somerville study, Joan McCord (1979) found that poor parental supervision in childhood was the best predictor of both violent and property crimes up to age 45.

Parental discipline refers to how parents react to a child's behavior. It is clear that harsh or punitive discipline (involving physical punishment) predicts a child's delinquency, as the review by Jaana Haapasalo and Elina Pokela (1999) showed. In a follow-up study of nearly 700 Nottingham, England, children, John and Elizabeth Newson (1989) found that physical punishment at ages 7 and 11 predicted later convictions; 40% of offenders had been smacked or beaten at age 11, compared with 14% of nonoffenders. In the Columbia County Study, Leonard Eron and his colleagues (1991) reported that parental punishment at age 8 predicted not only arrests for violence up to age 30 but also the severity of the man's punishment of his child at age 30, as well as his history of spouse assault.

Family factors may have different effects on African American and Caucasian children in the United States. It is clear that African American children are more likely to be physically punished, and that physical punishment is more related to antisocial behavior for Caucasian children than for African American children (see e.g., Deater-Deckard, Dodge, Bates, and Pettit, 1996; Kelley, Power, and Wimbush, 1992). In the Pittsburgh Youth Study, 21% of Caucasian boys who were physically punished (slapped or spanked) by their mothers were violent, compared with 8% of those not physically punished. In contrast, 32% of African American boys who were physically punished were violent, compared with 28% of those not physically punished (Farrington, Loeber, and Stouthamer-Loeber, 2003). It was suggested that physical punishment may have a different meaning in African American families. Specifically, in these families it may indicate warmth and concern for the child, whereas in Caucasian families it tends to be associated with a cold and rejecting parental attitude.

Erratic or inconsistent discipline also predicts delinquency (West and Farrington, 1973). This can involve either erratic discipline by one parent, sometimes turning a blind eye to bad behavior and sometimes punishing it severely, or inconsistency between two parents, with one parent being tolerant or indulgent and the other being harshly punitive. It is not clear whether unusually lax discipline predicts delinquency. Just as inappropriate methods of responding to bad behavior predict delinquency, low parental reinforcement (not praising) of good behavior is also a predictor (Farrington and Loeber, 1999).

Cold, rejecting parents tend to have delinquent children, as Joan McCord (1979) found almost 30 years ago in the Cambridge-Somerville study. More recently, she concluded that parental warmth could act as a protective factor against the effects of physical punishment (McCord, 1997). Whereas 51% of boys with cold physically punishing mothers were convicted in her study, only 21% of boys with warm physically punishing mothers were convicted, similar to the 23% of boys with warm nonpunitive mothers who were convicted. The father's warmth was also a protective factor against the father's physical punishment.

Low parental involvement in the child's activities predicts delinquency, as the Newsons found in their Nottingham survey (Lewis, Newson, and Newson, 1982). In the Cambridge Study, having a father who never joined in the boy's leisure activities doubled his risk of conviction

(West and Farrington, 1973), and this was the most important predictor of persistence in offending after age 21, as opposed to desistance (Farrington and Hawkins, 1991). Similarly, poor parent–child communication predicted delinquency in the Pittsburgh Youth Study (Farrington and Loeber, 1999), and low family cohesiveness was the most important predictor of violence in the Chicago Youth Development Study (Gorman-Smith, Tolan, Zelli, and Huesmann, 1996).

In psychology, there has been a great emphasis on parenting styles rather than parenting practices. Diana Baumrind (1966) originally distinguished three broad styles: authoritarian, authoritative, and permissive. Briefly, authoritarian parents are controlling, punitive, demanding and rather cold; authoritative parents set firm rules but are also warm and supportive and allow the child some autonomy; and permissive parents are rather lax, nonpunitive, and warm. Authoritative and permissive parents have good communication with their children, negotiating, explaining, and being sensitive to the child's needs. While parenting styles are influential in psychology, largely due to the work of Laurence Steinberg and his colleagues (1992; see also Darling and Steinberg, 1993), they have rarely been investigated in criminological research. However, in the Cambridge Study it was found that having authoritarian parents was the second most important predictor (after hyperactivity/poor concentration) of convictions for violence (Farrington, 1994a).

Most explanations of the link between child-rearing methods and delinquency focus on social learning or attachment theories. Social learning theory suggests that children's behavior depends on parental rewards and punishments and on the models of behavior that parents represent (see e.g., Patterson, 1995). Children will tend to become delinquent if parents do not respond consistently and contingently to their antisocial behavior and if parents behave in an antisocial manner. Attachment theory was inspired by the work of the British psychiatrist John Bowlby (discussed later) and suggests that children who are not emotionally attached to warm, loving, and law-abiding parents will tend to become delinquent (see e.g., Carlson and Sroufe, 1995). The sociological equivalent of attachment theory is social bonding theory, which suggests that delinquency depends on the strength or weakness of a child's bond to society (see e.g., Catalano and Hawkins, 1996).

Another possibility is that the link between child-rearing methods and delinquency merely reflects the genetic transmission of offending, as the University of Arizona psychologist David Rowe (1994) has argued. This idea was tested in the Cambridge Study. The specific hypothesis was that child-rearing factors (supervision, discipline, and warmth/coldness) would not predict offending after controlling for parental criminality. This was confirmed in a structural equation modeling analysis but not in a regression analysis (Rowe and Farrington, 1997). Thus, genetic factors could explain only part of the link between child-rearing factors and delinquency.

Child Abuse and Neglect

Children who are physically abused or neglected tend to become offenders later in life (Malinosky-Rummell and Hansen, 1993). Cathy Widom (1989) carried out the most famous study of this in Indianapolis. She used court records to identify over 900 children who had been abused or neglected before age 11, and compared them with a control group matched on age, race, gender, elementary school class, and place of residence. A 20-year follow-up showed that the children who were abused or neglected were more likely to be arrested as juveniles and as adults than were the controls, and they were more likely to be arrested for juvenile violence (Maxfield and Widom, 1996). Child abuse predicted later violence after controlling for other predictors such as gender, ethnicity, and age, and predictability was greater for females than for males (Widom and White, 1997). Child sexual abuse, and child physical abuse and neglect, predicted adult arrests for sex crimes (Widom and Ames, 1994).

Similar results have been obtained in other studies. In the Cambridge-Somerville study, Joan McCord (1983) found that about half of the abused or neglected boys were convicted for serious crimes, became alcoholics or mentally ill, or died before age 35. In the Rochester Youth Development Study, Carolyn Smith and Terence Thornberry (1995) showed that recorded child maltreatment under age 12 (physical, sexual, or emotional abuse or neglect) predicted later self-reported and official delinquency. Furthermore, these results held up after controlling for gender, race, socioeconomic status, and family structure. Similarly, child abuse and neglect predicted later violence in the "Young Lawbreakers as Adults" project in Stockholm, Sweden (Lang, Klinteberg, and Alm, 2002).

Cathy Widom (1994) reviewed possible environmental causal mechanisms linking childhood victimization and later violence. First, childhood victimization may have immediate but long-lasting consequences (e.g., shaking may cause brain injury). Second, childhood victimization may cause bodily changes (e.g., desensitization to pain) that encourage later violence. Third, child abuse may lead to impulsive or dissociative copying styles that, in turn, lead to poor problem-solving skills or poor school performance. Fourth, victimization may cause changes in self-esteem or in social information-processing patterns that encourage later violence. Fifth, child abuse may lead to changed family environments (e.g., being placed in foster care) that have deleterious effects. Sixth, juvenile justice practices may label victims, isolate them from prosocial peers, and encourage them to associate with delinquent peers.

Numerous theories have been put forward to explain the link between child abuse and later offending. Timothy Brezina (1998) has described three of the main ones. Social learning theory suggests that children learn to adopt the abusive behavior patterns of their parents through imitation, modeling, and reinforcement. Attachment or social bonding theory proposes that child maltreatment results in low attachment to parents and hence to low self-control. Strain theory posits that negative treatment by others generates negative emotions such as anger and frustration, which in turn lead to a desire for revenge and increased aggression. Based on the Youth in Transition study, Brezina found limited support for all three theories.

Ronald Symons and his colleagues (1995) tested a fourth theory, namely, that the link between child abuse and offending was one aspect of the intergenerational transmission of antisocial behavior from parents to children. Their findings in Iowa were most concordant with this theory.

Lisabeth DiLalla and Irving Gottesman (1991) more specifically suggested that the link reflected the genetic transmission of violent behavior. It is clear that the importance of genetic factors needs to be estimated in future studies of the effects of child abuse.

Parental Conflict and Disrupted Families

John Bowlby (1951) popularized the theory that broken homes cause delinquency. He argued that mother love in infancy and childhood was just as important for mental health as were vitamins and proteins for physical health. He thought that it was essential that a child should experience a warm, loving, and continuous relationship with a mother figure. If a child suffered a prolonged period of maternal deprivation during the first five years of life, this would have irreversible negative effects, including becoming a cold "affectionless character" and a delinquent.

Most studies of broken homes have focused on the loss of the father rather than the mother, because the loss of a father is much more common. In general, it is found that children who are separated from a biological parent are more likely to offend than children from intact families. For example, in the Newcastle (England) Thousand Family Study, Israel Kolvin and his colleagues (1988b) discovered that boys who experienced divorce or separation in their first five years of life had a doubled risk of conviction up to age 32 (53% as opposed to 28%). In the Dunedin study in New Zealand, Bill Henry and his colleagues (1996) found that boys from single-parent families were particularly likely to be convicted.

Joan McCord (1982) in Boston carried out an innovative study of the relationship between homes broken by loss of the biological father and later serious offending by boys. She found that the prevalence of offending was high for boys from broken homes without affectionate mothers (62%) and for those from unbroken homes characterized by parental conflict (52%), irrespective of whether they had affectionate mothers. The prevalence of offending was low for those from unbroken homes without conflict (26%) and—importantly—equally low for boys from broken homes with affectionate mothers (22%). These results suggest that it might not be the broken home that is criminogenic but the parental conflict that often causes it. They also suggest that a loving mother might in some sense be able to compensate for the loss of a father.

The importance of the cause of the broken home was also shown by Michael Wadsworth (1979) in the National Survey of Health and Development (UK). Illegitimate children were excluded from this survey, so all the children began life with two married parents. Boys from homes broken by divorce or separation had an increased likelihood of being convicted or officially cautioned up to age 21 (27%), in comparison with those from homes broken by death of the mother (19%) or death of the father (14%) and with those from unbroken homes (14%). Homes broken while the boy was between birth and age 4 especially predicted delinquency, while homes broken while the boy was between ages 11 and 15 were not particularly criminogenic. Remarriage (which happened more often after divorce or separation than after death) was also associated with an increased risk of delinquency, suggesting an undesirable effect of stepparents. This undesirable effect was confirmed in research in Montreal by Linda Pagani and her colleagues (1998). The meta-analysis by Edward Wells and Joseph Rankin (1991) also shows that broken homes are more strongly related to delinquency when they are caused by parental separation or divorce rather than by death.

There is no doubt that parental conflict and interparental violence predict antisocial behavior by a child (see e.g., Buehler et al., 1997; Kolbo, Blakely, and Engleman, 1996). In the Christchurch (New Zealand) Health and Development Study, David Fergusson and John Horwood (1998) found that children who witnessed violence between their parents were more likely to commit both violent and property offenses according to their self-reports. The importance of witnessing father-initiated violence held up after controlling for other risk factors such as parental criminality, parental substance abuse, parental physical punishment, a young mother, and low family income. Parental conflict also predicted delinquency in both the Cambridge and Pittsburgh studies (Farrington and Loeber, 1999).

Much research suggests that frequent changes of parent figures predict offending by children. For example, in a longitudinal survey of a birth cohort of over 500 Copenhagen males, Birgitte Mednick, Robert Baker, and Linn Carothers (1990) found that divorce followed by changes in parent figures predicted the highest rate of offending by children (65%), compared with divorce followed by stability (42%) and no divorce (28%). In the Dunedin study in New Zealand, Bill Henry and his colleagues (1993) reported that both parental conflict and many changes of the child's primary caretaker predicted the child's antisocial behavior up to age 11. However, in the Christchurch study in New Zealand, David Fergusson, John Horwood, and Michael Lynskey (1992) showed that parental transitions in the absence of parental conflict did not predict an increased risk of the child offending. In addition, in the Oregon Youth Study, Deborah Capaldi and Gerald Patterson (1991) concluded that antisocial mothers caused parental transitions, which in turn caused child antisocial behavior. In the Woodlawn longitudinal study in Chicago, the diversity and fluidity of children's living arrangements were remarkable (see e.g., Hunter and Ensminger, 1992; Kellam, Ensminger, and Turner, 1977).

Explanations of the relationship between disrupted families and delinquency fall into three major classes. Trauma theories suggest that the loss of a parent has a damaging effect on a child, most commonly because of the effect on attachment to the parent. Life-course theories focus on separation as a sequence of stressful experiences, and on the effects of multiple stressors such as parental conflict, parental loss, reduced economic circumstances, changes in parent figures, and poor child-rearing methods. Selection theories argue that disrupted families produce delinquent children because of preexisting differences from other families in risk factors such as parental conflict, criminal or antisocial parents, low family income, or poor child-rearing methods.

Hypotheses derived from the three theories were tested in the Cambridge Study (Juby and Farrington, 2001). While boys from broken homes (permanently disrupted families) were more delinquent than boys from intact homes, they were not more delinquent than boys from intact high conflict families. Interestingly, this result was replicated in Switzerland (Haas, Farrington, Killias, and Sattar, 2004). Overall, the most important factor was the postdisruption trajectory. Boys who remained with their mothers after the separation had the same delinquency rate as boys from intact low-conflict families. Boys who remained with their fathers, with relatives, or with others (e.g., foster parents) had high delinquency rates. It was concluded that the results favored life-course theories rather than trauma or selection theories.

Other Parental Features

Numerous other parental features predict delinquency and antisocial behavior of children. For example, early child-bearing or teenage pregnancy is a risk factor. Merry Morash and Lila Rucker (1989) analyzed results from four surveys in the United States and England (including the Cambridge Study) and found that teenage mothers were associated with low-income families, welfare support, and absent biological fathers, that they used poor child-rearing methods, and that their children were characterized by low school attainment and delinquency. However, the presence of the biological father mitigated many of these adverse factors and generally seemed to have a protective effect. Similarly, a large-scale study in Washington state showed that children of teenage or unmarried mothers had a significantly increased risk of offending (Conseur, Rivara, Barnoski, and Emanuel, 1997). Boys born to unmarried mothers aged 17 or less had an elevenfold increased risk of chronic offending, compared to boys born to married mothers aged 20 or more.

In the Cambridge and Pittsburgh studies, the age of the mother at her first birth was only a moderate predictor of the boy's later delinquency (Farrington and Loeber, 1999). In the Cambridge Study, for example, 27% of sons of teenage mothers were convicted as juveniles, compared with 18% of the remainder. More detailed analyses in this study showed that teenage mothers who went on to have large numbers of children were especially likely to have convicted children (Nagin, Pogarsky, and Farrington, 1997). It was concluded that the results were concordant with a diminished resources theory: the offspring of adolescent mothers were more crime prone because they lacked not only economic resources but also personal resources such as attention and supervision. Of course, it must be remembered that the age of the mother is highly correlated with the age of the father; having a young father may be just as important as having a young mother. In addition, since juvenile delinquency predicts causing an early pregnancy (Smith et al., 2000), the link between teenage parents and child delinquency may be one aspect of the link between criminal parents and delinquent children.

Recently, researchers have investigated factors that might mediate the link between young mothers and child delinquency. In the Dunedin study, Sara Jaffee and her colleagues (2001) concluded that the link between teenage mothers and violent children was mediated by maternal characteristics (e.g., intelligence, criminality) and family factors (e.g., harsh discipline, family size, disrupted families). In the Rochester Youth Development Study, Greg Pogarsky, Alan Lizotte, and Terence Thornberry (2003) found that the most important mediating factor was the number of parental transitions (frequent changes in care-givers). Interestingly, the link between young mothers and child delinquency was stronger for white and Hispanic families than for African American families. Pogarsky and his colleagues suggested that early child-bearing was less harmful when it was more common.

Parents' substance use predicts delinquency of children, as found in the Pittsburgh Youth Study (Loeber et al., 1998a). Smoking by the mother during pregnancy is a particularly important risk factor. The Northern Finland Birth Cohort study showed that mothers' smoking during pregnancy doubled the risk of violent or persistent offending by their sons, after controlling for other biopsychosocial risk factors (Rasanen et al., 1999). When maternal smoking was combined with a teenage mother, a single-parent family, and an unwanted pregnancy, risks of offending increased tenfold. A Copenhagen birth cohort study by Patricia Brennan, Emily Grekin, and Sarnoff Mednick (1999) obtained comparable results.

In the Pittsburgh Youth Study, parental stress and parental depression were only moderate predictors of the boy's delinquency (Loeber et al., 1998a). Rand Conger, Gerald Patterson, and Xiaojia Ge (1995) carried out an interesting study of parental stress (caused by negative life events) and delinquency based on two surveys in Iowa and Oregon. They concluded that parental stress produced parental depression, which in turn caused poor discipline, which in turn caused childhood antisocial behavior.

In the days when working mothers were statistically uncommon, it was often argued that they caused delinquency, presumably because it was expected that they would supervise their children less well than would nonworking mothers. However, in the Cambridge Study, having a working mother was associated with a relatively low risk of delinquency, possibly because full-time working mothers tended to have higher incomes and smaller families (West and Farrington, 1973).

Key Methodological Issues

It is difficult to determine what are the precise causal mechanisms that link family factors—such as parental criminality, young mothers, family size, parental supervision, child abuse, or disrupted families—to the delinquency of children. This is because these factors tend to be related not only to each other but also to other risk factors for delinquency such as low family income, poor housing, impulsiveness, low intelligence, and low school attainment. Just as it is hard to know what are the key underlying family constructs, it is equally hard to know what are the key underlying constructs in other domains of life. It is important to investigate which family factors predict delinquency independently of other family factors, independently of genetic and biological factors, and independently of other factors (e.g., individual, peer, neighborhood, and socioeconomic). In the Oregon Youth Study, Lew Bank and Bert Burraston (2001) found that child maltreatment predicted arrests for violent crimes after controlling for unskilled discipline, academic performance, and deviant peers.

Another important question focuses on the interactions between family and other factors in the prediction of delinquency. There are many examples of interactions between family and biological factors. For example, Adrian Raine and his colleagues (1997, p. 5) found that maternal rejection interacted with birth complications in predicting violence in a large birth cohort of Copenhagen males. The prevalence of violence was only high when both maternal rejection and birth complications were present. Family factors are likely to have different effects on children of different ages (Frick, Christian, and Wootton, 1999). Similarly, family and other risk factors may have different effects on offending in different neighborhoods (Wikström and Loeber, 2000).

It might be expected that family factors would have different effects on boys and girls, since there are well-documented gender differences in child-rearing experiences. In particular, boys are more likely to receive physical punishment from parents (see e.g., Lytton and Romney, 1991; Smith and Brooks-Gunn, 1997). However, in their extensive review of gender differences in antisocial behavior, University of London psychologist Terrie Moffitt and her colleagues (2001) concluded that boys were more antisocial essentially because they were exposed to more risk factors or a higher level of risk. Family risk factors did not seem to have different effects on antisocial behavior for boys and girls. It might also be expected that family factors would have different effects at different ages, and in the Rochester Youth Development Study (in New York state), Terence Thornberry, Timothy Ireland, and Carolyn Smith (2001) found that maltreatment during adolescence was more strongly related to delinquency than maltreatment during childhood.

While family influences are usually investigated as risk factors for delinquency, it is important also to investigate their effects as protective factors. In the Pittsburgh Youth Study, good supervision (compared with average levels) predicted nondelinquency, just as poor supervision (compared with average levels) predicted delinquency (Stouthamer-Loeber et al., 1993). In the Newcastle Thousand Family Study, Israel Kolvin and his colleagues (1988a) studied high-risk boys (from deprived backgrounds) who nevertheless did not become offenders. The most important protective factors included good maternal care and good maternal health for children under age 5 and good parental supervision at ages 11 and 15.

It is important to investigate sequential effects of risk factors on offending. Several researchers have concluded that socioeconomic factors have an effect on offending through their effects on family factors (see e.g., Bor et al., 1997; Dodge, Pettit, and Bates, 1994; Larzelere and Patterson, 1990; Stern and Smith, 1995). In the Pittsburgh Youth Study, it was proposed that socioeconomic and neighborhood factors (e.g., poor housing) influenced family factors (e.g., poor supervision), which in turn influenced child factors (e.g., lack of guilt), which in turn influenced offending (Loeber et al., 1998a, p. 10). There may also be sequential effects of some family factors on others, for example, if young mothers tend to use poor child-rearing methods (see Conger, Patterson, and Ge, 1995). There may also be effects of family factors on other risk factors; for example, if antisocial parents tend to have low incomes and choose to live in poor neighborhoods.

Just as parental child-rearing methods influence characteristics of children, so child characteristics may influence parenting, as Hugh Lytton (1990) suggested. For example, an antisocial child may provoke more punishment from a parent than a well-behaved child. In the New York State Longitudinal Study, Patricia Cohen and Judith Brook (1995) found that there were reciprocal influences between parental punishment and child behavior disorder. Similarly, several researchers have concluded that there are reciprocal relationships between parental supervision and delinquency (e.g., Jang and Smith, 1997; Paternoster, 1988).

It is also important to investigate the cumulative effects of family risk factors (and indeed of all risk factors) on delinquency. Rex Forehand, Heather Biggar, and Beth Kotchik (1998) showed how the probability of conduct disorder and delinquency increased with the number of family risk factors. A logical implication of the clustering of risk factors is that boys with multiple risk factors should be studied. As mentioned in chapter 2, Rolf Loeber and his colleagues (1998b) investigated how multiple risk factors were related to multiple types of child problems (including delinquency, substance use, hyperactivity, and depression) in the Pittsburgh Youth Study. Relationships were general rather than specific. Many types of risk factors predicted many types of problems, and the number of risk factors predicted the number of problems, rather than specific risk factors predicting specific problems.

These results are in agreement with the hypothesis that delinquency is one element of a larger syndrome of antisocial behavior, hence that predictors of one type of offending (e.g., violence) are similar to predictors of another (e.g., theft). Nevertheless, it is still useful to search for specific relationships between types of family factors and types of antisocial behavior.

Conclusions

It is clear that many family factors predict offending, but less clear what are the causes or key underlying family dimensions that should be measured or targeted in prevention programs. The strongest predictor is usually criminal or antisocial parents. Other quite strong and replicable predictors are large family size, poor parental supervision, parental conflict, and disrupted families. In contrast, child abuse and young mothers are relatively weak predictors. The obvious practical implication is that family-based programs targeting family risk factors might prevent delinquency. We review these programs in chapter 8.

In the next chapter, we review socioeconomic, peer, school, and community risk and protective factors.

Socioeconomic, Peer, School, and Community Factors

5

This chapter first assesses the importance of socioeconomic factors as predictors of offending. It then reviews peer, school, and community influences. As before, we focus as much as possible on results obtained in prospective longitudinal surveys. Unfortunately, these topics have not been addressed very extensively in the large-scale surveys on which we are focusing.

Socioeconomic Deprivation

Classic delinquency theories assume that offenders disproportionately come from lower class social backgrounds, and aim to explain why this is so. For example, Albert Cohen (1955) proposed that lower class boys found it hard to succeed according to the middle-class standards of their school, partly because lower class parents tended not to teach their children to delay immediate gratification in favor of long-term goals. Consequently, lower class boys joined delinquent subcultures by whose standards they could succeed. Richard Cloward and Lloyd Ohlin (1960) argued that lower class children could not achieve universal goals of status and material wealth by legitimate means and consequently had to resort to illegitimate means to achieve them.

Unfortunately, as Terence Thornberry and Margaret Farnworth (1982) pointed out, the voluminous literature on the relationship between socioeconomic status (SES) and offending is characterized by inconsistencies and contradictions, and some reviewers have concluded that there is no relationship between SES and either self-reported or official offending (e.g., Hindelang, Hirschi, and Weis, 1981). British studies have reported more consistent links between low social class and offending. In the National Survey of Health and Development (UK), Michael Wadsworth (1979) found that the prevalence of official offending by males up to age 21 varied considerably according to the occupational prestige and educational background of their parents at age 11, from 2% in the highest category to 19% in the lowest.

Numerous indicators of SES were measured in the Cambridge Study, both for the boy's family of origin and for the boy himself as an adult, including occupational prestige, family income, housing, and employment instability. Most of the measures of occupational prestige were not significantly related to offending. However, low SES of the family when the boy was aged 8–10 significantly predicted his later self-reported, but not his official, delinquency. More consistently, low family income and poor housing predicted official and self-reported juvenile and adult offending (Farrington, 1992a, 1992b).

It was interesting that the peak age of offending, at 17–18, coincided with the peak age of affluence for many convicted males. In the Cambridge Study, convicted males tended to come from low-income families at age 8 and later tended to have low incomes themselves at age 32. However, at age 18, they were relatively well paid in comparison with nondelinquents. Whereas convicted delinquents might be working as unskilled laborers on building sites and getting the full adult wage for this job, nondelinquents might be in poorly paid jobs with prospects, such as bank clerks, or might still be students. These results show that the link between income and offending is quite complex.

Socioeconomic deprivation of parents is usually compared to offending by children. However, when the children grow up, their own socioeconomic deprivation can be related to their own offending. In the

Cambridge Study, official and self-reported delinquents tended to have unskilled manual jobs and an unstable job record at age 18. Just as an erratic work record of his father predicted the later offending of the Cambridge Study boy, an unstable job record of the boy at age 18 was one of the best independent predictors of his convictions between ages 21 and 25 (Farrington, 1986). Between ages 15 and 18, the Cambridge Study boys were convicted at a higher rate when they were unemployed than when they were employed (Farrington et al., 1986), suggesting that unemployment in some way causes crime, and conversely that employment may lead to desistance from offending. Since crimes involving material gain (e.g., theft, burglary, robbery) especially increased during periods of unemployment, it seems likely that financial need is an important link in the causal chain between unemployment and crime.

In general, coming from a low SES family predicts violence. For example, in the U.S. National Youth Survey, Delbert Elliott, David Huizinga, and Scott Menard (1989) found that the prevalences of self-reported felony assault and robbery were about twice as high for lower class youth as for middle-class youth. Similar results have been obtained for official violence in Project Metropolitan in Stockholm (Wikström, 1985), Project Metropolitan in Copenhagen (Hogh and Wolf, 1983), and the Dunedin Study in New Zealand (Henry, Caspi, Moffitt, and Silva, 1996). Interestingly, all three of these studies compared the SES of the family at the boy's birth, based on the father's occupation, with the boy's later violent crimes. The strongest predictor of official violence in the Pittsburgh Youth Study was family dependence on welfare benefits (Farrington, 1998b). Low SES predicted violence more strongly for Caucasians than for African Americans in this project (Farrington, Loeber, and Stouthamer-Loeber, 2003).

As mentioned in chapter 4, several researchers have suggested that the link between a low SES family and antisocial behavior is mediated by family socialization practices. For example, Richard Larzelere and Gerald Patterson (1990), in the Oregon Youth Study, concluded that the effect of SES on delinquency was entirely mediated by parent management skills. In other words, low SES predicted delinquency because low SES families used poor child-rearing practices. In the Christchurch Health and Development Study, David Fergusson, Nicola Swain-Campbell, and John Horwood (2004) reported that living in a low SES family between birth and age 6 predicted self-reported and official delinquency between ages 15 and 21. However, this association disappeared after controlling for family factors (physical punishment, maternal care, and parental changes), conduct problems, truancy, and deviant peers, suggesting that these may have been mediating factors.

Peer Influences

The reviews by Franklin Zimring (1981) and Albert Reiss (1988) show that delinquent acts tend to be committed in small groups (of two or three people, usually) rather than alone. Large gangs are comparatively unusual. In the Cambridge Study, the probability of committing offenses with others decreased steadily with age (Reiss and Farrington, 1991). Whereas the average crime before age 17 was committed with others, the average crime after age 17 was committed alone. Boys tended to commit their crimes with other boys similar in age and living close by.

The major problem of interpretation is whether young people are more likely to commit offenses while they are in groups than while they are alone, or whether the high prevalence of co-offending merely reflects the fact that whenever young people go out, they tend to go out in groups. Do peers tend to encourage and facilitate offending, or is it just that most kinds of activities outside the home (both delinquent and nondelinquent) tend to be committed in groups? Another possibility is that the commission of offenses encourages association with other delinquents, perhaps because "birds of a feather flock together" or because of the stigmatizing and isolating effects of court appearances and institutionalization. Terence Thornberry and his colleagues (1994) in the Rochester Youth Development Study and Delbert Elliott and Scott Menard (1996) in the U.S. National Youth Survey concluded that there were reciprocal effects, with delinquent peer bonding causing delinquency and delinquency causing association with delinquent peers.

Associating with delinquent friends at age 14 was an important independent predictor of convictions at the young adult ages in the Cambridge Study (Farrington, 1986). In addition, the recidivists at age 19 who stopped offending differed from those who persisted, in that the desisters were more likely to have stopped going around in a group of male friends. Furthermore, spontaneous comments by the youths indicated that withdrawal from the delinquent peer group was seen as an important influence on ceasing to offend (West and Farrington, 1977). Therefore, continuing to associate with delinquent friends may be a key factor in determining whether juvenile delinquents persist in offending as young adults or desist.

It is clear that young people increase their offending after joining a gang. In the Seattle Social Development Project, Sara Battin and her colleagues (1998) found this, and showed that gang membership predicted delinquency above and beyond having delinquent friends. In the Pittsburgh Youth Study, Rachel Gordon and her colleagues (2004) reported not only a substantial increase in drug selling, drug use, violence, and property crime after a boy joined a gang but also that the frequency of offending decreased to pre-gang levels after a boy left a gang. Terence Thornberry and his colleagues (2003) in the Rochester Youth Development Study and Uberto Gatti and his colleagues (2005) in the Montreal longitudinal-experimental study also found that young people offended more after joining a gang. Several of these studies contrasted the "selection" and "facilitation" hypotheses mentioned in chapter 1 and concluded that future gang members were more delinquent to start with but became even more delinquent after joining a gang. Several other studies have investigated risk factors for joining a gang (e.g., Hill, Howell, Hawkins, and Battin-Pearson, 1999; Howell and Egley, 2005).

As mentioned in chapter 2, in the Pittsburgh Youth Study, peer delinquency did not predict a boy's delinquency within individuals (unlike poor parental supervision), suggesting that it was a correlate of offending rather than a cause (Farrington et al., 2002a). In the Cambridge Study, boys particularly tended to offend with their brothers, and a delinquent older sibling predicted youthful convictions for violence.

Sibling resemblance in delinquency held after controlling for numerous family factors in an Australian longitudinal survey (Fagan and Najman, 2003).

There is no doubt that highly aggressive children tend to be rejected by most of their peers (Coie, Dodge, and Kupersmidt, 1990; Dodge et al., 2003). In the Oregon Youth Study, Sarah Nelson and Thomas Dishion (2004) found that peer rejection at age 9–10 significantly predicted adult antisocial behavior at age 23–24. Low popularity at age 8–10 was only a weak predictor of adolescent aggression and teenage violence in the Cambridge Study (Farrington, 1989), but it significantly predicted chronic offending (Farrington and West, 1993). John Coie and Shari Miller-Johnson (2001) argued that it was the boys who were both aggressive and rejected by their classmates who tended to become the self-reported and official offenders. In addition, poor relationships with siblings predicted later adult arrests in the Oregon Youth Study (Bank, Patterson, and Reid, 1996).

School Influences

It is clear that the prevalence of offending varies dramatically between different secondary schools, as Michael Power and his colleagues (1967) showed many years ago in London. Characteristics of high delinquency-rate schools are well known (Graham, 1988). For example, such schools have high levels of distrust between teachers and students, low commitment to school by students, and unclear and inconsistently enforced rules. What is far less clear is how much of the variation between schools should be attributed to differences in school organization, climate, and practices and how much to differences in the composition of the student body. Reviews of American research show that schools with clear, fair, and consistently enforced rules tend to have low rates of student misbehavior (Gottfredson, 2001; Herrenkohl, Hawkins, Chung, Hill, and Battin-Pearson, 2001).

In the Cambridge Study, the effects of secondary schools on offending were investigated by following boys from their primary schools to their secondary schools (Farrington, 1972). The best primary school predictor of juvenile offending was the rating of the boy's troublesomeness at age 8–10 by peers and teachers, showing the continuity in antisocial behavior. The secondary schools differed dramatically in their official offending rates, from one school with 21 court appearances per 100 boys per year to another where the corresponding figure was less than 1. Moreover, going to a high delinquency-rate secondary school was a significant predictor of later convictions (Farrington, 1993a).

It was, however, very noticeable that the most troublesome boys tended to go to the high delinquency-rate schools, while the least troublesome boys tended to go to the low delinquency-rate schools. Furthermore, it was clear that most of the variation between schools in their delinquency rates could be explained by differences in their intakes of troublesome boys. The secondary schools themselves had only a very small effect on the boys' offending.

The most famous study of school effects on offending was also carried out in London, by the child psychiatrist Michael Rutter and his colleagues (1979). They studied 12 comprehensive schools, and again found big differences in official delinquency rates between them. High delinquency-rate schools tended to have high truancy rates, low-ability pupils, and low-social-class parents. However, the differences between the schools in delinquency rates could not be entirely explained by differences in the social-class and verbal reasoning scores of the pupils at intake (age 11). Therefore, some aspect of the schools themselves or other, unmeasured factors must have caused these differences.

In trying to discover which aspects of schools might be encouraging or inhibiting offending, Rutter and his colleagues found that the main school factors that were associated with delinquency were a high amount of punishment and a low amount of praise given by teachers in class. Unfortunately, it is difficult to know whether much punishment and little praise are causes or consequences of antisocial school behavior, which in turn is probably linked to offending outside school. In regard to other outcome measures, Michael Rutter (1983) argued that an academic emphasis, good classroom management, the careful use of praise and punishment, and student participation were important features of successful schools.

In the New York State Longitudinal Study, Stephanie Kasen, Jim Johnson, and Patricia Cohen (1990) investigated the effects of different dimensions of school climate on changes in children's conduct problems over time. They found that high school conflict (between students and teachers, or between students and other students) predicted increases in conduct problems. In contrast, a high academic focus in schools (e.g., emphasizing homework, academic classes, and task orientation) predicted decreases in conduct problems and hence might be regarded as a protective factor.

Community Influences

Offending rates vary systematically with area of residence. For example, the classic studies by Clifford Shaw and Henry McKay (1969) in Chicago and other American cities showed that juvenile delinquency rates (based on where offenders lived) were highest in inner-city areas characterized by physical deterioration, neighborhood disorganization, and high residential mobility. Crime rates decreased as the distance from the inner-city center increased, in concentric rings. A large proportion of all offenders came from a small proportion of areas, which tended to be the most deprived.

Furthermore, the relatively high delinquency rates of inner-city areas persisted over time, despite the effect of successive waves of immigration and emigration of different national and ethnic groups in different areas. Shaw and McKay concluded that the delinquency-producing factors were inherent in the community. Areas had persistently high offending rates partly because of the cultural transmission of antisocial values and norms from one generation to the next and partly because of the ineffective socialization processes children were exposed to in deprived areas. Both of these were consequences of the social disorganization of an area, or the poor ability of local institutions to control the behavior of local residents (Bursik, 1988).

Later work has tended to cast doubt on the consistency of offending rates over time. Robert Bursik and Jim Webb (1982) tested Shaw and McKay's cultural transmission hypothesis using more recent data in Chicago and more sophisticated quantitative methods. They concluded that the ordering of area delinquency rates was not stable after 1950 but reflected demographic changes. Variations in delinquency rates in different areas were significantly correlated with variations in the percentage of nonwhite residents, the percentage of foreign-born whites, and the percentage of overcrowded households. The greatest increase in offending in an area occurred when African Americans moved from the minority to the majority, as indeed Clifford Jonassen (1949) and James Short (1969) had noticed earlier. These results suggested that Shaw and McKay's ideas, about community values that persisted irrespective of successive waves of immigration and emigration, were incorrect. It was necessary to take account both of the type of area and of characteristics of individuals living in the area.

Most recently, Robert Sampson, Stephen Raudenbush, and Felton Earls (1997) studied community influences on violence in the Project on Human Development in Chicago Neighborhoods. The most important community predictors were concentrated disadvantage (poverty, female-headed families, African Americans), immigrant concentration (Latinos, foreign-born persons), residential instability, and low levels of informal social control and social cohesion. They concluded that the "collective efficacy" of a neighborhood, or the willingness of residents to intervene to prevent antisocial behavior, might act as a protective factor against crime. In the Family and Community Health Study in Iowa and Georgia, Ronald Simons and his colleagues (2005) found that increases in collective efficacy were associated with increases in authoritative parenting, decreases in affiliation with delinquent peers, and decreases in delinquent behavior.

The Yale sociologist Albert Reiss (1986) pointed out that a key question was why crime rates of communities changed over time, and to what extent this was a function of changes in the communities or in the individuals living in them. Answering this question requires longitudinal research in which both communities and individuals are followed up. The best way of establishing the impact of the environment is to follow people who move from one area to another. For example, in the Cambridge Study, Stephen Osborn (1980) found that moving out of London led to a significant decrease in convictions and self-reported offending. This decrease may have occurred because moving out led to a breaking up of co-offending groups, or because there were fewer opportunities for crime outside London.

The most important pioneering UK study of communities and crime was carried out in Sheffield by John Baldwin, Anthony Bottoms, and Monica Walker (1976). This study was important because they measured not only where offenders lived (offender rates) but also where offenses were committed (offense rates). In general, the two were closely related, with the exception of the central business district, which had high offense rates but low offender rates (partly because few people lived there). Baldwin and his colleagues did not find anything in Sheffield like the concentric rings of Shaw and McKay. Instead, the key factor that influenced offender rates was the type of housing. Offender rates were lowest in owner-occupied areas and highest in areas of public housing or private renting.

More recently, Anthony Bottoms and Paul Wiles (2002) focused on explaining community crime careers, and especially why some public housing estates have relatively high crime rates for many years, while other ostensibly similar estates have relatively low crime rates for many years. They concluded that public housing allocation policies were largely responsible. In Sheffield, problematic tenants tended to be allocated to high-crime estates, partly because they tended to have friends and relatives already living there. In Seattle, David Weisburd and his colleagues (2004) studied trajectories of crime in different places. They concluded that, while there was general consistency in whether places had high or low crime rates, an overall drop in crime occurred because a small number of places had strongly declining crime trajectories over time.

Generally, people living in urban areas are more violent than those living in rural ones. In the U.S. National Youth Survey, Delbert Elliott,

David Huizinga, and Scott Menard (1989) found that the prevalence of self-reported felony assault and robbery was considerably higher among urban youth. Within urban areas, people living in high-crime neighborhoods are more violent than those living in low-crime neighborhoods. In the Rochester Youth Development Study, Terence Thornberry, David Huizinga, and Rolf Loeber (1995) reported that living in a high-crime neighborhood significantly predicted self-reported violence. Similarly, in the Pittsburgh Youth Study, living in a bad neighborhood (either rated by the mother or based on census measures of poverty, unemployment, and female-headed households) significantly predicted official and re-ported violence (Farrington, 1998b). In Pittsburgh, boys who lived in public housing had a high level of violence but not of property crimes (Ireland, Thornberry, and Loeber, 2003). Interestingly, violence in afflu-ent neighborhoods seemed to be predicted mainly by individual factors, whereas violence in disadvantaged neighborhoods seemed to be predicted mainly by social and contextual factors (Beyers, Loeber, Wikström, and Stouthamer-Loeber et al., 2001). In the Pittsburgh Youth Study, living in a bad neighborhood, low SES, and welfare dependency were among the factors that best predicted homicide offenders out of other offenders (Loeber et al., 2005).

It is clear that offenders disproportionately live in inner-city areas characterized by physical deterioration, neighborhood disorganization, and high residential mobility (Shaw and McKay, 1969). Observed neigh-borhood physical disorder correlated with neighborhood crime rates in Pittsburgh (Wei, Hipwell, Pardini, Beyers, and Loeber, 2006). However, it is difficult to determine how much the areas themselves influence an-tisocial behavior and how much it is merely the case that antisocial people tend to live in deprived areas (e.g., because of their poverty or public housing allocation policies).

Interestingly, both neighborhood researchers, such as Denise Gottfredson, R. McNeil, and Gary Gottfredson (1991), and developmen-tal researchers, such as Michael Rutter (1981), have argued that neigh-borhoods have only indirect effects on antisocial behavior via their effects on individuals and families. In the Chicago Youth Development Study,

Patrick Tolan, Deborah Gorman-Smith, and David Henry (2003) concluded that the relationship between community structural characteristics (concentrated poverty, ethnic heterogeneity, economic resources, violent crime rate) and individual violence was mediated by parenting practices, gang membership, and peer violence.

In the Pittsburgh Youth Study, Per-Olof Wikström and Rolf Loeber (2000) found an interesting interaction between types of people and types of areas. Six individual, family, peer, and school variables were trichotomized into risk, middle, or protective scores and added up. Boys with the highest risk scores tended to be delinquent, irrespective of the type of area in which they were living. However, boys with high protective scores or balanced risk and protective scores were more likely to be delinquent if they were living in disadvantaged public housing areas. Hence the area risk was most important when other risks were not high.

Clearly, there is an interaction between individuals and the communities in which they live. Some aspect of an inner-city neighborhood may be conducive to offending, perhaps because the inner city leads to a breakdown of community ties or neighborhood patterns of mutual support, or perhaps because the high population density produces tension, frustration, or anonymity. There may be many interrelated factors. As Albert Reiss (1986) argued, high-crime-rate areas often have a high concentration of single-parent, female-headed households with low incomes, living in low-cost, poor housing. The weakened parental control in these families—partly caused by the fact that the mother has to work and leave her children largely unsupervised—means that the children tend to congregate on the streets. In consequence, they are influenced by a peer subculture that often encourages and reinforces offending. This interaction of individual, family, peer, and neighborhood factors may be the rule rather than the exception.

Conclusions

Offenders disproportionately come from deprived families, tend to have friends who are also delinquents, tend to attend high delinquency-rate schools, and tend to live in deprived areas. All these adversities tend to be associated with the individual and family adversities we described in the previous two chapters. It is very difficult to disentangle all these interrelationships and draw conclusions about which risk factors are causal. Nevertheless, in the present state of knowledge, it is reasonable to target all these types of risk factors in early prevention programs. Such programs might seek to improve a family's economic status, discourage a child's association with delinquent peers or encourage association with prosocial peers, change the climate of schools, or improve the social cohesiveness of areas.

In the next chapter, we discuss risk-focused prevention.

PART II

PREVENTION IN THE EARLY YEARS

Understanding Risk-Focused Prevention

There are many possible ways of classifying crime prevention programs. One of the first efforts drew upon the public health approach to preventing diseases and injuries (Brantingham and Faust, 1976; Moore, 1995). This divides crime prevention activities into three categories: primary, secondary, and tertiary. Primary prevention involves measures targeted on the whole community to prevent the onset of delinquency. Secondary prevention focuses on intervening with children and youth who are at risk for becoming offenders because of the presence of one or more risk factors. Tertiary prevention involves measures targeted on offenders.

In a similar three-part classification scheme, largely drawn from psychology, prevention methods can be viewed as universal, selected, or indicated. A universal program is one applied to a complete population, as in primary prevention. A selective program is one applied to a high-risk subgroup of the population, as in secondary prevention. An indicated program is one applied to identified cases such as offenders. Unfortunately, these terms are not used consistently in the literature. In particular, for a program targeted on children living in a high-crime area, Gail Wasserman and Laurie Miller (1998, p. 199) would term this "universal," whereas Richard Tremblay and Wendy Craig (1995, p. 167) would term this "selective." Wasserman and Miller restrict the term "selective" to programs where children are individually identified as high risk (e.g., possessing some combination of risk factors). Thus, in Wasserman and Miller's terms, targeting children according to family poverty would constitute a selective program but targeting children according to area-level poverty would not.

We prefer the Tremblay and Craig usage, since children living in low-income areas are just as clearly a high-risk group as are children living in low-income families; we have defined all these types of prevention programs as "selective," restricting the term "universal" to programs targeted at fairly representative samples of the general population. Actually, there are very few truly universal programs in this sense. Most prevention programs aim to reserve scarce public resources for children and families in greatest need, and these inevitably tend to be the high-risk children and families.

Another influential classification scheme distinguishes four major prevention strategies (Tonry and Farrington, 1995). Developmental prevention refers to interventions designed to prevent the development of criminal potential in individuals, especially those that target risk and protective factors discovered in studies of human development (Tremblay and Craig, 1995). Community prevention refers to interventions designed to change the social conditions and institutions (e.g., families, peers, social norms, clubs, organizations) that influence offending in residential communities (Hope, 1995). Situational prevention refers to interventions designed to prevent the occurrence of crimes by reducing opportunities for offending and increasing its risk and difficulty (Clarke, 1995). Criminal justice prevention refers to traditional deterrent, incapacitative, and rehabilitative strategies that law enforcement and criminal justice system agencies operate. The term "risk-focused prevention" is now used more generally than "developmental prevention," but the two terms have essentially the same meaning.

Risk-Focused Prevention

Beginning in the 1990s, there has been an enormous increase in the influence of the concept of risk-focused prevention in criminology. The basic idea of this approach is very simple: identify the key risk factors for offending and implement prevention methods designed to counteract them. There is often a related attempt to identify key protective factors against offending and to implement prevention methods designed to enhance them. Typically, longitudinal surveys provide knowledge about risk and protective factors, and experimental and quasi-experimental studies are used to evaluate the impact of prevention and intervention programs. Thus, risk-focused prevention links explanation and prevention, links fundamental and applied research, and links scholars, policymakers, and practitioners.

Pioneers such as David Hawkins and Richard Catalano (1992) from Seattle imported risk-focused prevention into criminology from medicine and public health. This approach has been used successfully for many years to tackle illnesses such as cancer and heart disease. For example, the identified risk factors for heart disease include smoking, a fatty diet, and lack of exercise. These can be tackled by encouraging people to stop smoking, to have a healthier, low-fat diet, and to exercise more. In the public health classification scheme we noted, risk-focused prevention spans primary and secondary prevention.

Typically, the effectiveness of risk-focused prevention in the medical field is evaluated using the "gold standard" of randomized controlled trials, and there has been increasing emphasis in medicine on cost-benefit analyses of interventions. Not surprisingly, therefore, there has been a similar emphasis in criminology in recent years on high-quality evaluations and on cost-benefit analyses (see Farrington and Welsh, in press; Sherman, Farrington, Welsh, and MacKenzie, 2002; Welsh, Farrington, and Sherman, 2001). We discuss these issues in more detail below.

Risk factors tend to be similar for many different outcomes, including violent and nonviolent offending, mental health problems, alcohol and drug problems, school failure, and unemployment. Therefore, a prevention program that succeeds in reducing a risk factor for offending will, in all probability, have wide-ranging benefits in reducing other types of social problems as well. As noted in chapter 2, because of the interest in linking risk factors with prevention programs, risk factors that cannot be changed feasibly in such programs (e.g., age, gender, race, biological factors) are excluded from consideration, except to the extent that they act as moderators (e.g., if the effect of a risk factor is different for males and females).

One methodological problem is that most knowledge about risk factors is based on variation between individuals, whereas prevention requires variation (change) within individuals over time. It is not always clear that findings within individuals would be the same as findings between individuals (see chapter 2). To take a specific example, unemployment is a risk factor for offending between individuals, since unemployed people are more likely than employed people to be offenders (West and Farrington, 1977). However, unemployment is also a risk factor for offending within individuals, since people are more likely to offend during their periods of unemployment than their periods of employment (Farrington et al., 1986). The within-individual finding has a much clearer implication for prevention, namely, that a reduction in unemployment should lead to a reduction in offending. This is because it is much easier to demonstrate that a risk factor is a cause in within-individual research. Since the same individuals are followed up over time, many extraneous influences on offending stay constant (Farrington, 1988).

A major problem of risk-focused prevention is to establish which risk factors are causes and which are merely markers or correlated with causes (Farrington, 2000). It is also desirable to establish mediators (intervening causal processes) between risk factors and outcomes (Baron and Kenny, 1986). Ideally, interventions should be targeted on risk factors that are causes; interventions targeted on risk factors that are markers will not necessarily lead to any decrease in offending. The difficulty of establishing causes, and the co-occurrence of risk factors, encourages the blunderbuss approach: interventions that target multiple risk factors. However, there is also evidence that integrated or multimodal intervention packages are more effective than interventions that target only a single risk factor (Tremblay and Craig, 1995; Wasserman and Miller, 1998).

In principle, a great deal can be learned about causes from the results of intervention experiments, to the extent that the experiments establish the impact of targeting each risk factor separately (Robins, 1992). For example, if an intervention that improves school success leads to a decrease in delinquency, this might be good evidence that school failure has a causal impact on delinquency (assuming that alternative hypotheses can be eliminated). Ideally, intervention experiments need to be designed to test causal hypotheses, as well as a particular intervention technology. However, there is a clear tension between maximizing the effectiveness of an intervention (which encourages a multiple component approach) and assessing the effectiveness of each element and hence drawing conclusions about causes (which requires disentangling of the different components).

Risk-focused prevention includes protective factors. Ideally, risk and protective factors should be identified and then risk factors should be reduced while protective factors are enhanced. However, as we discussed in chapter 2, both the definition and existence of protective factors are controversial. More research is needed to identify protective factors and to base interventions on this knowledge.

Other Key Issues

Assessing Research Evidence

As discussed in chapter 1, it is crucial to use the highest quality evaluation designs to investigate the effects of early prevention programs. It is also important that the most rigorous methods be used to assess or review the available evaluation research evidence. Efforts to assess whether a particular prevention strategy (e.g., developmental, community), intervention modality (e.g., parent training, home visitation), or some other grouping of prevention programs is effective in preventing delinquency or later criminal offending can take many different forms. The systematic review and the meta-analytic review (or meta-analysis) are the most rigorous methods for assessing effectiveness (Welsh and Farrington,

2006).[1] These are the sources we rely on most in our reviews of the effectiveness of early prevention programs in chapters 7–9.

Systematic Review

According to Byron Johnson and his colleagues (2000, p. 35), systematic reviews "essentially take an epidemiological look at the methodology and results sections of a specific population of studies to reach a research-based consensus on a given study topic." Such reviews use rigorous methods for locating, appraising, and synthesizing evidence from prior evaluation studies, and they are reported with the same level of detail that characterizes high-quality reports of original research. Some of the key features of a systematic review include the following.

- Eligibility criteria are explicit. The reviewers specify in detail why they included certain studies and rejected others. What was the minimum level of methodological quality? Did they consider only a particular type of evaluation design, such as randomized experiments?[2] Did the studies have to include a certain type of participant, such as children or adults? What types of interventions were included? What kinds of outcome data had to be reported in the studies? In the final report, the reviewers should explicitly present all the criteria or rules used in selecting eligible studies.
- The search for studies is designed to reduce potential bias. Because there are many possible ways bias can compromise the results of a review, reviewers must explicitly state how they conducted their search of potentially relevant studies to reduce such bias. How did they try to locate studies reported outside scientific journals? How did they try to locate studies reported in foreign languages? All bibliographic databases that were searched should be made explicit so that potential gaps in coverage can be identified.

- Each study is screened according to eligibility criteria, with exclusions justified. The searches will undoubtedly locate many citations and abstracts to potentially relevant studies. Each of the reports of these potentially relevant studies must be screened to determine if the study meets the eligibility criteria for the review. A full listing of all excluded studies and the justifications for exclusion should be made available to readers.
- The most complete data possible are assembled. The systematic reviewer will generally try to obtain all relevant evaluations meeting the eligibility criteria. In addition, all data relevant to the objectives of the review should be carefully extracted from each eligible report and coded and computerized. Sometimes original study documents lack important information. When possible, the systematic reviewer will attempt to obtain these data from the authors of the original report.
- Quantitative techniques are used, when appropriate and possible, in analyzing results. A systematic review may or may not include a meta-analysis (discussed later). The use of meta-analysis may not be appropriate due to a small number of studies, heterogeneity across studies, or different units of analysis of the studies (i.e., a mix of area- and individual-based studies). But when suitable, meta-analyses should be conducted as part of systematic reviews.
- The report is structured and detailed. The final report of a systematic review is structured and detailed so that the reader can understand each phase of the research, the decisions that were made, and the conclusions that were reached.

As noted by Anthony Petrosino and his colleagues (2001, p. 20), "the foremost advantage of systematic reviews is that when done well and with full integrity, they provide the most reliable and comprehensive statement about what works." Systematic reviews are not, however, without their limitations, although these limitations or challenges appear to be more closely linked with administrative and dissemination issues, such as getting them in the hands of decision-makers (see Petrosino, Boruch, Soydan, Duggan, and Sanchez-Mecca, 2001). Some of the challenges involving the "substance" of systematic reviews include the transparency of the process (e.g., the need to present the reasons why studies were included or excluded) and the need to reconcile differences in coding of study characteristics and outcomes by multiple researchers (e.g., by measuring interrater reliability).

Meta-Analytic Review

A meta-analysis addresses the question: How well does the program work? It involves the statistical or quantitative analysis of the results of prior research studies (Lipsey and Wilson, 2001). Since it involves the statistical summary of data (in particular, effect sizes), it requires a reasonable number of intervention studies that are sufficiently similar to be grouped together; there may be little point in reporting an average effect size based on a very small number of studies. Nevertheless, quantitative methods can be very important in helping the reviewer determine the average effect of a particular intervention.

One major product of a meta-analysis is a weighted average effect size. For example, the percentage reduction in offending would be one simple effect size. In calculating the average, each effect size is weighted according to the sample size on which it is based, with larger studies having greater weights. There is usually also an attempt to investigate factors (moderators) that predict larger or smaller effect sizes in different studies. This is to establish whether an intervention works better in certain contexts and which features of the intervention are related to a successful outcome.

Some of the strengths of the meta-analytic review method include its transparent nature—the explication of its methods and the studies involved—which makes it easily replicated by other researchers, its ability to handle a very large number of studies that may be overwhelming for other review methods, and the "statistical methods of meta-analysis help guard against interpreting the dispersion in results as meaningful when it can just as easily be explained as sampling error" (Wilson, 2001, p. 84). Limitations of meta-analysis include, on a practical side, its time-consuming nature and its inability to synthesize "complex patterns of effects found in individual studies" (p. 84). Another problem concerns how to select effect sizes for analysis in studies that measure many different outcomes.

Assessing Value for Money

A fair and reliable assessment of a prevention program's value for money is the purview of economic analysis. An economic analysis (e.g., cost-benefit analysis, cost-effectiveness analysis) can be described as a policy tool that allows choices to be made between alternative uses of resources or alternative distributions of services (Knapp, 1997, p. 11). Many criteria are used in economic analysis. The most common is efficiency, or value for money (achieving maximum outcomes from minimum inputs). However, the specific focus on economic efficiency is not meant to imply that early prevention programs should be continued only if their benefits outweigh their costs. There are many important noneconomic criteria on which these programs should be judged (e.g., equity in the distribution of services).

We report monetary costs and benefits (where available) in our reviews of early prevention programs in the next three chapters. Of the two main techniques of economic analysis—cost-benefit and cost-effectiveness analysis—only cost-benefit analysis allows for an assessment of both costs and benefits. A cost-effectiveness analysis can be referred to as an incomplete cost-benefit analysis. This is because no attempt is made to estimate the monetary value of program effects (benefits or disbenefits), only resources used (costs). For example, a cost-effectiveness analysis might specify how many crimes were prevented per $1,000 spent on a program. Another way to think about how cost-benefit and cost-effectiveness analysis differ is that "cost-effectiveness analysis may help one decide among competing program models, but it cannot show that the total effect was worth the cost of the program" (Weinrott, Jones, and Howard, 1982, p. 179), unlike cost-benefit analysis.

A cost-benefit analysis is a step-by-step process that follows a standard set of procedures. There are six main steps: (1) define the scope of the analysis; (2) obtain estimates of program effects; (3) estimate the monetary value of costs and benefits; (4) calculate present value and assess profitability; (5) describe the distribution of costs and benefits (an assessment of who gains and who loses, e.g., program participant, government/taxpayer, crime victim); and (6) conduct sensitivity analyses by varying the different assumptions made (Barnett, 1993, pp. 143–148).[3]

Two other key features of economic analysis require brief mention. First, an economic analysis is an extension of an outcome or impact evaluation, and is only as defensible as the evaluation it is based on. David Weimer and Lee Friedman (1979, p. 264) recommended that economic analyses be limited to programs that have been evaluated with an "experimental or strong quasi-experimental design." As mentioned, the most convincing method of evaluating early programs to prevent delinquency and later offending, and crime prevention programs in general, is to conduct a randomized experiment (see chapter 1).

Second, many perspectives can be taken in measuring program costs and benefits. Some cost-benefit analyses adopt a society-wide perspective that includes the major parties that can receive benefits or incur costs, such as the government or taxpayer, crime victim, and program participant. Other analyses may take a more narrow view, focusing on one or two of these parties. The decision about which perspective to take has important implications for evaluating the program, particularly if it is being funded by public money. That is, if conclusions are to be drawn about the monetary benefits or costs of a program to the public, the benefits or costs must be those that the public will either receive or incur. In reporting on the cost-benefit findings of the studies we review in the next three chapters, we have used, as far as possible, the middle-of-the-road approach—focusing on the costs and benefits for the government or taxpayer and for crime victims.

Conclusions

There are many possible ways to classify programs to prevent delinquency and later offending. Important to this book is a focus on prevention programs that begin early in life and are made available to the whole population (primary or universal prevention) or are targeted at children and youth who are at risk for becoming offenders (secondary or selective prevention). Also important to this book is risk-focused prevention, which serves as the leading conceptual, scientific, and practical approach to implementing more efficacious programs to save children from a life of crime.

As noted in chapter 1, the basic idea of risk-focused prevention is straightforward: identify the key risk factors for offending and implement effective prevention methods designed to counteract them. There should also be an attempt to identify key protective factors against offending and to implement effective prevention methods designed to enhance them. As simple as this approach to prevention may be, it very much represents the basic building block of evidence-based prevention. While risk-focused prevention makes clear that effective prevention methods (as demonstrated by the highest quality experimental or quasi-experimental evaluation designs) should be used to target scientifically identified risk factors, what is most important is that the accumulated scientific research evidence on effectiveness (and where possible economic efficiency) from systematic reviews is utilized.

In short, it may be enough for a community or government agency to implement an effective prevention method, as demonstrated through one or two experimental tests, but it is far more powerful to base this decision on the conclusions from a systematic review based on the totality of the highest quality available scientific evidence. In this regard, risk-focused prevention may be better thought of as risk-focused, evidence-based prevention.

In the next three chapters, we explore this evidence-based dimension of risk-focused prevention in an effort to identify early interventions that are effective in preventing delinquency and later offending, as organized around the three main categories of risk and protective factors: individual; family; and peer, school, and community. These three chapters follow a similar organization; they review evidence on the effectiveness of various intervention modalities—by drawing on the most rigorous reviews of the evaluation research—and they describe leading programs.

Individual Prevention 7

I ndividual-based prevention programs target risk factors for delinquency and later offending that are found within the individual. As we discussed in chapter 3, some of these risk factors include low intelligence and attainment, low empathy, impulsivity, and hyperactivity. These programs are targeted on the child. As noted by Greg Duncan and Katherine Magnuson (2004, p. 94), "individual interventions focus directly on the person whose development is targeted, and can occur very early in life, as with intensive preschool education." This is distinguished from family-based interventions, which are directed at both the child and parent or caregiver (see chapter 8).

Early childhood prevention programs have wide appeal across a large spectrum of constituencies (Karoly et al., 1998). The reasons for the widespread support can be found in any number of areas, from developmental theory to prevention science to the welfare of children. These programs help society's most vulnerable members. They have as explicit aims the betterment of children's immediate learning and social and emotional competencies, as well as the improvement of children's success over the life-course. In addition, they are implemented at a time when children are most impressionable and hence receptive to intervention (Duncan and Magnuson, 2004). With a primary emphasis on improving school readiness, providing families in need with various other services, and reaching about half of all impoverished children (Currie, 2001), Head Start is considered the nation's most important early childhood program (Ripple and Zigler, 2003).

This chapter reviews the scientific evidence on what works to prevent delinquency and later criminal offending through individual-based interventions that are delivered in the early years of life.

Evidence on What Works

The most rigorous methods of systematic and meta-analytic reviews find that two main types of individual-based programs—preschool intellectual enrichment and child skills training—are generally effective in preventing delinquency or later criminal offending (Farrington and Welsh, 2003; Lösel and Beelmann, 2003, 2006). A number of narrative reviews and one comprehensive vote-counting review of experimental and high-quality quasi-experimental evaluations provide further support for this finding (Currie, 2001; Duncan and Magnuson, 2004; Farrington and Welsh, 2002; Welsh and Farrington, 2004).

Preschool Intellectual Enrichment

Preschool intellectual enrichment programs are generally targeted on the risk factors of low intelligence and attainment. As noted by Duncan and Magnuson (2004, p. 105), "Child-focused early-education intervention programs are designed to provide economically disadvantaged children with cognitively stimulating and enriching experiences that their parents are unlikely to provide at home." Improved cognitive skills, school readiness, and social and emotional development are the main goals of these programs (Currie, 2001). Some of the key features of these programs include the provision of the following (Duncan and Magnuson, 2004, pp. 105–106).

- Developmentally appropriate learning curricula
- A wide array of cognitive-based enriching activities

- Activities for parents, usually of a less intensive nature, so that they may be able to support the school experience at home

As part of a meta-analysis of the effects of a larger range of early interventions on antisocial behavior, delinquency, and later offending, we found that a group of interventions that included both daycare and preschool programs was highly effective (Farrington and Welsh, 2003).[1] The mean effect size of these programs was .259, corresponding to a significant 13% reduction in offending (e.g., from 50% in the control group to 37% in the experimental group). (See table 7.1.)[2] Compared to the other five types of early intervention, daycare and preschool programs were in the midrange level of effectiveness, with a slightly larger mean effect size than home visiting programs and a somewhat lower effect than parent management training or multisystemic therapy programs (see table 7.1).

If we remove the three daycare programs (because the main intervention is parent education rather than intellectual enrichment of the children; we review these family-based programs in chapter 8), the mean effect size of two preschool programs was .316, corresponding to a sig-

Table 7.1 Meta-Analysis Results of Early Interventions on Offending

Program type	Low CI	Mean ES	High CI	Fraction significant
Home visiting	.111	.235	.360	2/4
Daycare/preschool	.147	.259	.371	4/5
Parent management training	.274	.395	.517	5/10
School-based programs	−.014	.068	.149	3/7
Home/community programs with older children	.056	.181	.306	3/8
Multisystemic therapy	.281	.414	.548	2/6

Note: weighted means are given. CI = confidence interval; ES = effect size; fraction significant = proportion of significant ES ($p < .05$).

Source: Adapted from Farrington and Welsh (2003, p. 144, table 4).

nificant 16% reduction in offending. These two studies are the Perry Pre-school project (the follow-up at age 27) of Lawrence Schweinhart, Helen Barnes, and David Weikart (1993) and the Chicago Child-Parent Center program of Arthur Reynolds and his colleagues (2001).

It is, of course, less than adequate to assess the effectiveness of preschool intellectual enrichment (or any other intervention type) on the basis of just two studies. A later article by Farrington and Welsh (2005; see also Farrington and Welsh, in press) identified two other preschool intellec-tual enrichment programs with offending outcomes (both evaluated with randomized experimental designs): the Abecedarian program of Frances Campbell and her colleagues (2002) and another by Paulette Mills and her colleagues (2002). We calculated the effect sizes of these programs to be .27 and -.11, respectively. This corresponds roughly to a 14% reduction in offending for the Abecedarian program and an undesirable 6% increase in offending for the other preschool program. Combining the effect sizes of the four preschool programs yields a mean effect size of .266, which corresponds to a 13% reduction in offending in the experimental group compared to the control group. If we use the most recent evaluation of the Perry program when the participants were age 40 (Schweinhart et al., 2005; see below), the mean effect size of the four preschool programs drops slightly to .242, for about a 12% reduction in offending.

Duncan and Magnuson's (2004) review of preschool education pro-grams distinguished between "intensive efficacy interventions" (or re-search and demonstration projects) and "more policy-relevant, less intensive interventions" (or routine practice). Their coverage of the former group of preschool intellectual enrichment programs is similar to those in our foregoing meta-analysis, and they, too, find that these programs have long-term beneficial effects on children's criminal behav-ior (as well as on other outcomes). On the matter of less intensive pre-school education interventions like Head Start (see below), the authors found that the evidence was less clear about the ability of these programs to produce results similar to the intensive efficacy ones. However, they concluded that "the weight of the evidence to date indicates that these programs may also improve children's life courses" (p. 105).

Janet Currie, an economist at the University of California, Los Angeles, reviewed early childhood education programs, defined more broadly than preschool programs. She, too, distinguished between "small-scale model programs" (or research and demonstration projects) and "large-scale public programs" (or routine practice), with the former "typically funded at higher levels and run by more highly trained staff" (2001, p. 217). The findings of the routine practice programs, specifically Head Start, are relevant here. As in Duncan and Magnuson's (2004) review, Currie (2001) found that the evidence in support of favorable long-term effects (e.g., on offending) of Head Start was less than conclusive. She attributed this result mostly to a paucity of well-designed studies that have measured long-term effects.

Child Social Skills Training

Social skills training or social competence programs for children are generally targeted on the risk factors of impulsivity, low empathy, and self-centeredness. As noted by Carolyn Webster-Stratton and Ted Taylor, this type of individual-based program is designed to "directly teach children social, emotional, and cognitive competence by addressing appropriate social skills, effective problem-solving, anger management, and emotion language" (2001, p. 178). A typical program includes one or more of these elements and is highly structured, with a limited number of sessions, thus lasting for a relatively short period of time (Lösel and Beelmann, 2003).

The criminologists Friedrich Lösel and Andreas Beelmann (2006; see also Lösel and Beelmann, 2003) carried out a systematic review of the effects of child social skills training on antisocial behavior (including delinquency). The review included 55 randomized controlled experiments with 89 separate experimental-control-group comparisons. A meta-analysis found that almost half of the comparisons produced desirable results favoring the children who received the treatment compared to those who did not, while less than 1 out of 10 revealed undesirable results (i.e., the control group fared better than the treatment group). Control participants typically received nonintensive, basic services.

Mixed results were found for temporal effects of child social skills training on delinquency (see table 7.2). At immediate outcome or postintervention (defined as within 2 months after treatment) the smallest effect size was for delinquency, although the mean effect sizes for all outcomes favored the treatment condition. At later follow-up (defined as 3 months or more after treatment) delinquency was the only outcome that was significantly affected. The meta-analysis also found that the most effective social skills training programs used a cognitive-behavioral approach and were implemented with older children (13 years and over) and higher risk groups who were already exhibiting some behavioral problems. On the basis of their findings, Lösel and Beelmann (2006) concluded that child social skills training represents a "promising approach to crime prevention."

Successful Case Studies

We now describe the highest quality individual-based prevention programs that have been effective in reducing delinquency or later offend-

Table 7.2 Meta-Analysis Results of Child Skills Training

Outcome measure	Postintervention		Follow-up	
	d	n	d	n
Aggressive behavior	0.24*	52	0.17	16
Oppositional/disruptive behavior	0.30*	28	1.03	2
Delinquent behavior	0.18*	11	0.19*	4
Antisocial behavior (unspecified)	0.36*	22	0.70	4

Note: postintervention = all effect sizes measured within 2 months after treatment; follow-up = all effect sizes measured 3 months or more after treatment; d = weighted mean effect size; n = number of treatment–control group comparisons.

*Effect size differs significantly from zero.

Source: Adapted from Lösel and Beelmann (2006, p. 42, table 3).

ing. These programs have been organized into two types: preschool intellectual enrichment and child social skills training. The focus is on what the programs did to improve the life chances of children, their impact on delinquency or later offending (as well as other important outcomes), and, where possible, their social rate of return or monetary value to society.

Preschool Intellectual Enrichment

The most famous preschool intellectual enrichment program is the Perry Preschool project carried out in Ypsilanti, Michigan, by Lawrence Schweinhart and David Weikart (1980). This was essentially a Head Start program targeted on disadvantaged African American children. A sample of 123 children were allocated (approximately at random) to experimental and control groups. The experimental children attended a daily preschool program, backed up by weekly home visits, usually lasting 2 years (covering ages 3–4). The aim of the "plan-do-review" program was to provide intellectual stimulation, to increase thinking and reasoning abilities, and to increase later school achievement.

This program had long-term benefits. John Berrueta-Clement and his colleagues (1984) showed that, at age 19, the experimental group was more likely to be employed, more likely to have graduated from high school, more likely to have received college or vocational training, and less likely to have been arrested. By age 27, the experimental group had accumulated only half as many arrests as the controls—an average of 2.3 compared to 4.6 arrests (Schweinhart, Barnes, and Weikart, 1993). In addition, they were more likely to have graduated from high school, had significantly higher earnings, and were more likely to be homeowners. More of the women in the experimental group were married, and fewer of their children were born out of wedlock. A cost-benefit analysis showed that for every $1 spent on the program, more than $7 were saved in the long run (Barnett, 1996). Other less comprehensive cost-benefit analyses of Perry also found that the program was worthwhile, but accrued fewer benefits per dollar of cost: $2.09, according to Peter Greenwood and his colleagues (2001; see also Karoly et al., 1998), and $1.50, according to Washington State Institute for Public Policy economist Steve Aos and his colleagues Polly Phipps, Robert Barnoski, and Roxanne Lieb (2001).[3]

The most recent follow-up of Perry, at age 40, which included 91% of the original sample (112 out of 123) found that the program continued to make an important difference in the lives of the participants (Schweinhart et al., 2005). In commenting on this latest follow-up, David Kirp, a professor of public policy at the University of California, Berkeley, said: "By almost any measure we might care about—education, income, crime, family stability—the contrast with those who didn't attend Perry is striking" (2004, p. 34). Compared to the control group, program group members had significantly fewer lifetime arrests for violent crimes (32% vs. 48%), property crimes (36% vs. 58%), and drug crimes (14% vs. 34%), and were significantly less likely to be arrested five or more times (36% vs. 55%). Improvements were also recorded in many other important life-course outcomes. For example, significantly higher levels of schooling (77% vs. 60% graduating from high school), better records of employment (76% vs. 62%), and higher annual incomes were reported by the program group compared to the controls. A cost-benefit analysis at age 40 found that Perry produced just over $17 of benefit per dollar of cost, with 76% of this being returned to the general public—in the form of savings in crime, education, and welfare, and increased tax revenue—and 24% benefiting each program participant.

Like Perry, the Child-Parent Center (CPC) program in Chicago (Reynolds, Temple, Robertson, and Mann, 2001) provided disadvantaged children, ages 3–4, with a high-quality, active learning preschool supplemented with family support. However, unlike Perry, CPC continued to provide the children with the educational enrichment component into elementary school, up to age 9. Begun in 1967, the CPC program is the second oldest federal preschool program in the United States (after Head Start) and the oldest "extended early intervention" program. It is located in 24 centers in high-poverty neighborhoods across Chicago (p. 2340).

This was not a randomized experiment. Children who were enrolled in the CPC program were matched with children who received regular preschool. Matching was done on "age of kindergarten entry, eligibility for and participation in government-funded programs, and neighborhood and family poverty" (Reynolds et al., 2001, p. 2340). The initial sample included more than 1,500 children (989 in the treatment group and 550 in the control group).

Just focusing on the effect of the preschool intervention, it was found that, compared to the control group, those who received the program were significantly less likely to be arrested for any offense (17% vs. 25%), multiple offenses (10% vs. 13%), and violent offenses (9% vs. 15%) by the time they were 18. Sample attrition was fairly low at this follow-up period, with 91% (n = 1,404) of the initial sample included. The CPC program also produced other benefits for those in the experimental compared to the control group, including a significantly higher rate of high school completion (50% vs. 39%).

A cost-benefit analysis of the program, which included some outcomes measured up to age 21 (crime was measured at age 18), found that for every dollar spent on the program, more than $7 was saved to society. These savings took the form of averted government expenditures on remedial education and the justice system, as well as increased economic well-being on the part of program participants (Reynolds, Temple, and Ou, 2003, p. 645). The latter benefit accounted for the largest share (46%) of total monetary benefits accrued by the program. Savings to crime victims and the criminal justice system accounted for the next largest share (28%) of monetary benefits.

A third successful preschool intellectual enrichment program is the Carolina Abecedarian Project of Frances Campbell and her colleagues (2002). This program was also targeted at children born to low-income, multirisk families. A sample of 111 children aged 3, mostly African American (98%), were randomly assigned either to receive full-time preschool childcare (focusing on the development of cognitive and language skills) or not. Families of children in both the experimental and control groups received supportive social services as needed.

At age 21, 104 of the participants were interviewed, and it was found that fewer of the experimentals, compared to the controls (but not significantly so), reported being convicted for a misdemeanor offense (14% vs. 18%) or a felony offense (8% vs. 12%) or incarcerated (14% vs. 21%). It was also found that significantly fewer of the experimental participants were regular marijuana users, significantly fewer had become teenage parents, significantly more had attended college or university and had significantly higher status jobs. A cost-benefit analysis of this program found that for every dollar spent on the program, $4 was saved to society (Masse and Barnett, 2002).

Child Social Skills Training

One of the most successful early skills training programs to have measured the effects on crime is the Montreal Longitudinal-Experimental Study of the psychologist Richard Tremblay and his colleagues (1995, 1996). This program combined child skills training and parent training. Tremblay and his colleagues (1996) identified disruptive (aggressive/hyperactive) boys at age 6 (from low socioeconomic neighborhoods in Montreal) and randomly allocated over 300 of these to experimental or control conditions.

Between ages 7 and 9, the experimental group received training designed to foster social skills and self-control. Coaching, peer modeling, role playing, and reinforcement contingencies were used in small group sessions on such topics as "how to help," "what to do when you are angry," and "how to react to teasing." In addition, the children's parents were trained using the parent management training techniques developed by Gerald Patterson (1982) at the Oregon Social Learning Center. Parents were taught how to provide positive reinforcement for desirable behavior, to use nonpunitive and consistent discipline practices, and to develop family crisis management techniques.

By age 12 (3 years after treatment), the experimental boys committed significantly less burglary and theft, were significantly less likely to get drunk, and were significantly less likely to be involved in fights than the controls. In addition, the experimental boys had significantly higher school achievement (McCord, Tremblay, Vitaro, and Desmarais-Gervais, 1994; Tremblay et al., 1992). At every age from 10 to 15, the experimental boys had significantly lower self-reported delinquency scores than the control boys. Interestingly, the differences in delinquency between experimental and control boys increased as the follow-up progressed. However, the experimental boys were only slightly less likely to have a juvenile court record up to age 15 (7% compared with 9% of the controls). The experimental boys were also less likely to be gang members, get drunk, or take drugs, but they were not significantly different from the controls on having sexual intercourse by age 15 (Tremblay, Pagani-Kurtz, Mâsse, Vitaro, and Pihl, 1995; Tramblay, Mâsse, Pagani, and Vitaro,1996). Later analyses have shown differences between experimental and control boys in trajectories of delinquency (Vitaro, Brendgen, and Tremblay, 2001) and aggression, vandalism, and theft (Lacourse et al., 2002). No economic analysis of this program has yet been carried out.

Another successful child skills training program also took place in Canada—in the nation's capital, Ottawa. Marshall Jones and Dan Offord (1989) evaluated this program. Known as Participate and Learn Skills (PALS), the program centered on nonschool skills, both athletic (e.g., swimming, ice hockey) and nonathletic (e.g., guitar, ballet). The aim of developing skills was to increase self-esteem, encourage children to use time constructively, and provide desirable role models. Implemented in a public housing complex in 1980, the program recruited low-income children (ages 5 to 15) to participate in these activities during the after-school hours.

This was not a randomized experiment. Another public housing complex that did not receive the program served as the control condition. The two complexes were the largest that were under the management of the city housing authority and had comparable sociodemographic characteristics. There were 417 age-eligible children at the experimental site and 488 at the control site. Children were recruited actively through direct contact, notices, and follow-up contacts made with those who did not participate in prior rounds of the program. In the first year, the rate of participating in at least one activity reached almost three-quarters (71%). In the program's second and third years, participation rates fell to 60% and 49%, respectively, largely because fewer activities were offered.

The program was successful, and its strongest effect was on juvenile delinquency. During the 32 months of the program, the monthly average number of juveniles (in the age-eligible program range) charged by the police at the experimental site compared to the control site was 80% lower (0.2 vs. 1.0). This statistically significant effect was diminished somewhat in the 16–month postintervention period: 0.5 juveniles were charged per month at the experimental site, compared to 1.1 at the control site. Possibly the effects of the intervention were wearing off. Gains were also observed in skill acquisition, as measured by the number of levels advanced in an activity, integration in the wider community, and self-esteem (but not in behavior at school or home) among experimental children compared with controls.

A cost-benefit analysis of the program, which covered the program and postintervention periods (48 months in total), found that for every dollar spent on the program about $2.6 was saved to society. An examination of the distribution of program benefits revealed that the city housing authority reaped the largest share of benefits (84%). These benefits were due to the reduced demand for private security services in the experimental housing site compared to the control site. The city fire department accrued the next largest share of program benefits (13%), followed by the youth liaison section of the police department (2%).

Discussion and Conclusions

In the case of preschool intellectual enrichment, it is important to note that one of the four programs noted here (Mills, Cole, Jenkins, and Dale, 2002) was not effective in preventing self-reported delinquency at age 15. This program's failure to produce a desirable effect on delinquency may have resulted, in part, from the control participants also receiving a high-quality intervention (direct instruction) as opposed to no preschool or the usual preschool services. The experimental group received a cognitively oriented, child-directed preschool model known as mediated learning.

On the other hand, a large-scale study of the long-term effects of Head Start, by Eliana Garces, Duncan Thomas, and Janet Currie (2002), found that children who attended Head Start (at ages 3–5) were significantly less likely to report being arrested or referred to court for a crime by ages 18–30, compared to their siblings who did not attend the program. However, these results are based on analyses of nonexperimental data drawn from a national panel survey of households.[4]

A simple cost-benefit analysis of Head Start by Janet Currie (2001), again using nonexperimental data, found that its short- and medium-term benefits could offset between 40% and 60% of its costs, and the addition of a small fraction of long-term benefits could make the program a worthwhile public investment. Steve Aos and his colleagues Roxanne Lieb, Jim Mayfield, Marna Miller, and Annie Pennucci (2004) conducted a cost-benefit analysis of Head Start and early education programs in general, which used the average effects of a number of experimental programs, and found that for every dollar spent on this group of programs, $2.36 was saved to the public in the long run.

Another observation that can be made about these two types of early intervention programs is that only a relatively small number of them have measured delinquency or later offending, which requires a long-term follow-up, and few have used high-quality experimental or quasi-experimental evaluation designs. These are well-known features of the early delinquency prevention literature (see e.g., Farrington, 1994b; Karoly et al., 1998; Tremblay and Craig, 1995). While we purposely limited our review of what works and our program profiles to those early interventions that have measured delinquency or later offending (and have the highest quality designs), one issue that further bolsters the claim of effectiveness of individual-based early interventions is the considerable continuity that exists between disruptive and antisocial behavior in childhood and later offending (see e.g., Farrington, 1998c). Therefore, programs that have short-term effects on disruptive or antisocial behavior are likely to have long-term effects on offending.

In the case of child skills training programs, Friedrich Lösel and Andreas Beelmann (2006; see table 7.2) found significantly desirable mean effect sizes at postintervention (or immediate outcome) and large but nonsignificantly desirable mean effect sizes at later follow-up on the outcomes of aggressive behavior, oppositional/disruptive behavior, and (unspecified) antisocial behavior. For example, the Canadian psychologist Debra Pepler and her colleagues (1995) found that the Earlscourt Social Skills Group program in Toronto, which combined home-school skills training and parent training, led to a decrease in teacher-rated externalizing behavior problems (at immediate outcome). The large-scale, multisite Fast Track prevention program in the United States implemented by the Conduct Problems Prevention Research Group (1999, 2002), which combined child skills training and parent training, found a smaller decrease in teacher-rated behavior problems (at immediate outcome) and conduct problems (at 3 years postintervention).[5] Both of these programs were evaluated using randomized experimental designs.

The effectiveness of preschool intellectual enrichment and child skills training programs is not limited to the prevention of delinquency and later offending. Results are highly favorable and robust for impacts on other important life-course outcomes, such as education, government assistance (e.g., welfare), employment, income, substance abuse, and family stability. This should not come as a surprise to many, given that the original impetus of the majority of these programs was to first and foremost improve early childhood outcomes well before delinquency or crime could be measured. Indeed, the desirable impact on delinquency and offending outcomes could be considered spinoff benefits. The noncrime benefits are also apparent from cost-benefit analyses of individual-based programs.

These individual-based early intervention programs very often involve other (secondary) interventions that are targeted at the parents or other caregivers. While the main focus is the child, the presence of these other interventions, as in the teacher visits to the parents of the Perry preschoolers (to provide the parents with educational information and encourage them to take an active role in their child's early education), makes it difficult to say with certainty that it is the individual-based intervention that caused the observed program effect. In many programs, including those reviewed above, it is clear from the research reports that the intervention targeted on the child is the primary or most important one. Of course, this problem of multimodal interventions and the difficulty in disentangling their independent effects also applies to other types of early interventions to prevent delinquency and later offending (see chapters 8 and 9).[6]

On the basis of the most rigorous reviews of the highest quality research evidence, we find that the two main individual-based interventions of preschool intellectual enrichment and child skills training are effective in preventing delinquency and later offending. Our assessment of effectiveness seems to be robust, in that both intervention types have reasonably large sample sizes and the mean effect sizes for delinquency or later offending outcomes are statistically significant.

In the next chapter, we review and assess the effectiveness of early family-based interventions in preventing delinquency and later offending.

Family Prevention   8

amily-based prevention programs target risk factors for delinquency
and later offending that are associated with the family, such as poor
child-rearing, poor supervision, and inconsistent or harsh discipline (see
chapter 4 for other family risk factors). Broadly speaking, family-based
prevention programs have developed along the lines of two major fields
of study: psychology and public health. When delivered by psychologists,
these programs are often classified into parent management training,
functional family therapy, or family preservation (Wasserman and Miller,
1998). Typically, they attempt to change the social contingencies in the
family environment so that children are rewarded in some way for appropriate or prosocial behaviors and punished in some way for inappropriate or antisocial behaviors.

Family-based programs delivered by health professionals such as
nurses are typically less behavioral, mainly providing advice and guidance to parents or general parent education. Home visiting with new
parents, especially mothers, is perhaps the most popular form of this
type of family intervention. In the early 1990s, Hawaii became the first
state to offer free home visits for all new mothers. A small number
of other states, with Colorado at the forefront, have more recently
implemented more intensive but targeted versions of home visiting
programs with the aim of eventually providing universal coverage
(Calonge, 2005).

This chapter reviews the scientific evidence on what works to prevent delinquency and later criminal offending through family-based interventions that are implemented in the early years of life.

Evidence on What Works

A recent meta-analysis found that two main types of family-based programs—general parent education (in the context of home visiting and parent education plus daycare services) and parent management—are effective in preventing delinquency or later criminal offending (Farrington and Welsh, 2003). Other reviews of the effectiveness of home visiting programs—one a systematic review (Bilukha et al., 2005) and the other a narrative review (Gomby, Culross, and Behrman, 1999)—found that the evidence on child behavior outcomes (from antisocial behavior to delinquency) was somewhat mixed. Another systematic review that assessed the effectiveness of parent education in the context of home visiting and combined with daycare services (Bernazzani and Tremblay, 2006) also found mixed results. Regarding parent management training, one other meta-analysis (Serketich and Dumas, 1996), a number of narrative reviews, and one comprehensive vote-counting review of experimental and high-quality quasi-experimental evaluations (Duncan and Magnuson, 2004; Farrington and Welsh, 2002; Kazdin, 1997; Kumpfer and Alvarado, 2003; Welsh and Farrington, 2004) provide further support for the finding that this is an effective early family-based intervention to prevent delinquency and offending.

Parent Education

Home Visiting

Home visiting with new parents, especially mothers, is a popular, although far from universal, method of delivering the family-based intervention known as general parent education. The main goals of home visiting programs center around educating parents to improve the life chances of children from a very young age, often beginning at birth and sometimes in the final trimester of pregnancy. Some of the main goals include the prevention of preterm or low-weight births, the promotion of healthy child development or school readiness, and the prevention of child abuse and neglect (Gomby, Culross, and Behrman, 1999, p. 4). Home visits very often also serve to improve parental well-being, linking parents to community resources to help with employment, educational, or addiction recovery. Home visitors are usually nurses or other health professionals with a diverse array of skills in working with families. In the words of Deanna Gomby, Patti Culross, and Richard Behrman (p. 5),

> home visitors can see the environments in which families live,
> gain a better understanding of the families' needs, and
> therefore tailor services to meet those needs. The relationships
> forged between home visitors and parents can break through
> loneliness and isolation and serve as the first step in linking
> families to their communities.

In a meta-analysis that included four home visitation programs, we found that this form of early intervention was effective in preventing antisocial behavior and delinquency (Farrington and Welsh, 2003).[1] As illustrated in table 8.1 (reproduced from table 7.1), the mean effect size of these programs was .235, corresponding to a significant 12% reduction in antisocial behavior/delinquency (e.g., from 50% in the control group to 38% in the experimental group). Compared to the other five types of early intervention that were examined in this meta-analysis, home visiting programs were at the midrange level of effectiveness, with a larger mean effect size than home/community parent training and a slightly smaller mean effect size than daycare/preschool programs (see table 8.1).

As part of the Task Force on Community Preventive Services, which receives support from the Centers for Disease Control and Prevention, Oleg Bilukha and his colleagues (2005) carried out a systematic review of the effectiveness of early childhood home visitation in preventing violence. Four studies were included that reported the effects of home visitation programs on violence by the visited children.[2] Mixed results were

Table 8.1 Meta-Analysis Results of Early Interventions on Offending

Program type	Low CI	Mean ES	High CI	Fraction significant
Home visiting	.111	.235	.360	2/4
Daycare/preschool	.147	.259	.371	4/5
Parent management training	.274	.395	.517	5/10
School-based programs	−.014	.068	.149	3/7
Home/community programs with older children	.056	.181	.306	3/8
Multisystemic therapy	.281	.414	.548	2/6

Note: weighted means are given. CI = confidence interval; ES = effect size; fraction significant = proportion of significant ES ($p < .05$).

Source: Adapted from Farrington and Welsh (2003, p. 144, table 4).

found for effects on criminal violence (in adolescence) and child externalizing behavior across the four programs: two reported desirable but nonsignificant effects; one reported a significant desirable effect; and one reported mixed results. On the basis of these results, the authors concluded that the "evidence is insufficient to determine the effectiveness of home visitation interventions in preventing child violence" (p. 17).

This systematic review also assessed, using these and many other studies, the effectiveness of early childhood home visitation on parental violence, intimate partner violence, and child maltreatment. For the first two outcomes, there was also insufficient evidence to make a determination of effectiveness. Strong evidence of effectiveness was, however, found for home visiting programs in preventing child abuse and neglect.

In an earlier narrative review of the effectiveness of early childhood home visiting programs by Deanna Gomby and her colleagues (1999), mixed results were found across a range of outcomes. The review included six programs of high quality (five using randomized experimental designs), but only two assessed children's behavior. One of these programs (by Olds et al., 1998; discussed later) reported desirable effects on child externalizing behavior, antisocial behavior, and delinquency, and the other reported no effects on child externalizing behavior.[3] Arguably, with just two studies it is difficult to draw a conclusion as to the effectiveness of this dimension of home visiting programs. The review found some benefits in "parenting practices, attitudes, and knowledge," but the authors concluded that these benefits were limited because "the benefits for children in the areas of health, development, and abuse and neglect rates that are supposed to derive from these changes have been more elusive" (Gomby et al., 1999, p. 10).

Parent Education Plus Daycare

A small number of parent education programs that include daycare services for the children of the participating parents have also measured delinquency. As noted in chapter 7, daycare programs are distinguished from preschool programs, in that the daycare programs are not focused on the child's intellectual enrichment or necessarily on readying the child for kindergarten and elementary school, but serve largely as an organized form of childcare to allow for parents (especially mothers) to return to work. Daycare also provides children with a number of important benefits, including social interaction with other children and stimulation of their cognitive, sensory, and motor control skills. In the United States and some other Western countries, daycare services are available to children as young as 6 weeks old (Michel, 1999).

In our meta-analysis discussed earlier, we found that parent education programs that include daycare services for the parents' children are effective in preventing child antisocial behavior and delinquency. This effect is independent of preschool intellectual programs, even though the two are combined in table 8.1. (As noted in chapter 7, two of the five daycare/preschool programs focus on preschool intellectual enrichment.) The mean effect size of the three parent education plus daycare programs was .138 (not shown in table 8.1), corresponding to a nonsignificant 7% reduction in antisocial behavior and delinquency (e.g., from 50% in the control group to 43% in the experimental group).[4] Aside from our previous narrative reviews, which include the same three studies (see Farrington and Welsh, 2002; Welsh and Farrington, 2004), we are not aware of any other systematic or other type of review that has examined specifically the effects of parent education plus daycare programs on delinquency or later offending.

Finally, it is important to note that the Canadian psychologists Odette Bernazzani and Richard Tremblay (2006; see also Bernazzani, Côté, and Tremblay, 2001) carried out a systematic review of the effectiveness of early parenting programs (for families with children up to age 3) in preventing child disruptive behavior (i.e., opposition to adults, truancy, aggression) and delinquency. Their review included parent education in the context of home visiting and parent education plus daycare (seven randomized experiments in total) but did not report results separately for these two types of intervention (as we do above).[5] Their review found mixed results: four studies reported no evidence of effectiveness; two reported beneficial effects; and one reported mainly beneficial effects. The only study that measured delinquency (the home visiting program by Olds et al., 1998) showed beneficial effects. The authors call for caution in interpreting these results, because of, for example, the limited number of high-quality studies and the modest effect sizes of the beneficial studies. It seems likely that the authors might have reached a more optimistic conclusion had they reported and analyzed (using a meta-analysis) the results separately for the two types of parent education.

Parent Management Training

Many different types of parent training have been used to prevent and treat child externalizing behavior problems and delinquency (Wasserman and Miller, 1998). Parent management training refers to "treatment procedures in which parents are trained to alter their child's behavior at home" (Kazdin, 1997, p. 1349). The Oregon psychologist Gerald Patterson (1982) developed behavioral parent management training. His careful observations of parent-child interaction showed that parents of antisocial children were deficient in their methods of child-rearing. These parents failed to tell their children how they were expected to behave, failed to monitor their behavior to ensure that it was desirable, and failed to enforce rules promptly and unambiguously with appropriate rewards and penalties. The parents of antisocial children used more punishment (such as scolding, shouting, or threatening) but failed to make it contingent on the child's behavior.

Patterson attempted to train these parents in effective child-rearing methods, namely, noticing what a child is doing, monitoring behavior over long periods, clearly stating house rules, making rewards and punishments contingent on behavior, and negotiating disagreements so that conflicts and crises do not escalate. His treatment was shown to be effective in reducing child stealing and antisocial behavior over short periods in small-scale studies (Patterson, Chamberlain, and Reid, 1982; Patterson, Reid, and Dishion, 1992).

In a meta-analysis that included 10 parent management training programs, we found that this form of early intervention was effective in preventing antisocial behavior and delinquency (Farrington and Welsh, 2003). As illustrated in table 8.1, the mean effect size of these programs was .395, corresponding to a significant 20% reduction in antisocial behavior/delinquency (e.g., from 50% in a control group to 30% in an experimental group). Compared to the other five types of early intervention that we examined in this meta-analysis, parent management training was second in effectiveness only to multisystematic therapy.

Each of the 10 parent management training programs included in this meta-analysis aimed to teach parents to use rewards and punishments consistently and contingently in child-rearing. The programs were usually delivered in guided group meetings of parents, including role-playing and modeling exercises, and three of the programs were delivered by videotape. Just 1 of the 10 programs combined parent management training with another intervention (child skills training).

The psychologists Wendy Serketich and Jean Dumas (1996) carried out a meta-analysis of 26 controlled studies of behavioral parent training (also called parent management training) with young children up to age 10. Most were based on small numbers (average total sample size was 29), and most were randomized experiments. They concluded that parent management training was effective in reducing child antisocial behavior, since the mean effect size was .86. However, d correlated -.52 with sample size, indicating that larger evaluations found smaller effect sizes, and .69 with age, indicating that parent management training was more effective for (relatively) older children.

In their narrative review of parent management training, Greg Duncan and Katherine Magnuson (2004) concluded that it is a "promising intervention strategy" for improving the behavior of children, especially for children with "severe behavior problems" (p. 123). The Yale psychologist Alan Kazdin's (1997) narrative review of this intervention strategy is more optimistic. He concluded that parent management training has led to "marked improvements in child behavior on parent and teacher reports of deviant behavior, direct observation of behavior at home and at school, and institutional records (e.g., school truancy, police contacts, arrest rates, institutionalization)" (p. 1351). He also noted that these programs had produced a number of spinoff benefits, including improvements in behaviors of siblings at home and maternal depression.

Successful Case Studies

We now describe the highest quality family-based prevention programs that have been effective in reducing delinquency or later offending. The programs have been organized into two main types: general parent education and parent management training. The focus is on what the programs did to improve the life chances of children, their impact on delinquency or later offending (as well as other important outcomes), and, where possible, their social rate of return or monetary value to society.

Parent Education

Home Visiting

The best known home visiting program (and the only one with a direct measure of delinquency) is the Prenatal/Early Intervention Project that David Olds and his colleagues (1998) carried out in the semirural community of Elmira, New York. This program was designed with three broad objectives: (1) to improve the outcomes of pregnancy; (2) to improve the quality of care that parents provide to their children; and (3) to improve the mothers' own personal life-course development (completing their education, finding work, and planning future pregnancies) (Olds, Henderson, Phelps, Kitzman, and Hanks, 1993, p. 158).

The program enrolled 400 women prior to their thirtieth week of pregnancy. Women were recruited if they had no previous live births and had at least one of the following high-risk characteristics, which tend to correlate with health and developmental problems in infancy: under 19 years of age, unmarried, or poor. The women were randomly assigned to a group who received home visits from nurses during pregnancy, a group who received visits both during pregnancy and the first 2 years of life, or a control group who received no visits. Each visit lasted about one and a quarter hours, and the mothers were visited on average every 2 weeks. The home visitors gave advice about prenatal and postnatal care of the child, about infant development, and about the importance of proper nutrition and avoiding smoking and drinking during pregnancy.

The results of this experiment showed that the postnatal home visits caused a significant decrease in recorded child physical abuse and neglect during the first 2 years of life, especially by poor, unmarried, teenage mothers; 4% of visited versus 19% of nonvisited mothers of this type were guilty of child abuse or neglect (Olds, Henderson, Chamberlin, and Tatelbaum, 1986). This result is important, partly because children who are physically abused or neglected have an enhanced likelihood of becoming violent offenders later in life (Widom, 1989). In a 15-year follow-up (13 years after program completion), which included 330 mothers and 315 children, significantly fewer experimental compared to control group mothers were identified as perpetrators of child abuse and neglect (29% versus 54%), and, for the higher risk sample only, significantly fewer treatment mothers, in contrast to the controls, had alcohol or substance abuse problems or were arrested (Olds et al., 1997). At the age of 15, children of the treatment mothers had incurred significantly fewer arrests than their control counterparts (20 as opposed to 45 per 100 children; Olds et al., 1998).

Several cost-benefit analyses show that the benefits of this program outweighed its costs for the higher risk mothers. The most important cost-benefit analyses are by Peter Greenwood and his colleagues (2001; see also Karoly et al., 1998) and Steve Aos and his colleagues (2004). Greenwood and his colleagues measured benefits to the government or taxpayer (welfare, education, employment, and criminal justice), not benefits to crime victims consequent upon reduced crimes. Aos and his colleagues measured a somewhat different range of benefits to the government (education, public assistance, substance abuse, teen pregnancy, child abuse and neglect, and criminal justice), as well as tangible benefits to crime victims. Both reported that for every dollar spent on the program, benefits were about three to four times greater; $4.06, according to Greenwood and his colleagues, and $2.88, according to Aos and his colleagues.

To test the generalizability of the results of the Elmira study, currently two urban replications are underway: one in Memphis, Tennessee (Olds et al., 2004a) and the other in Denver, Colorado (Olds et al., 2004b). Early follow-up results of both replications (4 and 2 years after program completion, respectively) show continued improvements on a wide range of outcomes for both nurse-visited mothers and their children, compared to their control counterparts.

Parent Education Plus Daycare

One of the most successful early family-based prevention programs to combine parent education and daycare services is the Syracuse University Family Development Research Project of Ronald Lally, Peter Mangione, and Alice Honig (1988). The project, which took place in Syracuse, New York, aimed to bolster family and child functioning through a comprehensive intervention strategy that focused on parent education, with childcare as supplementary. The researchers began with a sample of pregnant women (mostly poor African American single mothers) and gave them weekly help with child-rearing, health, nutrition, and other problems. In addition, their children received free full-time daycare, designed to develop their intellectual abilities, up to age 5. This was not a randomized experiment, but a matched control group was chosen when the children were aged 3. The experimental group consisted of 82 children and the control group of 74.

Ten years later, 119 children were followed up to about age 15. The strongest program effects were on delinquency. Significantly fewer of the experimental group children (2% as opposed to 17%) had been referred to the juvenile court for delinquency offenses, and the severity of offenses and degree of chronicity were much higher among control group children. Treated girls, compared to their control counterparts, showed better school attendance and school performance; no differences were found among the boys.

Lally and his colleagues did not carry out an economic analysis, but instead measured a number of costs associated with youth encounters with the juvenile justice system: court processing; placements administered by the county probation department (foster care and nonsecure and secure detention); and probation supervision. Total costs of the experimental group's (n = 65) involvement with the justice system were estimated at $12,111, while the control group (n = 54) amassed costs totaling $107,192. The estimated cost per treated child was $186, compared with $1,985 per control child. Very little can be said about how these savings would measure up to the costs of running the program and other costs, as well as other potential monetary benefits. At the very least, it could be said that if the program's effects on delinquency were sustained during the late teenage and early adult years, the program might save substantial governmental expenditure on the juvenile and adult justice systems.

A cost-benefit analysis of the Syracuse program by Steve Aos and his colleagues (2001) came to a different conclusion. They found that the costs of running the program exceeded program benefits—in the form of savings to the criminal justice system and crime victims—by a factor of 3 to 1; that is, for each dollar spent on the program, only $0.34 in benefits was produced. This was largely because of the high cost of the program ($45,000 per child in 1998 dollars, compared with $7,000 for Elmira); providing free full-time daycare up to age 5 was very expensive. Against this, it must be repeated that the early findings of Aos and his colleagues (2001) tend to underestimate the benefit-to-cost ratio.

Parent Management Training

Patricia Long and her colleagues (1994) carried out the longest follow-up of a parent management training program, tracking their experimental children for 14 years after the completion of the program. Seventy-three young children (between 2 and 7 years old) who were referred to the researcher's clinic for noncompliance (to parent requests) and their mothers were randomly allocated to an experimental group that received parent management training or to a control group that received no services. Over the course of 8 to 10 sessions, mothers were taught to attend to and reward appropriate behavior and to use clear commands and time-out for noncompliance.

At the completion of treatment, it was found that children in the experimental group, compared to the controls, were less likely to exhibit "deviant" behavior and were more compliant (Long, Forehand, Wierson, and Morgan, 1994, p. 101). At the latest follow-up, when the experimental group participants were between 16 and 21 years old, Long and her colleagues found that, as adults, they were similar on delinquency, emotional adjustment, and academic progress, compared to controls retrospectively matched on age, gender, ethnicity, and family socioeconomic status. In our meta-analysis of parent management training programs noted earlier, we calculated the effect size d to be .306 for the program's effect on delinquency. This corresponds roughly to a sizeable but non-significant 15% reduction (e.g., from 50% in the control group to 35% in the experimental group). Unfortunately, no economic analysis of this program has been conducted.

Alex Mason and his colleagues (2003) evaluated the effectiveness of an early family-based program that included, as a main component, parent management training. Known as "Preparing for the Drug Free Years" (PDFY), this universal program to "enhance family protection and reduce children's risk for early substance initiation" was designed to aid parents on many fronts: "teaching parents about the risk and protective factors for substance abuse and helping them to develop skills for establishing and communicating clear behavioral expectations, monitoring their children's behavior and enforcing norms, managing family conflict, promoting child involvement, and strengthening family bonds" (p. 206).

In their evaluation, the first to assess the program's impact on delinquency, 33 rural schools in 19 contiguous counties in the state of Iowa were randomly allocated—using a randomized block design that blocked on or grouped by "enrollment and on the proportion of lower income students"—to one of three groups. One group was in the PDFY program, another group was in what is known as the Iowa Strengthening Families Program, (which the authors did not evaluate as part of this study), and the control group was a minimal contact group (Mason, Kosterman, Hawkins, Haggerty, and Spoth, 2003, p. 205). Altogether, the study included 429 sixth-grade students (average age 11.3 years) and their families. The PDFY program was carried out in a group format and was fairly short in duration, involving five weekly parenting sessions, each lasting about 2 hours. Children were involved in one of the sessions.

At the latest follow-up (3.5 years postintervention), it was found that the experimental group had experienced a significantly slower rate of increase in delinquency and substance use compared to the control group.[6] The authors speculated that other comprehensive family-focused drug prevention programs should be able to produce "effects that generalize to nondrug-related delinquency" (Mason et al., 2003, p. 210). No economic analysis of this program has been conducted.

Discussion and Conclusions

Both general parent education and parent management training programs also produced a wide range of other important benefits for families, from improved school readiness and school performance on the part of children to greater employment and educational opportunities for parents, to greater family stability in general. This mirrors our finding in chapter 7 for child-focused early interventions. Again, this may not come as a surprise, because the original impetus of the majority of these programs was to improve family outcomes well before child delinquency or offending could be measured. This is evidenced in the cost-benefit analysis of the Elmira nurse home visitation program performed by Greenwood and his colleagues (2001). An analysis of the distribution of benefits accrued to government, which exceeded program costs by a ratio of 4.1 to 1, revealed that 57% of these benefits were due to a reduction in welfare costs, 23% were due to tax revenue from increased employment income, 20% were due to a reduction in juvenile and criminal justice costs, and less than 1% were due to a reduction in health care services.

Just as we noted in chapter 7 that very often individual-based early intervention programs involve other interventions targeted on parents or caregivers, family-focused programs sometimes involve other interventions targeted on children. Parent education plus daycare is one example. This can make it difficult to establish that it is the family-focused intervention that caused the observed program effects. In the programs reviewed in this chapter, it is clear from the research reports that the intervention targeted on the family is the most important one. Interestingly, in our meta-analysis of parent management training, only 1 out of the 10 programs included any other intervention.

Another observation that can be made about parent education and parent management training programs is that only a relatively small number of them have measured delinquency or later offending. This was another issue that came up in chapter 7. We purposely limited our review of what works and our program profiles to those early family-focused intervention programs that have measured delinquency or later offending (and had the highest quality designs). However, the considerable continuity that exists between child disruptive and antisocial behavior and later offending (see e.g., Farrington, 1998c) gives further support to the claim that parent education (in the context of home visiting and combined with daycare services) and parent management training are effective in preventing delinquency and later offending.

In the case of parent education plus daycare services, Dale Johnson and his colleagues (Johnson and Breckenridge, 1982; Johnson and Walker, 1987) found that the Houston Parent-Child Development Center, which provided services to disadvantaged families beginning when the children were 1 to 3 years old, led to a significant decrease in teacher-rated child destructive behavior (at 1 to 4 years postintervention) and child antisocial behavior in the form of fighting (at 5 to 8 years postintervention). In London, England, the child psychiatrist Stephen Scott and his colleagues (2001) evaluated a parent management training program for parents of children (ages 3 to 8) who were referred for antisocial behavior. They found that experimental children showed a large and significant decrease in antisocial behavior after the program.[7] Both of these programs had large sample sizes and were evaluated using randomized experimental designs.

While beyond the scope of this chapter and the book in general, it is noteworthy that various family-based interventions, parent management training included, have also demonstrated evidence of effectiveness in preventing delinquency and offending among adjudicated populations, both juvenile and adult. In our meta-analysis (see table 8.1), we found that the most effective family-based approach was multisystematic therapy (MST), an increasingly popular multimodal intervention that is designed for serious juvenile offenders (Henggeler, Schoenwald, Borduin, Rowland, and Cunningham, 1998). The particular type of treatment is chosen according to the needs of the young person, and it may include individual, family, peer, school, and community interventions (including parent training and skills training); more often, though, it is referred to as a family-based treatment. Unfortunately, two more recent meta-analyses of the effectiveness of MST reached diametrically opposite conclusions. Nicola Curtis, Kevin Ronan, and Charles Borduin (2004) found that it was effective, while Julia Littell (2005) found that it was not.

Susan Woolfenden and her colleagues K. Williams and J. Peat (2002a, 2002b) carried out a systematic review of the effectiveness of family and parenting interventions, including MST, multidimensional treatment foster care (MTFC), functional family therapy (FFT), and parent management training, with mostly delinquent children and adolescents (in seven of the eight randomized studies, all of the participants were chronic and/or serious offenders). Multidimensional treatment foster care involves individual-focused therapeutic care (e.g., skill building in problem solving) for the young person in an alternative, noncorrectional environment (foster care) and parent management training (Chamberlain and Reid, 1998). Functional family therapy involves modifying patterns of family interaction —by modeling, prompting, and reinforcement—to encourage clear communication of requests and solutions between family members, and to minimize conflict (Alexander and Parsons, 1973). Woolfenden and her colleagues found that family and parenting interventions for juvenile delinquents and their families led to a significant reduction in rearrest rates.

On the basis of the most rigorous reviews of the highest quality research evidence, we find that parent education plus daycare services and parent management training are effective in preventing delinquency and later offending. There is seemingly less consensus among evidence-based reviews on the effectiveness of parent education in the context of home visiting. Our meta-analytic review, based on four clearly defined, well-implemented, and methodologically rigorous home visitation programs, found that this form of early intervention was effective in preventing child antisocial behavior and delinquency. None of the other reviews (one a narrative review) utilized meta-analytic techniques to assess results, and in two of the reviews, programs other than home visiting were included. In our estimation, these differences go a long way toward explaining why these reviews found mixed results regarding the efficacy of home visiting.

In the next chapter, we review and assess the effectiveness of early peer, school, and community interventions in preventing delinquency and later offending.

Peer, School, and Community Prevention 9

Peer, school, and community prevention programs target environ-
mental-level risk factors for delinquency and later offending. As discussed in chapter 5, some of these risk factors include associating with
delinquent friends; attending high delinquency-rate schools, which have
high levels of distrust between teachers and students, low commitment
to the school by students, and unclear and inconsistently enforced rules;
and growing up in a poor, disorganized neighborhood.

School-based prevention programs have become increasingly popular in recent years. This is due in part to increased attention to school crime
that has come about in response to high-profile school shootings and other
violent incidents. Most of the programs that have been set up in the wake
of these tragic events focus on the safety of students within schools; fewer
focus on the prevention of delinquency in the wider community. Less can
be said about early intervention programs targeted on peer risk factors
to prevent delinquency. However, peer-based programs have been used
extensively to help children resist peer influences to initiate drug use.
Community-based prevention covers a wide array of programs, including after-school, mentoring, and youth and resident groups. These programs hold wide appeal among the public and political leaders alike, but
are often among the first programs to lose funding in times of federal or
state budget cuts (Butterfield, 2003). This state of affairs has hampered the
knowledge base on the effectiveness of this type of early intervention.

This chapter reviews the scientific evidence on what works to prevent delinquency and later criminal offending through peer-, school-, and community-based interventions that are delivered in the early years of life. Our examination of this group of preventive interventions together stems in large part from their shared focus on environmental factors.

Evidence on What Works

Peer-Based Programs

Peer-based programs to prevent delinquency and offending are ostensibly designed with two related aims: to reduce the influence of delinquent friends and increase the influence of prosocial friends. Teaching children to resist antisocial peer pressures that encourage delinquent activities can take many forms, including modeling and guided practice. Peers must be older, preferably in their later teens, and influential; such peers are sometimes known as high-status peer leaders.

Unfortunately, we have not found any systematic or meta-analytic review that has investigated the effects of peer-based programs on delinquency or later offending. The reviews that have been completed to date have focused on substance use. For example, a large-scale meta-analysis of 143 substance use prevention programs by Nancy Tobler (1986) concluded that programs using peer leaders were the most effective in reducing smoking, drinking, and drug use.

The National Research Council and Institute of Medicine's Panel on Juvenile Crime (McCord et al., 2001) reviewed four randomized experiments of peer-based interventions, two with delinquency measures.[1] The panel did not attempt to synthesize program effects on delinquency or other outcomes, but rather cautioned against the practice of grouping deviant or high-risk peers together during early adolescence (p. 138). This was largely because of the research of Joan McCord (the panel's cochair) on harmful effects of youth delinquency prevention programs (see Dishion, McCord, and Poulin, 1999; McCord, 2002, 2003), which began with her long-term follow-up of the famous Cambridge-Somerville Youth Study (McCord, 1978).

School-Based Programs

Schools are a critical social context for crime prevention efforts, from the early to the later grades (Elliott, Hamburg, and Williams, 1998). All schools work to produce vibrant and productive members of society. According to the Maryland criminologist Denise Gottfredson and her colleagues (2002b, p. 149), "students who are impulsive, are weakly attached to their schools, have little commitment to achieving educational goals, and whose moral beliefs in the validity of conventional rules for behavior are weak are more likely to engage in crime than those who do not possess these characteristics." The school's role in influencing these risk factors and preventing delinquency in both school and the wider community (the focus here) differs from situational and administrative measures taken to make the school a safer place (e.g., through metal detectors, police in school, or closed-circuit television surveillance cameras). As mentioned, we do not focus on situational interventions in this book.

In contrast to peer-based intervention strategies, there have been a number of comprehensive, evidence-based reviews on the effectiveness of early school-based programs to prevent delinquency and offending.[2] David Wilson, Denise Gottfredson, and Stacy Najaka (2001; see also Gottfredson et al., 2002a, 2002b) conducted a meta-analysis that included 165 randomized and quasi-experimental studies, with 216 comparisons of experimental group to control group. The effectiveness of school-based programs was assessed using four main outcomes: delinquency, alcohol/drug use, dropout/truancy, and other problem behavior. As illustrated in table 9.1, the meta-analysis identified four types of school-based programs as effective in preventing delinquency, as indicated by statistically significant mean effect sizes favoring the experimental compared to the control group.

With the exception of attempts to establish norms or expectations for behavior, environmentally focused school-based interventions were found to be effective in preventing delinquency, along with one individually focused intervention: fostering self-control or social competency using cognitive behavioral or behavioral instructional methods. Reorganization of grades or classes had the largest mean effect size ($d = .34$), corresponding to a significant 17% reduction in delinquency. Three of these four effective types of school-based programs (other than school and discipline management) were also effective in preventing alcohol and drug use, and fostering self-control or social competency with cognitive behavioral or behavioral instructional methods was effective in preventing other problem behaviors (not shown in table 9.1).

In an equally rigorous and comprehensive meta-analysis, the Vanderbilt University researchers Sandra Wilson and Mark Lipsey (2005) assessed the effectiveness of school-based violence prevention programs with a similar psychosocial orientation. The review included 219 randomized and quasi-experimental studies, with more than 600 comparisons of experimental group to control group. The effectiveness of school-based programs was assessed using three main outcomes: aggressive or violent behavior (e.g., fighting, bullying), disruptive behavior (e.g., conduct disorder, acting out), and other problem behavior. In reporting results, the authors used a slightly different method of categorizing programs: universal, selected/indicated, special schools/classes, and comprehensive.[3]

The authors found that universal, selected/indicated, and comprehensive programs were "generally effective at reducing the more common types of aggressive behavior seen in schools, including fighting, name-calling, intimidation, and other negative interpersonal behaviors, especially among higher risk students" (2005, p. 24). For aggressive behavior, selected/indicated programs had the largest mean effect size ($d = .29$), corresponding to a significant 15% reduction in aggressive behavior. Interestingly, the meta-analysis did not reveal any significant differences in effectiveness in reducing aggressive behavior among different treatment modalities (e.g., cognitively oriented, behavioral) within universal and selected/indicated program categories.

Julie Mytton and her colleagues (2002) conducted a systematic review and meta-analysis of school-based violence prevention programs,

Table 9.1 Meta-Analysis Results of School-Based Interventions on Delinquency

Intervention category	Delinquency	
	d	k
Environmentally focused interventions		
School and discipline management	.16*	2
Establish norms or expectations for behavior	−.07	2
Classroom or instructional management	.19*	5
Reorganization of grades or classes	.34*	2
Individually focused interventions		
Self-control or social competency (instructional)		
With cognitive behavioral or behavioral instructional methods	.10*	9
Without cognitive behavioral or behavioral instructional methods	−.00	12
Other instructional	−.08	3
Cognitive behavioral, behavioral modeling, or behavior modification	.06	4
Counseling, social work, and other therapeutic interventions	−.17*	3
Mentoring, tutoring, and work study	−.02	5

Note: d = covariance adjusted mean effect size (method and sample equated); k = number of effect sizes contributing to each analysis.

* $p \leq .05$.

Source: Adapted from Wilson, Gottfredson, and Najaka (2001, p. 266, table 8).

but focused more narrowly on programs for children identified as at risk for aggressive behavior (secondary or selected programs) and included only randomized experiments. On the basis of a total of 28 studies, the authors found a mean effect size of $d = .36$, corresponding to a significant 18% reduction in aggressive behavior. Subgroup analyses showed that interventions implemented in primary and secondary grades were similarly effective ($d = .33$ and .43, respectively). The authors did not examine in any detail effects across different intervention modalities, so it is not known if one particular type of program is more effective than another. However, the main conclusion is consistent with Sandra Wilson and Mark Lipsey's (2005) finding that the most effective school-based programs are those that target the highest risk children.

Community-Based Programs

More often than not, community-based efforts to prevent delinquency and later offending are some combination of developmental prevention, with its focus on reducing the development or influence of early risk factors—or "root causes"—for delinquency and later offending (Tremblay and Craig, 1995), and situational prevention, with its focus on reducing opportunities for crime (Clarke, 1995). Unlike these two general crime prevention strategies, there is little agreement in the academic literature on the definition of community prevention and the types of programs that fall within it (Bennett, 1996). Tim Hope (1995, p. 21) defined community crime prevention as "actions intended to change the social conditions that are believed to sustain crime in residential communities." Local social institutions (e.g., community associations, churches, youth clubs) are usually the means by which these programs are delivered, in an attempt to address delinquency and crime problems (Hope, 1995, p. 21).

The most rigorous reviews of the effectiveness of community-based crime prevention find that two main types of programs—after-school and community-based mentoring—can be classified as promising in preventing delinquency or later criminal offending (Sherman, 1997; Welsh and Hoshi, 2002; see also Welsh, 2003).[4] Promising programs are those where the level of certainty from the available scientific evidence is too low to support generalizable conclusions, but where there is some empirical basis for predicting that further research could support such conclusions (Farrington et al., 2002b, p. 18).

After-School Programs

This type of program is premised on the belief that providing prosocial opportunities for young people in the after-school hours can reduce their involvement in delinquent behavior in the community. After-school programs target a range of risk factors for delinquency, including alienation and association with delinquent peers. There are many different types of after-school programs, including recreation-based programs, drop-in clubs, dance groups, and tutoring services.

As part of an effort to update Lawrence Sherman's (1997) review, Brandon Welsh and Akemi Hoshi (2002) identified three high-quality after-school programs with an evaluated impact on delinquency. Each program produced desirable effects on delinquency, and one program also reported lower rates of drug activity for program participants compared to controls. The desirable aggregate effect of these programs was weakened somewhat by one program not reporting significance tests. Welsh and Hoshi concurred with Sherman's assessment that community-based after-school programs (on the basis of the same three programs) represent a promising approach to preventing juvenile offending, but this only applies to areas immediately around recreation centers.

Denise Gottfredson and her colleagues (2004; see also Gottfredson, Gottfredson, and Weisman, 2001), as part of a larger study to investigate the effects of after-school programs on delinquency in the state of Maryland, reported on a brief review of the effectiveness of these programs. They concluded that there is insufficient evidence at present to support claims that after-school programs are effective in preventing delinquency or other problem behaviors. However, they noted that, among a small number of experimental and quasi-experimental studies (which included two of the three programs in Welsh and Hoshi's review), after-school programs that "involve a heavy dose of social competency skill development . . . may reduce problem behavior" (p. 256). In the Maryland study, which used randomized experimental and quasi-experimental methods with statistical matching designs to evaluate the effects of 14 after-school programs, it was found that participation in the programs reduced delinquent behavior among children in middle school but not elementary school. Increasing intentions not to use drugs and positive peer associations were identified as the mechanisms for the middle school programs' favorable effects on delinquency, while decreasing time spent unsupervised or increasing involvement in constructive activities played no significant role (pp. 263–264).

Community-Based Mentoring

This type of program usually involves nonprofessional adult volunteers spending time with young people at risk for delinquency, dropping out of school, school failure, and other social problems. Mentors behave in a "supportive, nonjudgmental manner while acting as role models" (Howell, 1995, p. 90). In many cases, mentors work one-on-one with young people, often forming strong bonds. Care is taken in matching the mentor and the young person.

Welsh and Hoshi (2002), again as part of an effort to update Sherman's (1997) review, identified seven community-based mentoring programs (of which six were high quality) that evaluated the impact on delinquency and other problem behaviors. Two programs had a direct measure of delinquency and showed mixed results: one found desirable effects on delinquency for youths with prior offenses but undesirable effects on delinquency for youths with no prior offenses;[5] the other found desirable effects on delinquency. On the basis of these two programs and the evidence provided by the four programs that measured outcomes related to offending (e.g., disruptive and aggressive behavior), which mostly found favorable results, the authors concluded that community-based mentoring represents a promising approach to preventing delinquency.

David DuBois and his colleagues (2002) conducted a meta-analysis to investigate the effects of mentoring programs on a wide range of outcomes, covering "emotional and behavioral functioning, academic achievement, and employment or career development" (pp. 161–162). Programs that involved peers working together (e.g., peer tutoring, peer mentoring; these would be classified as peer-based) were not included; the mentor needed to be an adult or a teenager serving younger children. The meta-analysis included 55 studies, ranging from randomized experiments to before-after, no control group designs, with 59 independent samples for analysis. Community-based mentoring programs made up about half (29) of the total sample.

The average effect size across the full complement of evaluations on the full range of outcomes was $d = .14$, corresponding to a modest but significant 7% benefit for youths participating in mentoring programs. The same average (and also statistically significant) effect size was found for the 29 community-based mentoring program samples. The settings of "workplace" and "other" (14 program samples in total) had much larger average effect sizes ($d = .24$ and $.28$, respectively), while the average effect size of school-based mentoring programs was only $d = .07$. For the 15 program samples that measured "problem/high-risk behavior" (the closest outcome measure to delinquency), the average effect size was $d = .19$, corresponding to a modest but significant 10% reduction in offending. Of the five types of outcomes investigated, mentoring programs had the largest effects on "problem/high-risk behavior" and "career/employment" (the average effect size was also $d = .19$).[6] Unfortunately, the authors did not investigate the effect of community-based mentoring programs on problem/high-risk behavior.

Successful Case Studies

We now describe the highest quality peer-, school-, and community-based programs that have been effective in preventing delinquency or later offending. The focus is on what the programs did to ameliorate negative influences associated with peers, schools, and communities (respectively), their impact on delinquency and later offending (as well as other important outcomes), and, where possible, their monetary value to society.

Peer-Based Programs

There are no outstanding examples of effective intervention programs for delinquency and later offending based on peer risk factors. The most hopeful programs involve using high-status conventional peers to teach children ways of resisting peer pressure; this is effective in reducing drug use (Tobler, Lessard, Marshall, Ochshorn, and Roona, 1999). In addition, in a randomized experiment in St. Louis, Ronald Feldman, John Wodarski, and Timothy Caplinger (1983) showed that placing antisocial adolescents in activity groups dominated by prosocial adolescents led to a reduction in their antisocial behavior (compared with antisocial adolescents placed in antisocial groups). Over 400 boys around the age of 11 were included in the study, and the focus was on group-level behavior modification. The findings of this study suggest that the influence of prosocial peers can be harnessed to reduce offending.

The most important intervention program whose success seems to be based mainly on reducing peer risk factors is the Children at Risk program, reported on by Adele Harrell, Shannon Cavanagh, and Sanjeev Sridharan (1999), which targeted high-risk adolescents (average age 12) in poor neighborhoods of five cities across the United States. Eligible youths were identified in schools and were randomly assigned to experimental or control groups. The program was a multicomponent, community-based, prevention strategy targeting risk factors for delinquency, including case management and family counseling, family skills training, tutoring, mentoring, after-school activities, and community policing. The program was different in each neighborhood.

The initial results of the program were disappointing (Harrell, Cavanagh, Harmon, Koper, and Sridharan, 1997), but a one-year follow-up showed that (according to self-reports) experimental youths were less likely to have committed violent crimes and used or sold drugs (Harrell, Cavanagh, and Sridharan, 1999). The process evaluation showed that the greatest change was in peer risk factors. Experimental youths associated less often with delinquent peers, felt less peer pressure to engage in delinquency, and had more positive peer support. In contrast, there were few changes in individual, family, or community risk factors, possibly linked to the low participation of parents in parent training and of youths in mentoring and tutoring (Harrell et al., 1997, p. 87). In other words, there were problems of implementation of the program, linked to the serious and multiple needs and problems of the families. No cost-benefit analysis of this program has been carried out.

Peer tutoring was also involved in the Quantum Opportunities Program, which was implemented in five sites across the United States and evaluated by Andrew Hahn (1994, 1999). It aimed to improve the life-course opportunities of disadvantaged, at-risk youth during the high school years and included peer tutoring for educational development and adult assistance with life skills, career planning, and community service. Participants received cash incentives to stay in the program, and staff received cash incentives for keeping youth in the program.

Fifty adolescents aged about 14 were randomly assigned to experimental or control conditions in each site, making an initial sample size of 250. Experimental adolescents were more likely to graduate from high school (63% versus 42%) and were less likely to be arrested (17% versus 58%). During the six-month follow-up period, experimental adolescents were more likely to have volunteered as a mentor or tutor themselves (28% versus 8%) and were less likely to have claimed welfare benefits.

A cost-benefit analysis of the Quantum Opportunities Program (Hahn, 1994) revealed substantial benefits for both participants and tax-payers. The program produced $3.70 in benefits per dollar of cost. Monetary benefits were limited to gains from education and fewer children, with the benefits from fewer children accruing from reduced costs for health and welfare services for teenage mothers. However, an independent cost-benefit analysis by Steve Aos and his colleagues (2004) found that the program failed to pay for itself, producing just $0.42 in benefits per dollar of cost. The main reason for this poor cost-benefit result was that fewer outcomes were included in this analysis.

School-Based Programs

David Wilson, Denise Gottfredson, and Stacy Najaka's (2001) meta-analysis showing that specific school-based intervention modalities are effective in preventing delinquency is of particular interest in relation to the purposes of this book. Therefore, we describe an effective program in each of the four intervention areas: school and discipline management; classroom or instructional management; reorganization of grades or classes; and increasing self-control or social competency using cognitive behavioral or behavioral instruction methods.

School and Discipline Management

One example of an effective program that used school and discipline management to improve the school environment to prevent delinquent and criminal behavior is Project PATHE (Positive Action Through Holistic Education; Gottfredson, 1986). This project was implemented in four middle schools and three high schools in Charleston County, South Carolina. The main elements included increasing shared decision-making in schools, increasing the competence of teachers, increasing the academic competence of students (e.g., through teaching study skills), and improving the school climate (e.g., through a school pride campaign). By increasing students' sense of belonging and usefulness, the project sought to promote a positive school experience. An evaluation of the program in seven schools (compared with two control schools) found that it produced a significant 16% reduction in crime. The evaluation also found a significant reduction in alcohol or other drug use (17%) and antisocial behavior (8%) (Gottfredson et al., 2002a, p. 75, table 4.5). No cost-benefit analysis of this program has been carried out.

Classroom or Instructional Management

One of the most important early school-based prevention experiments was carried out in Seattle by David Hawkins and his colleagues (1991). They implemented a multicomponent program (known as the Seattle Social Development Project) combining parent training, teacher training, and skills training. About 500 first-grade children (aged 6) in 21 classes were randomly assigned to be in experimental or control classes. The children in the experimental classes received special treatment at home and a school that was designed to increase their attachment to their parents and their bonding to the school, in accordance with the assumption that delinquency is inhibited by the strength of social bonds. In addition, the treated children were trained in interpersonal cognitive problem-solving. Their parents were trained to notice and reinforce socially desirable behavior in a program called "Catch Them Being Good." Their teachers were trained in classroom management, for example, to provide clear instructions and expectations to children, to reward children for participation in desired behavior, and to teach children prosocial (socially desirable) methods of solving problems.

In an evaluation of this program 18 months later, when the children were in different classes, Hawkins and his colleagues (1991) found that the boys who received the experimental program were significantly less aggressive than the control boys, according to teacher ratings. This difference was particularly marked for Caucasian rather than African American boys. The experimental girls were not significantly less aggressive, but they were less self-destructive, anxious, and depressed. Julie O'Donnell and her colleagues (1995) focused on children in low-income families and reported that, in the sixth grade (age 12), experimental boys were less likely to have initiated delinquency, while experimental girls were less likely to have initiated drug use. In the latest follow-up of offending outcomes, at age 18, David Hawkins and his colleagues (1999) found that the full intervention group (those receiving the intervention from grades 1–6) admitted less violence, less alcohol abuse, and fewer sexual partners than the late intervention group (grades 5–6 only) or the controls. A cost-benefit analysis of the program by Steve Aos and his colleagues (2004) found that for every dollar spent on the program, more than $3 was saved to government and crime victims.

Reorganization of Grades or Classes

One example of an effective program that used the reorganization of grades or classes to improve the school environment to prevent criminal and other problem behaviors is Student Training Through Urban Strategies (STATUS), which was evaluated by Denise Gottfredson (1990). The main component of the program was referred to as "school-within-a-school" scheduling, whereby high-risk students were brought together for a 2-hour period each day to receive an "integrated social studies and English program which involved a law-related education curriculum and used instructional methods emphasizing active student participation"

(Gottfredson et al., 2002a, p. 92). The program lasted 1 academic year and was implemented in one junior and one senior high school (grades 7 to 9) in Pasadena, California. Randomized assignment of students (n = 247) to experimental and control conditions was attempted but proved unsuccessful, resulting in nonequivalent experimental and control groups. Pooled results of the evaluations of the program in the two schools showed that the experimental students, compared to their control counterparts, had significantly lower rates of criminal activity (18%) and alcohol or other drug use (20%), as well as impressive but nonsignificantly lower rates of school dropout or truancy (12%) and antisocial behavior (12%) (p. 95, table 4.8). No cost-benefit analysis of this program has been carried out.

Increasing Self-Control or Social Competency Using Cognitive Behavioral or Behavioral Instructional Methods

General instruction of students is the most common school-based delinquency prevention strategy. It involves a wide range of functions, including "to teach [students] factual information, increase their awareness of social influences to engage in misbehavior, expand their repertoires for recognizing and appropriately responding to risky or potentially harmful situations, increase their appreciation for diversity in society, improve their moral character" (Gottfredson et al., 2002a, p. 63, box 4.3). The addition of a cognitive-behavioral dimension (e.g., the use of cues, feedback, rehearsal, role-playing) seems to be crucial to the efficacy of self-control or social competency instruction programs.[7]

One example of an effective program that used this individually focused school-based strategy to reduce delinquency is Responding in Peaceful and Positive Ways (RIPP) by Albert Farrell and Aleta Meyer (1997). Targeted at sixth-grade students, mostly African-American children from low-income families, in six public middle schools in Richmond, Virginia, RIPP involved an 18–session violence prevention curriculum, divided into seven instructional topics: building trust; respect for individual differences; the nature of violence and risk factors; anger management; personal values; precipitants and consequences of fighting; and nonviolent alternatives to fighting (Farrell and Meyer, 1997, p. 980). Almost 1,300 students participated in the program.

This was not a randomized experiment. Instead, the researchers used a quasi-experimental design with matching, comparing before and after measures of delinquency (and other outcomes) for those who received the program in the first semester (experimental group) with those scheduled to receive the program in the second semester (wait-list control group). At the end of the program, it had produced a nonsignificant reduction in violence in general, physical fighting, problem behavior, and drug use. An analysis of treatment effects by gender showed that boys, but not girls, were significantly less likely to engage in each one of these activities. In a randomized experiment on RIPP modified for seventh graders, Farrell and his colleagues (2003) observed a significant reduction in disciplinary code violations for violent offenses among the experimental group compared to the control group one year after the program ended. A cost-benefit analysis has not been carried out for either of these programs.

Community-Based Programs

After-School Programs

The Boys and Girls Clubs of America (BGC) plays an important role in the provision of after-school services for children and youths. Founded in 1902, the BGC is a nonprofit organization with a membership of more than 1.3 million young people nationwide. The clubs provide programs in six main areas: cultural enrichment; health and physical education; social recreation; personal and educational development; citizenship and leadership development; and environmental education. Steven Schinke, Mario Orlandi, and Kristin Cole (1992) evaluated the impact of BGCs in public housing sites in five cities. The usual services of BGCs, which include reading classes, sports, and homework assistance, were offered, as well as a program to prevent substance abuse, known as SMART Moves (Self-Management and Resistance Training). This program targets the pressures that young people face to try drugs and alcohol. It also provides education to parents and the community at large to assist young people in learning about the dangers of substance abuse and strategies for resisting the pressures to use drugs and alcohol (p. 120).

This was not a randomized experiment. The researchers used a pre-post, experimental-control group design using matching with 10 experimental sites and 5 control sites. Five sites had a traditional BGC program, five sites received the BGC program in combination with SMART Moves, and five sites had no intervention (the control condition). Police records were available in two cities and showed that housing projects with BGCs (with and without SMART Moves), compared with housing projects without clubs, had significantly less juvenile criminal activity (70 as opposed to 80 juvenile arrests per year). The study also found that housing sites with BGCs, compared to sites without, had fewer damaged units, lower rates of substance abuse, and less drug trafficking. No cost-benefit analysis of this program has been carried out.

Community-Based Mentoring

Big Brothers Big Sisters (BBBS) of America is a national youth mentoring organization that was founded in 1904 and is committed to improving the life chances of at-risk children and teens. One BBBS program brought together unrelated pairs of adult volunteers and youths ages 10 to 16. Rather than trying to address particular problems facing a youth, the program focused on providing a youth with an adult friend. The premise behind this is that the "friendship forged with a youth by the Big Brother or Big Sister creates a framework through which the mentor can support and aid the youth" (Grossman and Tierney, 1998, p. 405). The program also stressed that this friendship needs to be long lasting. To this end, mentors met with youths on average three or four times a month (for 3 to 4 hours each time) for at least 1 year.

An evaluation of the BBBS program, by Jean Grossman and Joseph Tierney (1998), took place at eight sites across the country and involved randomly assigning more than 1,100 youths to the program or to a control group that did not receive mentoring. At program completion, it was found that those youths who received the program, compared to their control counterparts, were significantly (32%) less likely to have hit some-one, initiated illegal drug use (46% less), initiated alcohol use (27% less), or been truant from school (30% less). The program group members were also more likely (but not significantly) than the controls to do better in school and have better relationships with their parents and peers. A cost-benefit analysis of the program by Steve Aos and his colleagues (2004) found that for every dollar spent on the program, more than $3 was saved to the government and crime victims.

Discussion and Conclusions

A wide range of environmentally and individually focused programs have been implemented in schools to prevent delinquency and other problem behaviors. The meta-analysis by David Wilson and his colleagues (2001) identified four intervention modalities that were effective in preventing delinquency among youths in middle school and high school: school and discipline management, classroom or instructional management, reorga-nization of grades or classes, and increasing self-control or social compe-tency with cognitive behavioral or behavioral instructional methods. Three of these four types of school-based programs (other than school and dis-cipline management) also produced benefits on other fronts, such as al-cohol and drug use and other problem behavior in general.

Importantly, each of the three meta-analyses of school-based programs reviewed above—despite looking at the topic in a slightly different way—found that the most effective programs in preventing delinquency and related externalizing behavior problems (i.e., aggressive or violent behav-ior) were those that targeted the highest risk students. From these meta-analyses, there was also some evidence to show that effective delinquency prevention programs can produce similar results when implemented in primary or secondary grades. The famous Seattle Social Development Project of David Hawkins and his colleagues (1999) is one example dem-onstrating that early school-based programs can produce benefits.

Unlike school-based programs, little can be said about the effec-tiveness of peer-based programs to prevent delinquency. As already noted, this is because of the state of evaluation research on the topic. Even among the two peer-based programs highlighted in this chapter, peer risk factors were not the sole focus of these multicomponent programs. Ideally, programs focusing more clearly and more narrowly on peer risk factors should be implemented and evaluated, rather than multimodal programs, so that it is easier to assess the effectiveness of the peer-based components. Future programs may benefit by drawing upon the lessons learned from effective peer-based substance abuse programs.

The state of evaluation research is somewhat better with respect to after-school and community-based mentoring programs, and in each case there are a small number of high-quality programs that demonstrate evidence of effectiveness in preventing delinquency. We therefore conclude that each of these approaches is promising.

However, the fact that not one community-based approach could be said to be effective in the early prevention of delinquency or later offending is cause for concern. Disappointingly, the words of Dennis Rosenbaum, almost two decades ago, still seem applicable today: "the primary reason we do not know 'what works' in community crime prevention is the quality of the evaluation research" (1988, p. 381). Some of the key methodological issues that hamper evaluations include mixed units of analysis, heterogeneity of effect across different populations, and systematic attrition, accretion, and ecological validity (Catalano, Arthur, Hawkins, Berglund, and Olson, 1998, pp. 278–280).

Random assignment is also problematic in the design of community-based crime prevention programs. This difficulty stems from the need to randomize a large enough number of communities to "gain the benefits of randomization in equating experimental and control communities on all possible extraneous variables" (Farrington, 1997a, p. 160). This number is relatively easy to achieve with individuals but very difficult to achieve with larger units such as communities. For larger units such as communities, the best and most feasible design usually involves before-and-after measures in experimental and control communities, together with statistical control of extraneous variables.

Psychologists Abraham Wandersman and Paul Florin (2003) also point to other key factors that may explain the lack of results from community-level interventions, including the complexities involved in the implementation process and the difficulties involved in developing and sustaining the coalition of agencies that is often involved in such programs.

Advancing knowledge about the effectiveness of community-based programs to prevent delinquency and later offending should begin with attention to these key issues, together with a rigorous program of replications and evaluations of the promising approaches of after-school and mentoring approaches. This would be of great benefit to community crime prevention science and policy.

Finally, because of our coverage of key socioeconomic risk factors for delinquency in chapter 5, brief mention is warranted of the few (and largely ineffective) interventions in this area. Since low family income and economic deprivation are risk factors for delinquency, it might be thought that giving poor families extra money might reduce the delinquency of their children. However, the results of income maintenance experiments in the United States do not confirm this prediction. In Seattle and Denver, James Short and his colleagues found that there were no significant differences between experimental families (who received extra income) and control families (who did not) in the later official offending records of their children who were aged 9–12 at the time of the experiment (see Groeneveld, Short, and Thoits, 1979).

Since living in a deprived area is a risk factor for delinquency, it might be thought that moving families from poor areas to more affluent areas would lead to a decrease in the delinquency of their children. Economists Jeffrey Kling, Jens Ludwig, and Lawrence Katz (2005) evaluated the impact of the large-scale Moving to Opportunity program, which gave vouchers to low socioeconomic status (often minority) families to enable them to move to better areas. The authors investigated the impact of this move on the offending of the children and found that there was little effect on the prevalence of arrests overall, but there were desirable effects on the number of arrests of females for violent and property crimes and undesirable effects on the number of arrests of males for property crimes. The authors speculated that brothers and sisters might have responded differently to new neighborhood environments; possibly, females reacted to their more affluent schoolmates by trying harder in school, while males reacted with resentment, stealing from their classmates and not trying in school.

On the basis of the most rigorous reviews of the highest quality research evidence of the effects of peer-, school-, and community-based prevention programs on delinquency and later offending, we find that only a handful of school-based intervention modalities are effective. Owing to a paucity of evaluations of peer-based programs and (perhaps not surprisingly) the absence of evidence-based reviews on the topic, we are left to conclude that, at present, a peer-based approach is of unknown effectiveness in preventing delinquency or later offending. After-school and community-based mentoring programs hold promise as efficacious approaches to preventing delinquency or later offending, but further evaluation research is needed.

In chapter 10, we bring together the leading scientific evidence on the early risk factors for and what works best to prevent delinquency and later offending to assess the merits of a national strategy to save children from a life of crime.

PART III

TOWARD A NATIONAL STRATEGY

Never Too Early

10

A Comprehensive National Prevention Strategy

After decades of rigorous research in the United States and across the Western world—using large-scale prospective longitudinal studies—a great deal is now known about early risk factors for delinquency and later criminal offending, especially family and individual factors. Less is known about protective factors against offending, but recent empirical research provides some important insights.

Among the most important individual factors that predict offending are low intelligence and attainment, personality and temperament, empathy, and impulsiveness. Just as low intelligence is a risk factor for offending, it has been suggested that high intelligence might be a protective factor.

The strongest family factor that predicts offending is usually criminal or antisocial parents. Other quite strong and replicable family factors that predict offending are large family size, poor parental supervision, parental conflict, and disrupted families. One of the best family protective factors is good parental supervision.

At the environmental level, the strongest factors that predict offending are growing up in a low socioeconomic status household, associating with delinquent friends, attending high-delinquency-rate schools, and living in deprived areas. However, all of these adversities tend to be associated with individual and family adversities. One of the best environmental protective factors is high academic focus in schools (e.g., emphasizing homework, academic classes, and task orientation).

There is a growing body of high-quality scientific evidence on the effectiveness of early interventions to tackle these risk factors to prevent delinquency and later offending. At the individual level, preschool intellectual enrichment and child skills training programs are effective in preventing delinquency and later offending. Results are also highly favorable and robust for impacts on other important life-course outcomes, such as education, government assistance (e.g., welfare), employment, income, substance abuse, and family stability. There is some evidence that these programs not only pay back their costs but also produce substantial monetary benefits for the government and taxpayers.

At the family level, parent education plus daycare services and parent management training programs are effective in preventing delinquency and later offending. There is seemingly less consensus among evidence-based reviews on the effectiveness of parent education in the context of home visiting. According to our meta-analytic review—based on four clearly defined, well-implemented, and methodologically rigorous studies—home visiting programs are effective in preventing child antisocial behavior and delinquency. Both general parent education (daycare and home visits) and parent management training programs also produce a wide range of other important benefits for families, from improved school readiness and school performance on the part of children, to greater employment and educational opportunities for parents, to greater family stability in general. There is some evidence that home visiting programs can pay back program costs and produce substantial monetary benefits for the government and taxpayers. Little is known about the economic efficiency of the other family programs.

At the environmental level, there are mixed results across peer, school, and community programs. A peer-based approach is presently of unknown effectiveness in preventing delinquency or later offending. This is because of the very few evaluations of peer-based programs and the absence of evidence-based reviews on the topic. After-school and community-based mentoring programs hold promise as efficacious approaches to preventing delinquency or later offending, but further evaluation research is needed on them. Four types of school-based interventions are effective in preventing delinquency among youths in middle school and high school: school and discipline management, classroom or instructional management, reorganization of grades or classes, and increasing self-control or social competency with cognitive behavioral or behavioral instructional methods. Three of these four types of school-based programs (other than school and discipline management) also produced benefits on other fronts, such as alcohol and drug use and other problem behavior in general. The most effective programs in preventing delinquency and related externalizing behavior problems (i.e., aggressive or violent behavior) were those that targeted the highest risk students.

Against the backdrop of these key conclusions from our reviews on early risk and protective factors and prevention programs, this chapter describes key elements of a comprehensive national strategy for the early prevention of delinquency and later offending. The strategy is particularly targeted on the United States, but could be implemented in the United Kingdom or other Western countries.

Why a National Strategy?

The delivery of early intervention programs to prevent delinquency and later offending is primarily a matter for local government, community groups, and individual citizens. This has long been recognized as a key principle of early intervention and crime prevention in general. The "Agenda for Safer Cities," the consensus statement of the first European and North American Conference on Urban Safety and Crime Prevention, held in Montreal in 1989, enunciated four key crime prevention principles, the first being that "the community is the focal point of crime prevention" (European Forum for Urban Safety et al., 1989, p. 2).[1] This important principle is also contained in the United Nations' (2002) "Guidelines for the Prevention of Crime."

Such statements—similar ones followed at other international conferences—and guidelines also called for other levels of government (i.e., federal/central and state/provincial) to support local crime prevention efforts. Federal or central governments (hereafter referred to as federal governments) have the ability to mobilize a diverse array of partners, governmental and nongovernmental, offer a vision for the nation over the short- and long-term, and contribute sizable financial resources to state and local governments. In commenting on the federal role in early childhood prevention initiatives in the United States, Yale scholars Carol Ripple and Edward Zigler (2003, p. 482) note:

> Federal policy has the ability to shape programs and approaches to prevention nationwide and can direct considerable federal funds toward primary prevention initiatives. Even when it does not provide significant funding, federal policy is a potent voice in setting the national agenda (education is an example, in which the federal government seeks to set national education policy despite paying just 7% of costs).

A national strategy is one way of harnessing the influential role of the federal government. At its most basic level, a national prevention strategy sets out the ideological orientation or vision of the country's approach to preventing crime. This orientation, whether it is directed at early intervention, situational prevention, or some other approach or combination of approaches, then becomes the guiding principle for more practical operations, including funding, technical assistance, research and evaluation, and so on. On the one hand, a national strategy is symbolic; on the other hand, it is the organizing principle from which all policy and programmatic action can flow.

Lessons from Western Countries

A national strategy very often involves the federal government establishing a permanent structure, such as an agency, council, or secretariat. In Sweden, this is known as the National Council for Crime Prevention (established in 1974), and in Canada, it is the National Crime Prevention Centre (formerly the National Crime Prevention Council, established in 1994). The need for and key roles of a national structure of this sort were outlined in the "Final Declaration" of the second international crime prevention conference, held in Paris in 1991:

> Governments must establish national crime prevention structures to recommend improved national policies, undertake research and development, and foster the implementation of effective crime prevention programmes, particularly by cities. (European Forum for Urban Safety et al., 1991, p. 2)

As part of a larger project on crime prevention internationally, the Canadian criminologist Irvin Waller and his colleagues (Waller and Welsh, 1999; Waller, Welsh, and Sansfaçon, 1997; see also Sansfaçon and Waller, 2001; Sansfaçon and Welsh, 1999; Waller and Sansfaçon, 2000) examined the crime prevention efforts of the federal governments of seven industrialized countries (Australia, Belgium, Canada, England/ Wales, France, the Netherlands, and the United States).[2] Six elements were identified as important for the success of a national strategy designed to foster effective crime prevention activities at the local level. These six elements can be divided into two categories and include:

Characteristics of a national secretariat or agency:

  (a) staff, reporting to a senior official, with a budget for development;
  (b) capacity to mobilize key partners, harness effective methods and set priorities; and
  (c) able to propose strategies based on analysis of crime problems and prevention practices.
Delivery possible through:
  (d) collaboration with other government departments;
  (e) development of local problem-solving partnerships;[3] and
  (f) involvement of citizens. (Waller and Welsh, 1999, p. 197)

Point (a) speaks to the need for permanency and influence within the government hierarchy. It goes without saying that a government agency that reports directly to a high-ranking public official, such as the U.S. attorney general or secretary of health and human services, will have a great deal more influence in shaping national policy and obtaining resources to pursue the agency's objectives than one that does not. In the seven-country study, it was found that national crime prevention agencies reported to an official between two and four levels down from the top public servant. In Sweden, a director general heads the National Council and reports to a government-appointed management board. The board in turn reports to the minister of justice. In Canada, an executive director (equivalent to a director general) heads the National Crime Prevention Centre and reports to the assistant deputy minister of the Community Safety and Partnerships Branch[4] of the Department of Public Safety and Emergency Preparedness. The assistant deputy minister in turn reports to the deputy minister, who reports to the minister in charge of the department.

On the matter of permanency, Sweden's National Council for Crime Prevention employs about 60 full-time staff, including criminologists, sociologists, psychologists, economists, lawyers, statisticians, and administrators, who work in nine divisions.[5] There is also an advisory group and scientific board attached to the Council (Andersson, 2005, p. 75; National Council for Crime Prevention, 2001, p. 14). Canada's National Centre employs about 85 full-time staff with similar professional backgrounds.[6] Two affiliated groups provide management and strategic advice on the implementation of the National Crime Prevention Strategy: Joint Management Committees and the Federal-Provincial-Territorial Working Group on Crime Prevention (Irving, 2006).

A national prevention agency also requires a capacity to influence other federal agencies or departments whose policies impact on crime levels, such as health, education, social services, and employment. This is a key feature of point (b). Daniel Sansfaçon and Brandon Welsh noted that "crime prevention policies will have optimal impacts if other ministries [or departments] include crime prevention as a consideration in developing their policies and programs" (1999, p. 77).

Point (b) also recognizes the need to develop the capacity to support an evidence-based approach: to use the best available research evidence on what works in preventing crime. A national prevention agency can serve as a research clearinghouse on what works, commission systematic reviews on important prevention measures and emerging issues, and produce guidelines on effective practice, all in an effort to aid prevention initiatives at the local level. Setting clear priorities for action, especially in the beginning years of an agency, is crucial to developing political capital within government and being able to produce tangible products to aid local officials in implementing effective prevention measures.

In the seven-country study, it was common for national crime prevention agencies either to be doing too little (often a function of a limited budget) or to be too overextended to support an evidence-based approach (Waller and Welsh, 1999). This cannot be said about Sweden, which was not among the countries in this study. Sweden's National Council publishes a series of "best practice" manuals "intended to have immediate relevance for those engaged in local crime prevention activities" (National Council for Crime Prevention, 2001, p. 11). These best practice manuals focus on a range of crime problems and bring together the leading research on effective programs in Sweden and, in many cases, other countries.

The Government of Canada, too, has long recognized the importance of having "access to experience and research from around the world" (2003, p. 2) to aid in the development of more efficacious and cost-beneficial crime prevention measures for Canadian communities. This has included providing funding for the International Centre for the Prevention of Crime and the Campbell Collaboration Crime and Justice Group (Farrington and Petrosino, 2001), among other efforts. With the Crime and Justice Group at the forefront of the development of evidence-based crime prevention internationally, this support has contributed to fostering new systematic reviews that may hold relevance to the Canadian situation.

Point (c), the ability to propose strategies based on analysis of crime problems and prevention practices, is concerned with research and strategic analysis capabilities on a national level. Here, the national agency is interested in identifying national trends in crime and related social problems and the effects of different national policies (e.g., early intervention, imprisonment) aimed at reducing crime. Sweden's National Council has a division—the crime studies division—for this sole purpose.

Points (d), (e), and (f)—collaboration with other government departments, development of local problem-solving partnerships, and involvement of citizens—pertain to the effective implementation or delivery of evidence-based programs at the local level. These points specify the pivotal role of the translation of evidence-based results (i.e., from systematic reviews) into local practice. Each point specifies concrete steps that a national agency can have some influence over at the local level, but program success, ultimately, will depend on persons at the local level. The influence a national agency can have on these implementation issues has a number of features; for example, developing guidelines on effective practice and making project funding conditional on the use of evidence-based programs.

In both Sweden and Canada, the national agencies play an important role in fostering the implementation of proven prevention programs at the local level. Just focusing on Sweden, this role took on more importance in recent years, with the government launching (in 1996) a national crime prevention policy called "Our Collective Responsibility" (Ministry of Justice, 1997).[7] At the heart of this policy was the importance of establishing crime prevention councils at the municipal level. These councils are meant to bring together the key local stakeholders that can influence the factors that cause crime and implement programs to successfully tackle these factors. The promotion of greater citizen involvement in crime prevention activities is also central to the work of the councils.

By the beginning of 2005 (the most recent data available), local councils were operating in more than 80% of the country's 290 municipalities. As noted by the Swedish criminologist Jan Andersson, "local crime prevention councils have come to assume a central and strategic role in the work of crime prevention" (2005, p. 82). The National Council has a budget of about 7.2 million Swedish krona (approximately 1 million U.S. dollars) to support the work of local crime prevention councils. This support comes in the form of disseminating knowledge on effective practice, training, and guidance in crime analysis and evaluation (p. 82).

A Comprehensive National Prevention Strategy for America

We believe the time is right for the U.S. federal government to mount a national prevention strategy. Its focus should be on intervening early to save children from a life of crime. Its prevention plans should be grounded in the leading scientific evidence on the causes of offending and what works to prevent delinquency and later offending. It should also be comprehensive. We discuss these and the other main elements of a proposed national strategy here.

Vision

The national strategy needs to have a clear vision of intent. The vision should be that early prevention of delinquency and later offending saves lives. It saves lives by diverting the very children who may embark on a life of crime and endure its consequences—incarceration, various social ills that face offenders later in life, injury, even death—and producing instead productive, law-abiding citizens.

This vision may be grand, but it need not be viewed as unrealistic. The scientific evidence on the early causes of crime establishes that identifying at an early age those children who are at greatest risk for offending is no guarantee that they will not later become criminals. Likewise, the scientific evidence on the efficacy of early prevention programs establishes that prevention work is not a panacea for keeping children out of a life of crime. But in each case, the scientific evidence, as we have shown in the previous chapters, provides guidance on the most important early crime risk factors to target and demonstrates that impressive results can be achieved by using a number of early prevention programs that target these risk factors.

Risk-Focused, Evidence-Based Prevention

Underlying the vision for the national strategy are the substantive concepts that are needed to make it happen: risk-focused prevention and evidence-based prevention. As we discussed in chapter 6, these two concepts are closely related and should be thought of in combination: risk-focused, evidence-based prevention. By identifying the key risk factors for offending and implementing effective prevention methods designed to counteract them (and, albeit to a lesser extent, identifying key protective factors against offending and implementing effective prevention methods designed to enhance them), risk-focused prevention represents the basic building block of evidence-based prevention. What evidence-based prevention adds is the utilization of accumulated scientific research evidence on effectiveness (and, where possible, economic efficiency) from systematic reviews.

We believe that it is crucial that a national strategy should make use of and promote risk-focused, evidence-based prevention at the local and state levels. Colorado is one example of a state that has adopted this approach. The state's focus is on home visiting services to prevent child maltreatment by targeting "first-time mothers with incomes below 200% of the federal poverty level" (Calonge, 2005, p. 5). This initiative, known as the Nurse Home Visitor Program (NHVP), was created by state law in 2000 and was based on the evidence-based early childhood home visiting program developed by David Olds and his colleagues (see chapter 8).[8] Importantly, NHVP was not funded as a one-off program or designed to be limited to the most at-risk families. As noted by Ned Calonge, chief medical officer of the Colorado Department of Public Health and Environment, "the intention of the legislation is that the program be expanded annually so that the services will be available for all eligible mothers who choose to participate in all parts of the state" (2005, p. 5).

National Council on Early Prevention

We believe that the federal government should establish a council to support a national early crime prevention strategy in the United States. This council should be permanent and have similar characteristics to its counterparts in other Western industrialized countries. It should provide technical assistance, skills, and knowledge to state and local agencies in implementing prevention programs, should provide funding for such programs, and should ensure continuity, coordination, and monitoring of local programs. It should provide training in prevention science for people in local agencies, and should maintain high standards for evaluation research. It should also act as a center for the discussion of how policy initiatives of different government agencies influence crime and associated social problems. It should set a national and local agenda for research and practice in the early prevention of crime, as well as drug and alcohol abuse, mental health problems, and associated social problems. Furthermore, the national council should provide support for systematic reviews of the evaluation literature on the effectiveness of early interventions that may impact delinquency and later offending.

An important consideration in setting up such a council is where in the federal government it should be located. In his new book, Peter Greenwood (2006) excellently reviews the pros and cons of different government departments that could have primary responsibility for delinquency prevention programs in general (Justice, Education, and Health and Human Services, or HHS). Ultimately, he argues that HHS should be the lead department for early prevention programs, while Justice is the more appropriate department for serving the needs of high-risk and adjudicated youths. Greenwood summarizes his arguments in favor of HHS with the following principle: "*Primary responsibility for developing and operating delinquency-prevention programs should be as-*

signed to an appropriate agency in HHS unless immediate public protection is an overriding concern" (p. 179, emphasis in original).

We concur with Greenwood's recommendation to place responsibility for early prevention in a government department other than Justice and, preferably, in HHS. One argument in favor of HHS is that the benefits of early prevention are not restricted to crime but include many other aspects of a successful or healthy lifestyle (including education, employment, substance use, relationships, and mental health). Instead of establishing this council as yet another agency in this government department's bewildering bureaucracy, we believe it should come under the immediate control of the Office of the Secretary of HHS. Furthermore, the council should be chaired either by the secretary or the under secretary of HHS. This is in accordance with the fact that national crime prevention agencies in other countries have a fairly high degree of influence with the top government official. In short, it speaks to the national importance of the issue and the ability to get things done.

Prevention at the Local Level

Crucial to the success of a national early prevention strategy is the ability of a national agency or council to foster and support the implementation or delivery of evidence-based programs at the local level. As discussed earlier, national crime prevention councils in other countries that have shown some success in doing this have done so because they emphasized three main mechanisms: collaboration with other government departments, development of local problem-solving partnerships, and involvement of citizens. In Sweden, for example, this has come about through federal government support for the establishment of crime prevention councils at the municipal level. These councils bring together the key local agencies that can influence the factors that cause crime and implement programs to successfully tackle these factors.

We must not be so foolhardy as to think that local crime prevention councils or partnerships have all the answers—they have both strengths and limitations. According to the Cambridge University criminologist

Per-Olof Wikström (in press, p. 8), "the idea with local crime prevention partnerships is fundamentally a good one because effective delivery of crime prevention requires the active involvement and contribution of a large range of local actors (parents, teachers, neighbours, police officers, social workers, doctors, shop-keepers, city planners, etc.)." The main problem, however, is that local persons are likely to lack knowledge and expertise. Wikström (p. 9) has found that, "as a rule, most partnerships lack such knowledge [about the causes of crime and effective programs] and therefore the starting point for their crime prevention policy and practise is often flawed." Technical assistance from a national agency is vital.

In the interests of achieving maximum effectiveness, what is needed is a comprehensive, locally driven program including several of the effective and promising individual, family, school, and community programs reviewed in chapters 7, 8, and 9. Communities That Care (CTC) has many attractions to serve as the model for delivering these early prevention programs. It is both risk-focused and evidence-based. While the effectiveness of the overall CTC strategy has not yet been demonstrated, the effectiveness of its individual components is clear (see Harachi et al., 2003).

Communities That Care

Communities That Care was developed as a risk-focused prevention strategy by the social work professors David Hawkins and Richard Catalano (1992), and it is a core component of the U.S. Office of Juvenile Justice and Delinquency Prevention's Comprehensive Strategy for Serious, Violent, and Chronic Juvenile Offenders (Wilson and Howell, 1993). This prevention strategy is based on a theory (the social development model) that organizes risk and protective factors. The intervention techniques are tailored to the needs of each particular community. The "community" could be a city, a county, a small town, or even a neighborhood or a public housing community.

This strategy aims to reduce delinquency and later offending by implementing particular prevention strategies that have demonstrated effectiveness in reducing risk factors or enhancing protective factors. It is modeled on large-scale community-wide public health programs designed to reduce illnesses such as coronary heart disease by tackling key risk factors (Farquhar et al., 1985; Perry, Klepp, and Sillers, 1989). There is great emphasis in CTC on enhancing protective factors and building on strengths, partly because this is more attractive to communities than tackling risk factors.Furthermore, to take a public health perspective, it is generally true that health promotion is more effective than disease prevention (Kaplan, 2000).

Communities That Care programs begin with community mobilization. Key community leaders (e.g., elected representatives, education officials, police chiefs, business leaders) are brought together, with the aim of getting them to agree on the goals of the prevention strategy and to implement CTC. The key leaders then set up a community board that is accountable to them, consisting of neighborhood residents and representatives from various agencies (e.g., school, police, social services, probation, health, parents, youth groups, business, church, media). The community board takes charge of prevention on behalf of the community.

The community board then carries out a risk and protective factor assessment, identifying key risk factors in that particular community that need to be tackled and key protective factors that need to be enhanced. This risk assessment might involve the use of police, school, social or census records, or local neighborhood or school surveys. After identifying key risk and protective factors, the community board assesses existing resources and develops a plan of intervention strategies. With specialist technical assistance and guidance, they choose programs from a menu of strategies that have been shown to be effective in well-designed evaluation research. The choice of prevention strategies is based on empirical evidence about effective methods of tackling each particular risk factor, but it also depends on what are identified as the particular problems and strengths of the community.

As a risk-focused, evidence-based prevention model, CTC continues to be supported at the local level across the United States, at the last count in several hundred communities (Harachi et al., 2003). It has also been implemented in over 20 sites in England, Scotland, and Wales, and in the Netherlands and Australia (France and Crow, 2001; Utting, 1999). With support from a national agency, the CTC model could be implemented in all communities across the United States.

Conclusions

We hope that this chapter has demonstrated that there are great merits in having a national strategy to guide early prevention policy and practice in the United States; that there are important lessons the United States could learn from other Western countries about how to support and foster more effective early prevention programs at the local level; and, in many respects, that the elements of a United States–based model are already in place to help achieve this goal. The time is right to implement a national risk-focused, evidence-based strategy for early prevention in the United States. This would lead to enormous benefits in saving children from a life of crime and contribute to a safer, more sustainable society for all.

NOTES

1. Descriptive validity, which refers to the adequacy of reporting of information, could be added as a fifth criterion of the methodological quality of evaluation research (Farrington, 2003c; see also Lösel and Koferl, 1989).
2. This is the probability of correctly rejecting the null hypothesis when it is false.

CHAPTER 6

1. While not as rigorous as these two methods, another widely used and robust review method is vote-counting. In short, it adds a quantitative element to the narrative review by considering statistical significance.
2. The criterion of methodological quality that is used for including (or excluding) studies is perhaps the "most important and controversial" issue in conducting systematic reviews (Farrington and Petrosino, 2001, p. 42). How high to set the "bar" of methodological rigor as part of a review of the literature, systematic or other, is a question that all researchers face. For a brief discussion of this issue in the context of one review method, see MacKenzie (2000).
3. It is beyond the scope of this chapter to discuss each step, but interested readers should consult the reviews of this methodology as applied in the context of early prevention programs (see Barnett, 1996; Barnett and

Escobar, 1987, 1990). In addition, for methodological features of cost-benefit analysis in general, see Layard and Glaister (1994) and Welsh, Farrington, and Sherman (2001).

CHAPTER 7

1. In selecting evaluations for inclusion, we used the following criteria: (1) the family (parent/guardian and/or child) and family factors (e.g., child-rearing methods) were a focus of the intervention; (2) there was an outcome measure of delinquency or antisocial child behavior; (3) the evaluation design was of high quality methodologically (i.e., a randomized experiment or an experiment with a matched control group); and (4) the original sample size (experimental and control groups combined) was at least 50 individuals.

2. The main measure of effect size was the standardized mean difference d, which summarizes the difference between the experimental and control groups in standard deviation units. Since these are mean offending scores, a positive value of d indicates a desirable effect of the intervention. Confidence intervals indicate the range within which the population mean (the mean of the included studies) is likely to be, based on the observed data (Lipsey and Wilson, 2001, p. 114). As is standard practice in meta-analyses, we used a 95% confidence interval.

3. Peter Greenwood and his colleagues' (2001) benefit-to-cost ratio was less than Steven Barnett's (1996) because the former examined benefits from the perspective of government only; savings to crime victims, which accounted for the majority (65%) of Perry's benefits in the cost-benefit analysis by Barnett (1996), were not included. In the case of the analysis by Steve Aos et al. (2001), the benefit-to-cost ratio was lower than Barnett's because crime victim costs were limited to tangible costs (e.g., property loss) and no other outcomes except crime were assessed.

4. In recognizing that a randomized experiment is the best method to evaluate the long-term effects of Head Start (but none have yet been carried out), the authors say: "We view our analysis of these nonexperimental data as an important complement to random assignment evaluations" (Garces et al., 2002, p. 1000).

5. We calculated d effect sizes for these programs: Earlscourt, .412 ($p = .077$); Fast Track: behavior problems, .002 (n.s.); conduct problems, .010 (n.s.) (Farrington and Welsh, 2003, pp. 135, 137).

6. From a policy (as opposed to a theoretical or research) perspective, the inability to say whether it was intervention X or Y that caused a program's successful result may not be so relevant, so long as there is a good understanding of the combination of the two interventions to facilitate replicating this result in other situations and contexts. This is a matter we return to in the final chapter.

CHAPTER 8

1. The four programs are the Elmira (New York) Prenatal/Early Intervention Project (PEIP) of David Olds and his colleagues (1998); the replication of PEIP in Memphis by Harriet Kitzman and her colleagues (1997); the Mailman Center program of Wendy Stone, Debra Bendell, and Tiffany Field (1988); and the Busselton (Western Australia) prevention study of Kevin Cullen (1976). Each used a randomized experimental design to assess program impact.
2. One of these programs (Olds et al., 1998) was included in our meta-analysis (Farrington and Welsh, 2003) and another (Lally et al., 1988) is one that we judge to have more to do with the provision of parent education and daycare services. Of the four included programs, two used randomized experimental designs, and the other two used quasi-experimental designs.
3. "Externalizing" behavior includes aggression, delinquency, and hyperactivity.
4. We calculated d effect sizes for these three programs: Houston Parent-Child Development Center (Johnson and Walker, 1987), .475 ($p = .007$); Syracuse University Family Development Research Project (Lally et al., 1988), 1.406 ($p = .017$); Infant Health and Development Program (McCarton et al., 1997), -.093 (ns). These effect sizes are based on the longest follow-up data using the most relevant outcomes of fighting, delinquency, and behavior problems, respectively.
5. Five of the seven programs focused on parent education in the context of home visiting (three were included in our meta-analysis of this intervention) and the other two on parent education plus daycare. (Both were included in our meta-analysis of this intervention.)
6. Data were analyzed using the statistical technique of latent growth curve modeling, controlling for delinquency or substance use (respectively, at pretest), age, and gender.
7. We calculated d effect sizes for these programs: Houston: destructive behavior, .643 ($p < .001$); fighting, .475 ($p = .007$); London, 1.06 ($p < .001$)

(Farrington and Welsh, 2003, pp. 135, 137). The latter was the largest effect size of the 10 parent management training programs included in our meta-analysis.

CHAPTER 9

1. The four studies were: the Adolescent Transitions Program (Dishion and Andrews, 1995); the Cambridge-Somerville Youth Study (McCord, 1978); Guided Group Interaction: Peer Culture Development (Gottfredson, 1987); and the St. Louis Experiment (Feldman, Wodarski, and Caplinger, 1983).

2. It is important to note that we have purposely not reported on the results of our meta-analysis of school-based programs here (see tables 7.1 and 8.1). This is because the seven programs included were selected on the basis of having a family-based intervention as a major component. In addition, these programs were categorized as school-based because they took place in schools, not because they targeted school-level risk factors for delinquency.

3. Universal programs are delivered to the entire classroom; selected/indicated programs are delivered to selected children because of the presence of some risk factor; special schools/classes programs are for children who possess "some behavioral or school difficulty that is judged to warrant their placement outside of mainstream classrooms"; and comprehensive programs involve multiple treatment modalities and formats (Wilson and Lipsey, 2005, pp. 10–11).

4. These reviews cannot be classified as systematic or meta-analytic reviews. Instead, they are comprehensive vote-counting reviews that consider statistical significance and integrate the Scientific Methods Scale, which ranks evaluation studies on overall internal validity (Farrington, Gottfredson, Sherman, and Welsh, 2002b). These reviews also identified gang member intervention programs (i.e., those focused on reducing cohesion among youth gangs and individual gang members) as another promising community-based effort to preventing criminal offending. We purposely left gang programs out of this discussion because this book's focus is on preventive interventions that take place early in life and are targeted at children or adolescents before they become involved in a life of crime. Furthermore, these reviews identified after-school recreation as promising. The recreation component had more to do with the location or setting (recreation center) in which the after-school programs were implemented than with the provision of recreation activities, which was not always the main intervention. Hence we do not consider recreation programs.

5. One explanation for this outcome could be that mentees with no prior offenses formed relationships with delinquent youngsters. Unfortunately, the study authors (Fo and O'Donnell, 1975) did not investigate this.

6. The other three outcomes were "emotional/psychological," "social competence," and "academic/educational."

7. Drug Abuse Resistance Education (D.A.R.E.) is an example of a noncognitive behavioral instruction program used in schools. Denise Gottfredson and her colleagues (2002a) found that D.A.R.E. was ineffective in preventing delinquency and drug use.

CHAPTER 10

1. The other three principles are: (1) any response to crime needs to go beyond the criminal justice system and be part of a long-range approach that is also responsive to immediate needs; (2) crime prevention must bring together those responsible for housing, social services, schools, policing, and justice to tackle the crime risk factors; and (3) partnerships need to be developed at local and national levels (European Forum for Urban Safety et al., 1989).

2. A later project expanded the number of countries to nine, by adding Sweden and New Zealand (Sansfaçon and Welsh, 1999).

3. These involve "measures developed as a result of a careful effort to identify causal factors while mobilizing the agencies able to influence those factors" (Waller and Welsh, 1999, p. 191).

4. This branch includes the National Crime Prevention Centre, the Corrections Policy Directorate, and the Aboriginal Policing Directorate.

5. These divisions are: local crime prevention; reform evaluation; evaluation of individual measures; crime studies; statistics; methodology and development; information and publications; administration; and international (National Council for Crime Prevention, 2001, p. 14).

6. Half of the staff are located at the Centre's main office in the nation's capital (Ottawa), and the other half are dispersed among the regional offices across the country. Almost three-quarters (62) of the staff are involved in program delivery, and the remainder (23) work in policy, research, and evaluation.

7. Not all were convinced of the value of Sweden's new national crime prevention policy, which also had the effect of greatly reducing government support for crime prevention research and vesting greater autonomy in municipalities over decisions about what works in preventing crime. As noted

by Per-Olof Wikström and Marie Torstensson: "We fear that prevention once again, as was much the case in the 1970s, will become increasingly dominated by slogans, such as that 'crime prevention is our collective responsibility,' the idea that crime prevention is best served by letting [a] 'thousand flowers bloom' (basically that all crime prevention ideas are equally valid until proven otherwise) and the view that 'locals' know best what to do about their crime problem" (1999, p. 460, n. 1).

8. In fiscal year 2002–3, 49 of the state's 64 counties participated in the program, and by the end of the fiscal year, services had been provided to 1,384 families with 1,019 children at a cost of $5,560,660 (Calonge, 2005, p. 5), or about $4,000 per family. No evaluation of the program's effects on child maltreatment is known to have been carried out.

REFERENCES

Alexander, James F., and Bruce V. Parsons. 1973. "Short-Term Behavioral Intervention with Delinquent Families: Impact on Family Process and Recidivism." *Journal of Abnormal Psychology* 81: 219–225.

Andersson, Jan. 2005. "The Swedish National Council for Crime Prevention: A Short Presentation." *Journal of Scandinavian Studies in Criminology and Crime Prevention* 6: 74–88.

Aos, Steve, Roxanne Lieb, Jim Mayfield, Marna Miller, and Annie Pennucci. 2004. *Benefits and Costs of Prevention and Early Intervention Programs for Youth.* Olympia: Washington State Institute for Public Policy.

Aos, Steve, Polly Phipps, Robert Barnoski, and Roxanne Lieb. 2001. "The Comparative Costs and Benefits of Programs to Reduce Crime: A Review of Research Findings with Implications for Washington State." In *Costs and Benefits of Preventing Crime*, Brandon C. Welsh, David P. Farrington, and Lawrence W. Sherman, eds. Boulder, Colo.: Westview Press.

Baldwin, John, Anthony E. Bottoms, and Monica A. Walker. 1976. *The Urban Criminal.* London: Tavistock.

Bank, Lew, and Bert Burraston. 2001. "Abusive Home Environments as Predictors of Poor Adjustment during Adolescence and Early Adulthood." *Journal of Community Psychology* 29: 195–217.

Bank, Lew, Gerald R. Patterson, and John B. Reid. 1996. "Negative Sibling Interaction Patterns as Predictors of Later Adjustment Problems in Adolescent and Young Adult Males." In *Sibling Relationships: Their Causes and Consequences*, Gene H. Brody, ed. Norwood, N.J.: Ablex.

Barnett, W. Steven. 1993. "Cost-Benefit Analysis." In *Significant Benefits: The High/Scope Perry Preschool Study through Age 27*, Lawrence J. Schweinhart, Helen V. Barnes, and David P. Weikart. Ypsilanti, Mich.: High/Scope Press.

Barnett, W. Steven. 1996. *Lives in the Balance: Age–27 Benefit-Cost Analysis of the High/Scope Perry Preschool Program*. Ypsilanti, Mich.: High/Scope Press.

Barnett, W. Steven, and Colette M. Escobar. 1987. "The Economics of Early Educational Intervention: A Review." *Review of Educational Research* 57: 387–414.

Barnett, W. Steven, and Colette M. Escobar. 1990. "Economic Costs and Benefits of Early Intervention." In *Handbook of Early Childhood Intervention*, Samuel J. Meisels and Jack P. Shonkoff, eds. New York: Cambridge University Press.

Baron, Reuben M., and David A. Kenny. 1986. "The Moderator-Mediator Variable Distinction in Social Psychological Research: Conceptual, Strategic, and Statistical Considerations." *Journal of Personality and Social Psychology* 51: 1173–1182.

Bates, John E. 1989. "Applications of Temperament Concepts." In *Temperament in Childhood*, G. A. Kohnstamm, John E. Bates, and Mary K. Rothbart, eds. Chichester, England: Wiley.

Battin, Sara R., Karl G. Hill, Robert D. Abbott, Richard F. Catalano, and J. David Hawkins. 1998. "The Contribution of Gang Membership to Delinquency beyond Delinquent Friends." *Criminology* 36: 93–115.

Baumrind, Diana. 1966. "Effects of Authoritative Parental Control on Child Behavior." *Child Development* 37: 887–907.

Bennett, Trevor H. 1996. "Community Crime Prevention in Britain. In *Kommunale Kriminalprävention: Paradigmenwechsel und Wiederentdeckung alter Weisheiten*, Thomas Trenczek and Hartmut Pfeiffer, eds. Bonn: Forum Verlag Godesberg.

Bernazzani, Odette, Catherine Côté, and Richard E. Tremblay. 2001. "Early Parent Training to Prevent Disruptive Behavior Problems and Delinquency in Children." *Annals of the American Academy of Political and Social Science* 578: 90–103.

Bernazzani, Odette, and Richard E. Tremblay. 2006. "Early Parent Training." In *Preventing Crime: What Works for Children, Offenders, Victims, and Places*, Brandon C. Welsh and David P. Farrington, eds. Dordrecht: Springer.

Berrueta-Clement, John R., Lawrence J. Schweinhart, W. Steven Barnett, Ann

S. Epstein, and David P. Weikart. 1984. *Changed Lives: The Effects of the Perry Preschool Program on Youths through Age 19*. Ypsilanti, Mich.: High/Scope Press.

Beyers, Jennifer M., Rolf Loeber, Per-Olof H. Wikström, and Magda Stouthamer-Loeber. 2001. "Predictors of Adolescent Violence by Neighborhood." *Journal of Abnormal Child Psychology* 29: 369–381.

Bilukha, Oleg, Robert A. Hahn, Alex Crosby, Mindy T. Fullilove, Akiva Liberman, Eve Moscicki, Susan Snyder, Farris Tuma, Phaedra Corso, Amanda Schofield, and Peter A. Briss. 2005. "The Effectiveness of Early Childhood Home Visitation in Preventing Violence: A Systematic Review." *American Journal of Preventive Medicine* 28 (2S1): 11–39.

Blackburn, Ronald. 1993. *The Psychology of Criminal Conduct*. Chichester, England: Wiley.

Blokland, Arjan A. J., and Paul Nieuwbeerta. 2005. "The Effects of Life Circumstances on Longitudinal Trajectories of Offending." *Criminology* 43: 1203–1240.

Bor, William, Tara R. McGee, and Abigail A. Fagan. 2004. "Early Risk Factors for Adolescent Antisocial Behaviour: An Australian Longitudinal Study." *Australian and New Zealand Journal of Psychiatry* 38: 365–372.

Bor, William, Jake M. Najman, Margaret J. Andersen, Michael O'Callaghan, Gail M. Williams, and Brett C. Behrens. 1997. "The Relationship between Low Family Income and Psychological Disturbance in Young Children: An Australian Longitudinal Study." *Australian and New Zealand Journal of Psychiatry* 31: 664–675.

Bottoms, Anthony E., and Paul Wiles. 2002. "Environmental Criminology." In *The Oxford Handbook of Criminology*, Mike Maguire, Rod Morgan, and Robert Reiner, eds. Oxford: Oxford University Press.

Bowlby, John. 1951. *Maternal Care and Mental Health*. Geneva: World Health Organization.

Brantingham, Paul J., and Frederick L. Faust. 1976. "A Conceptual Model of Crime Prevention." *Crime and Delinquency* 22: 284–296.

Brennan, Patricia A., Emily R. Grekin, and Sarnoff A. Mednick. 1999. "Maternal Smoking during Pregnancy and Adult Male Criminal Outcomes." *Archives of General Psychiatry* 56: 215–219.

Brennan, Patricia A., Birgitte R. Mednick, and Sarnoff A. Mednick. 1993. "Parental Psychopathology, Congenital Factors, and Violence." In *Mental Disorder and Crime*, Sheilagh Hodgins, ed. Newbury Park, Calif.: Sage.

Brennan, Patricia A., Sarnoff A. Mednick, and Sheilagh Hodgins. 2000. "Major Mental Disorders and Criminal Violence in a Danish Birth Cohort." *Archives of General Psychiatry* 57: 494–500.

Brezina, Timothy. 1998. "Adolescent Maltreatment and Delinquency: The Question of Intervening Processes." *Journal of Research in Crime and Delinquency* 35: 71–99.

Brownfield, David, and Ann M. Sorenson. 1994. "Sibship Size and Sibling Delinquency." *Deviant Behavior* 15: 45–61.

Buehler, Cheryl, Christine Anthony, Ambika Krishnakumar, Gaye Stone, Jean Gerard, and Sharon Pemberton. 1997. "Interparental Conflict and Youth Problem Behaviors: A Meta-analysis." *Journal of Child and Family Studies* 6: 233–247.

Bursik, Robert J. 1988. "Social Disorganization and Theories of Crime and Delinquency: Problems and Prospects." *Criminology* 26: 519–551.

Bursik, Robert J., and Jim Webb. 1982. "Community Change and Patterns of Delinquency." *American Journal of Sociology* 88: 24–42.

Butterfield, Fox. 2003. "Proposed White House Budget Cuts Imperil a Lifeline for Troubled Oregon Teenagers." *New York Times*, June 7; available at: www.nytimes.com.

Calonge, Ned. 2005. "Community Interventions to Prevent Violence: Translation into Public Health Practice." *American Journal of Preventive Medicine* 28 (2S1): 4–5.

Campbell, Donald T., and Julian C. Stanley. 1966. *Experimental and Quasi-experimental Designs for Research*. Chicago: Rand McNally.

Campbell, Frances A., Craig T. Ramey, Elizabeth Pungello, Joseph Sparling, and Shari Miller-Johnson. 2002. "Early Childhood Education: Young Adult Outcomes from the Abecedarian Project." *Applied Developmental Science* 6: 42–57.

Canada. Government of Canada (2003). *National Crime Prevention Centre Strategic Plan 2002/03–2005/06*. Ottawa: Author.

Capaldi, Deborah M., and Gerald R. Patterson. 1991. "Relation of Parental Transitions to Boys' Adjustment Problems." *Developmental Psychology* 27: 489–504.

Capaldi, Deborah M., and Gerald R. Patterson. 1996. "Can Violent Offenders be Distinguished from Frequent Offenders? Prediction from Childhood to Adolescence." *Journal of Research in Crime and Delinquency* 33: 206–231.

Carlson, Elizabeth A., and L. Alan Sroufe. 1995. "Contribution of Attachment Theory to Developmental Psychopathology." In *Developmental Psychopa-*

thology, vol. 1, *Theory and Methods*, Dante Cicchetti and Donald J. Cohen, eds. New York: Wiley.

Caspi, Avshalom. 2000. "The Child Is Father of the Man: Personality Continuities from Childhood to Adulthood." *Journal of Personality and Social Psychology* 78: 158–172.

Catalano, Richard F., Michael W. Arthur, J. David Hawkins, Lisa Berglund, and Jeffrey J. Olson. 1998. "Comprehensive Community- and School-Based Interventions to Prevent Antisocial Behavior." In *Serious and Violent Juvenile Offenders: Risk Factors and Successful Interventions*, Rolf Loeber and David P. Farrington, eds. Thousand Oaks, Calif.: Sage.

Catalano, Richard F., and J. David Hawkins. 1996. "The Social Development Model: A Theory of Antisocial Behavior." In *Delinquency and Crime: Current Theories*, J. David Hawkins, ed. Cambridge: Cambridge University Press.

Chamberlain, Patricia, and John B. Reid. 1998. "Comparison of Two Community Alternatives to Incarceration for Chronic Juvenile Offenders." *Journal of Consulting and Clinical Psychology* 66: 624–633.

Chess, Stella, and Alexander Thomas. 1984. *Origins and Evolution of Behavior Disorders: From Infancy to Early Adult Life*. New York: Brunner/Mazel.

Clarke, Ronald V. 1995. "Situational Crime Prevention." In *Building a Safer Society: Strategic Approaches to Crime Prevention*, Michael Tonry and David P. Farrington, eds. Chicago: University of Chicago Press.

Clarke, Ronald V., and Derek B. Cornish. 1985. "Modelling Offenders' Decisions: A Framework for Research and Policy." In *Crime and Justice*, vol. 6, Michael Tonry and Norval Morris, eds. Chicago: University of Chicago Press.

Clarke, Ronald V., ed. 1997. *Situational Crime Prevention: Successful Case Studies*, 2nd ed. Guilderland, N.Y.: Harrow and Heston.

Cloward, Richard A., and Lloyd E. Ohlin. 1960. *Delinquency and Opportunity*. New York: Free Press.

Cohen, Albert K. 1955. *Delinquent Boys: The Culture of the Gang*. Glencoe, Ill.: Free Press.

Cohen, Patricia. 1996. "Childhood Risks for Young Adult Symptoms of Personality Disorder: Method and Substance." *Multivariate Behavioral Research* 31: 121–148.

Cohen, Patricia, and Judith S. Brook. 1995. "The Reciprocal Influence of Punishment and Child Behavior Disorder." In *Coercion and Punishment in Long-Term Perspectives*, Joan McCord, ed. Cambridge: Cambridge University Press.

Coie, John D., Kenneth A. Dodge, and Janice Kupersmidt. 1990. "Peer Group Behavior and Social Status." In *Peer Rejection in Childhood*, Stephen R. Asher and John D. Coie, eds. Cambridge: Cambridge University Press.

Coie, John, and Shari Miller-Johnson. 2001. "Peer Factors and Interventions." In *Child Delinquents: Development, Intervention, and Service Needs*, Rolf Loeber and David P. Farrington, eds. Thousand Oaks, Calif.: Sage.

Conduct Problems Prevention Research Group. 1999. "Initial Impact of the Fast Track Prevention Trial for Conduct Problems: I. The High-Risk Sample." *Journal of Consulting and Clinical Psychology* 67: 631–647.

Conduct Problems Prevention Research Group. 2002. "Evaluation of the First Three Years of the Fast Track Prevention Trial with Children at High Risk for Adolescent Conduct Problems." *Journal of Abnormal Child Psychology* 30: 19–35.

Conger, Rand D., Gerald R. Patterson, and Xiaojia Ge. 1995. "It Takes Two to Replicate: A Mediational Model for the Impact of Parents' Stress on Adolescent Adjustment." *Child Development* 66: 80–97.

Conseur, Amy, Frederick P. Rivara, Robert Barnoski, and Irvin Emanuel. 1997. "Maternal and Perinatal Risk Factors for Later Delinquency." *Pediatrics* 99: 785–790.

Cook, Thomas D., and Donald T. Campbell. 1979. *Quasi-experimentation: Design and Analysis Issues for Field Settings*. Chicago: Rand McNally.

Cullen, Kevin J. 1976. "A Six-Year Controlled Trial of Prevention of Children's Behaviour Disorders." *Journal of Paediatrics* 88: 662–666.

Currie, Janet. 2001. "Early Childhood Education Programs." *Journal of Economic Perspectives* 15: 213–238.

Curtis, Nicola M., Kevin R. Ronan, and Charles M. Borduin. 2004. "Multisystemic Treatment: A Meta-analysis of Outcome Studies." *Journal of Family Psychology* 18: 411–419.

Darling, Nancy, and Laurence Steinberg. 1993. "Parenting Style in Context: An Integrative Model." *Psychological Bulletin* 113: 487–496.

Deater-Deckard, Kirby, Kenneth A. Dodge, John E. Bates, and Gregory S. Pettit. 1996. "Physical Discipline among African American and European American Mothers: Links to Children's Externalizing Behaviors." *Developmental Psychology* 32: 1065–1072.

Denno, Deborah W. 1990. *Biology and Violence: From Birth to Adulthood*. Cambridge: Cambridge University Press.

DiLalla, Lisabeth F., and Irving I. Gottesman. 1991. "Biological and Genetic Contributions to Violence: Widom's Untold Tale." *Psychological Bulletin* 109: 125–129.

Dishion, Thomas J., and D. Andrews. 1995. "Preventing Escalation in Problem Behaviors with High-Risk Young Adolescents: Immediate and 1-Year Outcomes." *Journal of Consulting and Clinical Psychology* 63: 538–548.

Dishion, Thomas J., Joan McCord, and François Poulin. 1999. "When Interventions Harm: Peer Groups and Problem Behavior." *American Psychologist* 54: 755–764.

Dodge, Kenneth A. 1991. "The Structure and Function of Reactive and Proactive Aggression." In *The Development and Treatment of Childhood Aggression*, Debra J. Pepler and Kenneth H. Rubin, eds. Hillsdale, N.J.: Erlbaum.

Dodge, Kenneth A., Jennifer E. Lansford, Virginia S. Burks, John E. Bates, Gregory S. Pettit, Reid Fontaine, and Joseph M. Price. 2003. "Peer Rejection and Social Information-Processing Factors in the Development of Aggressive Behavior Problems in Children." *Child Development* 74: 374–393.

Dodge, Kenneth A., Gregory S. Pettit, and John E. Bates. 1994. "Socialization Mediators of the Relation between Socioeconomic Status and Child Conduct Problems." *Child Development* 65: 649–665.

DuBois, David L., Bruce E. Holloway, Jeffrey C. Valentine, and Harris Cooper. 2002. "Effectiveness of Mentoring Programs for Youth: A Meta-analytic Review." *American Journal of Community Psychology* 30: 157–197.

Duncan, Greg J., and Katherine Magnuson. 2004. "Individual and Parent-Based Intervention Strategies for Promoting Human Capital and Positive Behavior." In *Human Development across Lives and Generations: The Potential for Change*, P. Lindsay Chase-Lansdale, Kathleen Kiernan, and Ruth J. Friedman, eds. New York: Cambridge University Press.

Eggleston, Elaine P., and John H. Laub. 2002. "The Onset of Adult Offending: A Neglected Dimension of the Criminal Career." *Journal of Criminal Justice* 30: 603–622.

Eklund, Jenny, and Britt af Klinteberg. 2003. "Childhood Behaviour as Related to Subsequent Drinking Offenses and Violent Offending: A Prospective Study of Eleven to Fourteen-Year-Old Youths into Their Fourth Decade." *Criminal Behaviour and Mental Health* 13: 294–309.

Elliott, Delbert S. 1994. "Serious Violent Offenders: Onset, Developmental Course, and Termination." *Criminology* 32: 1–21.

Elliott, Delbert S., Beatrix A. Hamburg, and Kirk R. Williams. 1998. "Violence in American Schools: An Overview." In *Violence in American Schools: A New Perspective*, Delbert S. Elliott, Beatrix A. Hamburg, and Kirk R. Williams, eds. New York: Cambridge University Press.

Elliott, Delbert S., David Huizinga, and Scott Menard. 1989. *Multiple Problem Youth: Delinquency, Substance Use, and Mental Health Problems*. New York: Springer-Verlag.

Elliott, Delbert S., and Scott Menard. 1996. "Delinquent Friends and Delinquent Behavior: Temporal and Developmental Patterns." In *Delinquency and Crime: Current Theories*, J. David Hawkins, ed. Cambridge: Cambridge University Press.

Ellis, Lee. 1988. "The Victimful—Victimless Crime Distinction, and Seven Universal Demographic Correlates of Victimful Criminal Behavior." *Personality and Individual Differences* 3: 525–548.

Eron, Leonard D., L. Rowell Huesmann, and Arnaldo Zelli. 1991. "The Role of Parental Variables in the Learning of Aggression." In *The Development and Treatment of Childhood Aggression*, Debra J. Pepler and Kenneth J. Rubin, eds. Hillsdale, N.J.: Lawrence Erlbaum.

European Forum for Urban Safety, Federation of Canadian Municipalities, and United States Conference of Mayors. 1989. "Agenda for Safer Cities: Final Declaration." European and North American Conference on Urban Safety and Crime Prevention, October 10–13, 1989, Montreal.

European Forum for Urban Safety, Federation of Canadian Municipalities, and United States Conference of Mayors. 1991. "Final Declaration." Second International Conference on Urban Safety, Drugs, and Crime Prevention, November 18–20, 1991, Paris.

Eysenck, Hans J. 1996. "Personality and Crime: Where do we Stand?" *Psychology, Crime and Law* 2: 143–152.

Fagan, Abigail A., and Jake M. Najman. 2003. "Sibling Influences on Adolescent Delinquent Behavior: An Australian Longitudinal Study." *Journal of Adolescence* 26: 547–559.

Farquhar, John W., Stephen P. Fortmann, Nathan MacCoby, William L. Haskell, Paul T. Williams, June A. Flora, C. Barr Taylor, Byron W. Brown, Douglas S. Solomon, and Stephen B. Hulley. 1985. "The Stanford Five-City Project: Design and Methods." *American Journal of Epidemiology* 122: 323–334.

Farrell, Albert D., and Aleta L. Meyer. 1997. "The Effectiveness of a School-Based

Curriculum for Reducing Violence among Urban Sixth-Grade Students."
American Journal of Public Health 87: 979–984.

Farrell, Albert D., Aleta L. Meyer, Terri N. Sullivan, and Eva M. Kung. 2003. "Evaluation of the Responding in Peaceful and Positive Ways (RIPP) Seventh Grade Violence Prevention Curriculum." *Journal of Child and Family Studies* 12: 101–120.

Farrington, David P. 1972. "Delinquency Begins at Home." *New Society* 21: 495–497.

Farrington, David P. 1979a. "Experiments on Deviance with Special Reference to Dishonesty." In *Advances in Experimental Social Psychology*, vol. 12, Leonard Berkowitz, ed. New York: Academic Press.

Farrington, David P. 1979b. "Longitudinal Research on Crime and Delinquency." In *Crime and Justice: An Annual Review of Research*, vol. 1, Norval Morris and Michael Tonry, eds. Chicago: University of Chicago Press.

Farrington, David P. 1983. "Randomized Experiments on Crime and Justice." In *Crime and Justice: An Annual Review of Research*, vol. 4, Michael Tonry and Norval Morris, eds. Chicago: University of Chicago Press.

Farrington, David P. 1986. "Stepping Stones to Adult Criminal Careers." In *Development of Antisocial and Prosocial Behavior*, Dan Olweus, Jack Block, and Marian R. Yarrow, eds. New York: Academic Press.

Farrington, David P. 1988. "Studying Changes Within Individuals: The Causes of Offending." In *Studies of Psychosocial Risk: The Power of longitudinal Data*, Michael Rutter, ed. New York: Cambridge University Press.

Farrington, David P. 1989."Early Predictors of Adolescent Aggression and Adult Violence." *Violence and Victims* 4: 79–100.

Farrington, David P. 1990. "Implications of Criminal Career research for the Prevention of Offending." *Journal of Adolescence* 13: 93–113.

Farrington, David P. 1991. "Childhood Aggression and Adult Violence: Early Precursors and Later Life Outcomes." In *The Development and Treatment of Childhood Aggression*, Debra J. Pepler and Kenneth H. Rubin, eds. Hillsdale, N.J.: Erlbaum.

Farrington, David P. 1992a. "Explaining the Beginning, Progress and Ending of Antisocial Behavior from Birth to Adulthood." In *Facts, Frameworks and Forecasts: Advances in Criminological Theory*, vol. 3, Joan McCord, ed. New Brunswick, N.J.: Transaction.

Farrington, David P. 1992b. "Juvenile Delinquency." In *The School Years*, 2nd ed., John C. Coleman, ed. London: Routledge.

Farrington, David P. 1993a. "Childhood Origins of Teenage Antisocial Behavior and Adult Social Dysfunction." *Journal of the Royal Society of Medicine* 86: 13–17.

Farrington, David P. 1993b. "Understanding and Preventing Bullying." In *Crime and Justice*, vol. 17, Michael Tonry and Norval Morris, eds. Chicago: University of Chicago Press.

Farrington, David P. 1994a. "Childhood, Adolescent and Adult Features of Violent Males." In *Aggressive Behavior: Current Perspectives*, L. Rowell Huesmann, ed. New York: Plenum.

Farrington, David P. 1994b. "Early Developmental Prevention of Delinquency." *Criminal Behaviour and Mental Health* 4: 209–227.

Farrington, David P. 1995. "The Development of Offending and Antisocial Behavior from Childhood: Key Findings from the Cambridge Study in Delinquent Development." *Journal of Child Psychology and Psychiatry* 36: 929–964.

Farrington, David P. 1997a. "Evaluating a Community Crime Prevention Program." *Evaluation* 3: 157–173.

Farrington, David P. 1997b. "Human Development and Criminal Careers." In *The Oxford Handbook of Criminology*, 2nd. ed., Mike Maguire, Rod Morgan, and Robert Reiner, eds. Oxford: Clarendon Press.

Farrington, David P. 1997c. "The Relationship between Low Resting Heart Rate and Violence." In *Biosocial Bases of Violence*, Adrian Raine, Patricia A. Brennan, David P. Farrington, and Sarnoff Mednick, eds. New York: Plenum.

Farrington, David P. 1998a. "Individual Differences and Offending." In *The Handbook of Crime and Punishment*, Michael Tonry, ed. New York: Oxford University Press.

Farrington, David P. 1998b. "Predictors, Causes, and Correlates of Youth Violence." In *Youth Violence*, Michael Tonry and Mark H. Moore, eds. Chicago: University of Chicago Press.

Farrington, David P. 1998c. "Youth Crime and Antisocial Behaviour." In *The Social Child*, Anne Campbell and Steven Muncer, eds. Hove, England: Psychology Press.

Farrington, David P. 2000. "Explaining and Preventing Crime: The Globalization of Knowledge." *Criminology* 38: 1–24.

Farrington, David P. 2002. "Families and Crime." In *Crime: Public Policies for Crime Control*, James Q. Wilson and Joan Petersilia, eds. Oakland, Calif.: Institute for Contemporary Studies Press.

Farrington, David P. 2003a. "Developmental and Life-Course Criminology: Key Theoretical and Empirical Issues." *Criminology* 41: 221–255.

Farrington, David P. 2003b. "Key Results from the First 40 Years of the Cambridge Study in Delinquent Development." In *Taking Stock of Delinquency: An Overview of Findings from Contemporary Longitudinal Studies*, Terence P. Thornberry and Marvin D. Krohn, eds. New York: Kluwer/ Plenum.

Farrington, David P. 2003c. "Methodological Quality Standards for Evaluation Research." *Annals of the American Academy of Political and Social Science* 587: 49–68.

Farrington, David P. 2005. "The Integrated Cognitive Antisocial Potential (ICAP) Theory." In *Integrated Developmental and Life-Course Theories of Offending*, David P. Farrington, ed. New Brunswick, N.J.: Transaction.

Farrington, David P. 2006. "Key Longitudinal-Experimental Studies in Criminology." *Journal of Experimental Criminology* 2: 121–141.

Farrington, David P., Geoffrey Barnes, and Sandra Lambert. 1996. "The Concentration of Offending in Families." *Legal and Criminological Psychology* 1: 47–63.

Farrington, David P., Louise Biron, and Marc LeBlanc. 1982. "Personality and Delinquency in London and Montreal." In *Abnormal Offenders, Delinquency, and the Criminal Justice System*, John Gunn and David P. Farrington, eds. Chichester, England: Wiley.

Farrington, David P., Bernard Gallagher, Lynda Morley, Raymond St. Ledger, and Donald J. West. 1986. "Unemployment, School Leaving, and Crime." *British Journal of Criminology* 26: 335–356.

Farrington, David P., Bernard Gallagher, Lynda Morley, Raymond St. Ledger, and Donald J. West. 1990. "Minimizing Attrition in Longitudinal Research: Methods of Tracing and Securing Cooperation in a Twenty-Four-Year Follow-up." In *Data Quality in Longitudinal Research*, David Magnusson and Lars Bergman, eds. Cambridge: Cambridge University Press.

Farrington, David P., Denise C. Gottfredson, Lawrence W. Sherman, and Brandon C. Welsh. 2002b. "The Maryland Scientific Methods Scale." In *Evidence-Based Crime Prevention*, Lawrence W. Sherman, David P. Farrington, Brandon C. Welsh, and Doris Layton MacKenzie, eds. New York: Routledge.

Farrington, David P., and J. David Hawkins. 1991. "Predicting Participation, Early Onset, and Later Persistence in Officially Recorded Offending." *Criminal Behavior and Mental Health* 1: 1–33.

Farrington, David P., Darrick Jolliffe, Rolf Loeber, Magda Stouthamer-Loeber, and Larry M. Kalb. 2001. "The Concentration of Offenders in Families, and Family Criminality in the Prediction of Boys' Delinquency." *Journal of Adolescence* 24: 579–596.

Farrington, David P., and Rolf Loeber. 2000. "Some Benefits of Dichotomization in Psychiatric and Criminological Research." *Criminal Behavior and Mental Health* 10: 100–122.

Farrington, David P., and Rolf Loeber. 1999. "Transatlantic Replicability of Risk Factors in the Development of Delinquency." In *Historical and Geographical Influences on Psychopathology*, Patricia Cohen, Cheryl Slomkowski and Lee N. Robins, eds. Mahwah, N.J.: Erlbaum.

Farrington, David P., Rolf Loeber, and Magda Stouthamer-Loeber. 2003. "How Can the Relationship between Race and Violence be Explained?" In *Violent Crime: Assessing Race and Ethnic Differences*, Darnell F. Hawkins, ed. Cambridge: Cambridge University Press.

Farrington, David P., Rolf Loeber, and Welmoet van Kammen. 1990. "Long-Term Criminal Outcomes of Hyperactivity-Impulsivity-Attention Deficit and Conduct Problems in Childhood." In *Straight and Devious Pathways from Childhood to Adulthood*, Lee N. Robins and Michael Rutter, eds. Cambridge: Cambridge University press.

Farrington, David P., Rolf Loeber, Yanming Yin, and Stewart Anderson. 2002a. "Are Within-Individual Causes of Delinquency the Same as Between-Individual Causes?" *Criminal Behavior and Mental Health* 12: 53–68.

Farrington, David P., and Anthony Petrosino. 2001. "The Campbell Collaboration Crime and Justice Group." *Annals of the American Academy of Political and Social Science* 578: 35–49.

Farrington, David P., Robert J. Sampson, and Per-Olof H. Wikström, eds. 1993. *Integrating Individual and Ecological Aspects of Crime*. Stockholm: National Council for Crime Prevention.

Farrington, David P., and Brandon C. Welsh. 2002. "Family-Based Crime Prevention." In *Evidence-Based Crime Prevention*, Lawrence W. Sherman, David P. Farrington, Brandon C. Welsh, and Doris Layton MacKenzie, eds. New York: Routledge.

Farrington, David P., and Brandon C. Welsh. 2003. "Family-Based Prevention of Offending: A Meta-analysis." *Australian and New Zealand Journal of Criminology* 36: 127–151.

Farrington, David P., and Brandon C. Welsh. 2005. "Randomized Experiments in Criminology: What Have We Learned in the Last Two Decades?" *Journal of Experimental Criminology* 1: 9–38.

Farrington, David P., and Brandon C. Welsh. In press. "A Half-Century of Randomized Experiments on Crime and Justice." In *Crime and Justice: A Review of Research*, vol. 34. Chicago: University of Chicago Press.

Farrington, David P., and Donald J. West. 1993. "Criminal, Penal and Life Histories of Chronic Offenders: Risk and Protective Factors and Early Identification." *Criminal Behavior and Mental Health* 3: 492–523.

Farrington, David P., and Donald J. West. 1995. "Effects of Marriage, Separation and Children on Offending by Adult Males." In *Current Perspectives on Aging and the Life Cycle*, vol. 4, *Delinquency and Disrepute in the Life Course*, John Hagan, ed. Greenwich, Conn.: JAI Press.

Feldman, Ronald A., John S. Wodarski, and Timothy E. Caplinger. 1983. *St. Louis Conundrum: The Effective Treatment of Antisocial Youth*. Englewood Cliffs, N.J.: Prentice-Hall.

Fergusson, David M., and L. John Horwood. 1998. "Exposure to Interparental Violence in Childhood and Psychosocial Adjustment in Young Adulthood." *Child Abuse and Neglect* 22: 339–357.

Fergusson, David M., L. John Horwood, and Michael T. Lynskey. 1992. "Family Change, Parental Discord and Early Offending." *Journal of Child Psychology and Psychiatry* 33: 1059–1075.

Fergusson, David M., L. John Horwood, and Michael T. Lynskey. 1994. "The Childhoods of Multiple Problem Adolescents: A Fifteen-Year Longitudinal Study." *Journal of Child Psychology and Psychiatry* 35: 1123–1140.

Fergusson, David M., Nicola Swain-Campbell, and L. John Horwood. 2004. "How Does Childhood Economic Disadvantage Lead to Crime?" *Journal of Child Psychology and Psychiatry* 45: 956–966.

Fischer, Dean G. 1984. "Family Size and Delinquency." *Perceptual and Motor Skills* 58: 527–534.

Fo, Walter S. O., and Clifford R. O'Donnell. 1975. "The Buddy System: Effect of Community Intervention on Delinquent Offenses." *Behavior Therapy* 6: 522–524.

Forehand, Rex, Heather Biggar, and Beth A. Kotchick. 1998. "Cumulative Risk across Family Stressors: Short and Long Term Effects for Adolescents." *Journal of Abnormal Child Psychology* 26: 119–128.

France, Alan, and Iain Crow. 2001. *CTC—The Story So Far: An Interim Evaluation of Communities That Care*. York, England: Joseph Rowntree Foundation.

Frick, Paul J., Rachel E. Christian, and Jane M. Wootton. 1999. "Age Trends in the Association between Parenting Practices and Conduct Problems." *Behavior Modification* 23: 106–128.

Garces, Eliana, Duncan Thomas, and Janet Currie. 2002. "Longer-Term Effects of Head Start." *American Economic Review* 92: 999–1012.

Gatti, Uberto, Richard E. Tremblay, Frank Vitaro, and Pierre McDuff. 2005. "Youth Gangs, Delinquency and Drug Use: A Test of the Selection, Facilitation and Enhancement Hypotheses." *Journal of Child Psychology and Psychiatry* 46: 1178–1190.

Gest, Ted. 2001. *Crime and Politics: Big Government's Erratic Campaign for Law and Order.* New York: Oxford University Press.

Gomby, Deanna S., Patti L. Culross, and Richard E. Behrman. 1999. "Home Visiting: Recent Program Evaluations—Analysis and Recommendations." *Future of Children* 9 (1): 4–26.

Gordon, Rachel A., Benjamin B. Lahey, Eriko Kawai, Rolf Loeber, Magda Stouthamer-Loeber, and David P. Farrington. 2004. "Antisocial Behavior and Youth Gang Membership: Selection and Socialization." *Criminology* 42: 55–87.

Gorman-Smith, Deborah, Patrick H. Tolan, Arnaldo Zelli, and L. Rowell Huesmann. 1996. "The Relation of Family Functioning to Violence among Inner-City Minority Youths." *Journal of Family Psychology* 10: 115–129.

Gottfredson, Denise C. 1986. "An Empirical Test of School-Based Environmental and Individual Interventions to Reduce the Risk of Delinquent Behavior." *Criminology* 24: 705–731.

Gottfredson, Denise C. 1990. "Changing School Structures to Benefit High-Risk Youths." In *Understanding Troubled and Troubling Youth*, Peter E. Leone, ed. Newbury Park, Calif.: Sage.

Gottfredson, Denise C. 2001. *Schools and Delinquency.* Cambridge: Cambridge University Press.

Gottfredson, Denise C., Stephanie A. Gerstenblith, David A. Soulé, Shannon C. Womer, and Shaoli Lu. 2004. "Do After School Programs Reduce Delinquency?" *Prevention Science* 5: 253–266.

Gottfredson, Denise C., Gary D. Gottfredson, and Stephanie A. Weisman. 2001. "The Timing of Delinquent Behavior and Its Implications for After-School Programs." *Criminology and Public Policy* 1: 61–86.

Gottfredson, Denise C., R. J. McNeil, and Gary D. Gottfredson. 1991. "Social Area

Influences on Delinquency: A Multilevel Analysis." *Journal of Research in Crime and Delinquency* 28: 197–226.

Gottfredson, Denise C., David B. Wilson, and Stacey S. Najaka. 2002a. "School-Based Crime Prevention." In *Evidence-Based Crime Prevention*, Lawrence W. Sherman, David P. Farrington, Brandon C. Welsh, and Doris L. MacKenzie, eds. New York: Routledge.

Gottfredson, Denise C., David B. Wilson, and Stacey S. Najaka. 2002b. "The Schools." In *Crime: Public Policies for Crime Control*, 2nd ed., James Q. Wilson and Joan Petersilia, eds. Oakland, Calif.: Institute for Contemporary Studies Press.

Gottfredson, Gary D. 1987. "Peer Group Interventions to Reduce the Risk of Delinquent Behavior: A Selective Review and a New Evaluation." *Criminology* 25: 671–714.

Gottfredson, Michael, and Travis Hirschi. 1990. *A General Theory of Crime.* Stanford, Calif.: Stanford University Press.

Graham, John. 1988. *Schools, Disruptive Behaviour and Delinquency.* Home Office Research Study No. 96. London: Her Majesty's Stationery Office

Greenwood, Peter W. 2006. *Changing Lives: Delinquency Prevention as Crime-Control Policy.* Chicago: University of Chicago Press.

Greenwood, Peter W., Lynn A. Karoly, Susan S. Everingham, Jill Houbé, M. Rebecca Kilburn, C. Peter Rydell, Matthew Sanders, and James Chiesa. 2001. "Estimating the Costs and Benefits of Early Childhood Interventions: Nurse Home Visits and the Perry Preschool." In *Costs and Benefits of Preventing Crime*, Brandon C. Welsh, David P. Farrington, and Lawrence W. Sherman, eds. Boulder, Colo.: Westview Press.

Groeneveld, L. P., James F. Short, and P. Thoits. 1979. *Design of a Study to Assess the Impact of Income Maintenance on Delinquency.* Washington, D.C.: National Institute of Juvenile Justice and Delinquency Prevention.

Grossman, Jean B., and Joseph P. Tierney. 1998. "Does Mentoring Work? An Impact Study of the Big Brothers Big Sisters Program." *Evaluation Review* 22: 403–426.

Grove, William M., Elke D. Eckert, Leonard Heston, Thomas J. Bouchard, Nancy Segal, and David T. Lykken. 1990. "Heritability of Substance Abuse and Antisocial Behavior: A Study of Monozygotic Twins Reared Apart." *Biological Psychiatry* 27: 1293–1304.

Guerin, D. W., A. W. Gottfried, and C. W. Thomas. 1997. "Difficult Tempera-

ment and Behavior Problems: A Longitudinal Study from 1.5 to 12 Years."
International Journal of Behavioral Development 21: 71–90.

Haapasalo, Jaana, and Elina Pokela. 1999. "Child-Rearing and Child Abuse Antecedents of Criminality." *Aggression and Violent Behavior* 4: 107–127.

Haas, Henriette, David P. Farrington, Martin Killias, and Ghazala Sattar. 2004. "The Impact of Different Family Configurations on Delinquency." *British Journal of Criminology* 44: 520–532.

Hahn, Andrew. 1994. "Evaluation of the Quantum Opportunities Program (QOP): Did the Program Work?" Unpublished report, Brandeis University, Waltham, Massachusetts.

Hahn, Andrew. 1999. "Extending the Time of Learning." In *America's Disconnected Youth: Toward a Preventive Strategy*, Douglas J. Besharov, ed. Washington, D.C.: Child Welfare League of America Press.

Harachi, Tracy W., J. David Hawkins, Richard F. Catalano, Andrea M. Lafazia, Brian H. Smith, and Michael W. Arthur. 2003. "Evidence-Based Community Decision Making for Prevention: Two Case Studies of Communities That Care." *Japanese Journal of Sociological Criminology* 28: 26–37.

Harrell, Adele V., Shannon E. Cavanagh, Michele A. Harmon, Christopher S. Koper, and Sanjeev Sridharan. 1997. *Impact of the Children at Risk Program: Comprehensive Final Report.* Vol. 2. Washington, D.C.: Urban Institute.

Harrell, Adele V., Shannon E. Cavanagh, and Sanjeev Sridharan. 1999. *Evaluation of the Children at Risk Program: Results 1 Year after the End of the Program.* Research in Brief. Washington, D.C.: U.S. Department of Justice, National Institute of Justice.

Hart, Stephen, D., and Robert D. Hare. 1994. "Psychopathy and the Big Five: Correlations between Observers' Ratings of Normal and Pathological Personality." *Journal of Personality Disorders* 8: 32–40.

Hawkins, J. David, and Richard F. Catalano. 1992. *Communities That Care: Action for Drug Abuse Prevention.* San Francisco: Jossey-Bass.

Hawkins, J. David, Richard F. Catalano, Rick Kosterman, Robert Abbott, and Karl G. Hill. 1999. "Preventing Adolescent Health Risk Behaviors by Strengthening Protection during Childhood." *Archives of Pediatric and Adolescent Medicine* 153: 226–234.

Hawkins, J. David, Brian H. Smith, Karl G. Hill, Rick Kosterman, Richard F. Catalano, and Robert D. Abbott. 2003. "Understanding and Preventing Crime and Violence: Findings from the Seattle Social Development Project." In *Taking Stock of Delinquency: An Overview of Findings from Contemporary*

Longitudinal Studies, Terence P. Thornberry and Marvin D. Krohn, eds. New York: Kluwer/Plenum.

Hawkins, J. David, Elizabeth von Cleve, and Richard F. Catalano. 1991. "Reducing Early Childhood Aggression: Results of a Primary Prevention Program." *Journal of the American Academy of Child and Adolescent Psychiatry* 30: 208–217.

Heaven, Patrick C. L. 1996. "Personality and Self-reported Delinquency: Analysis of the 'Big Five' Personality Dimensions." *Personality and Individual Differences* 20: 47–54.

Henggeler, Scott W., Sonja K. Schoenwald, Charles M. Borduin, Melisa D. Rowland, and Phillippe B. Cunningham. 1998. *Multisystemic Treatment of Antisocial Behavior in Children and Adolescents.* New York: Guilford Press.

Henry, Bill, Avshalom Caspi, Terrie E. Moffitt, and Phil A. Silva. 1996. "Temperamental and Familial Predictors of Violent and Nonviolent Criminal Convictions: Age Three to Age Eighteen." *Developmental Psychology* 32: 614–623.

Henry, Bill, Terrie E. Moffitt, Lee Robins, Felton Earls, and Phil Silva. 1993. "Early Family Predictors of Child and Adolescent Antisocial Behavior: Who Are the Mothers of Delinquents?" *Criminal Behavior and Mental Health* 3: 97–118.

Herrenkohl, Todd I., J. David Hawkins, Ick-Jung Chung, Karl G. Hill and Sarah Battin-Pearson. 2001. "School and Community Risk Factors and Interventions." In *Child Delinquents: Development, Intervention and Service Needs*, Rolf Loeber and David P. Farrington, eds. Thousand Oaks, Calif.: Sage.

Hill, Karl G., James C. Howell, J. David Hawkins, and Sara R. Battin-Pearson. 1999. "Childhood Risk Factors for Adolescent Gang Membership: Results from the Seattle Social Development Project." *Journal of Research in Crime and Delinquency* 36: 300–322.

Hindelang, Michael J., Travis Hirschi, and Joseph G. Weis. 1981. *Measuring Delinquency.* Beverly Hills, Calif.: Sage.

Hogh, Erik, and Preben Wolf. 1983. "Violent Crime in a Birth Cohort: Copenhagen 1953–1977." In *Prospective Studies of Crime and Delinquency*, Katherine T. van Dusen and Sarnoff A. Mednick, eds. Boston: Kluwer-Nijhoff.

Hope, Tim. 1995. "Community Crime Prevention." In *Building a Safer Society: Strategic Approaches to Crime Prevention*, Michael Tonry and David P. Farrington, eds. Chicago: University of Chicago Press.

Howell, James C., and Arlen Egley. 2005. "Moving Risk Factors into Developmental Theories of Gang Membership." *Youth Violence and Juvenile Justice* 3: 334–354.

Howell, James C., ed. 1995. *Guide for Implementing the Comprehensive Strategy for Serious, Violent, and Chronic Juvenile Offenders*. Washington, D.C.: U.S. Department of Justice, Office of Juvenile Justice and Delinquency Prevention.

Huesmann, L. Rowell, and Leonard D. Eron. 1984. "Individual Differences and the Trait of Aggression." *European Journal of Personality* 3: 95–106.

Huizinga, David, Anne W. Weiher, Rachel Espiritu, and Finn Esbensen. 2003. "Delinquency and Crime: Some Highlights from the Denver Youth Survey." In *Taking Stock of Delinquency: An Overview of Findings from Contemporary Longitudinal Studies*, Terence P. Thornberry and Marvin D. Krohn, eds. New York: Kluwer/Plenum.

Hunter, Andrea G., and Margaret E. Ensminger. 1992. "Diversity and Fluidity in Children's Living Arrangements: Family Transitions in an Urban Afro-American Community." *Journal of Marriage and the Family* 54: 418–426.

Ireland, Timothy O., Terence P. Thornberry, and Rolf Loeber. 2003. "Violence among Adolescents Living in Public Housing: A Two-Site Analysis." *Criminology and Public Policy* 3: 3–38.

Irving, Mark H. 2006. Electronic Communication with the Acting Chief of the Research and Knowledge Unit, National Crime Prevention Centre, Canada, March 17.

Jaffee, Sara, Avshalom Caspi, Terrie E. Moffitt, Jay Belsky, and Phil A. Silva. 2001. "Why Are Children born to Teen Mothers at Risk for Adverse Outcomes in Young Adulthood? Results from a 20-year Longitudinal Study." *Development and Psychopathology* 13: 377–397.

Jang, Soon J., and Carolyn A. Smith. 1997. "A Test of Reciprocal Causal Relationships among Parental Supervision, Affective Ties, and Delinquency." *Journal of Research in Crime and Delinquency* 34: 307–336.

John, Oliver P., Avshalom Caspi, Richard W. Robins, Terrie E. Moffitt, and Magda Stouthamer-Loeber. 1994. "The 'Little Five': Exploring the Nomological Network of the Five-Factor Model of Personality in Adolescent Boys." *Child Development* 65: 160–178.

Johnson, Byron R., Spencer De Li, David B. Larson, and Michael McCullough. 2000. "A Systematic Review of the Religiosity and Delinquency Literature: A Research Note." *Journal of Contemporary Criminal Justice* 16: 32–52.

Johnson, Dale L., and James N. Breckenridge. 1982. "The Houston Parent-Child Development Center and the Primary Prevention of Behavior Problems in Young Children." *American Journal of Community Psychology* 10: 305–316.

Johnson, Dale L., and Todd Walker. 1987. "Primary Prevention of Behavior Problems in Mexican-American Children." *American Journal of Community Psychology* 15: 375–385.

Johnson, Jeffrey G., Elizabeth Smailes, Patricia Cohen, Stephanie Kasen, and Judith S. Brook. 2004. "Antisocial Parental Behavior, Problematic Parenting, and Aggressive Offspring Behavior during Adulthood." *British Journal of Criminology*, 44, 915–930.

Jolliffe, Darrick, and David P. Farrington. 2004. "Empathy and Offending: A Systematic Review and Meta-analysis." *Aggression and Violent Behavior* 9: 441–476.

Jolliffe, Darrick, and David P. Farrington. In press-a. "Development and Validation of the Basic Empathy Scale." *Journal of Adolescence.*

Jolliffe, Darrick, and David P. Farrington. In press-b. "Examining the Relationship between Low Empathy and Self-Reported Offending." *Legal and Criminological Psychology.*

Jonassen, C. T. 1949. "A Re-Evaluation and Critique of the Logic and Some Methods of Shaw and McKay." *American Sociological Review* 14: 608–614.

Jones, Marshall B., and David R. Offord. 1989. "Reduction of Antisocial Behaviour in Poor Children by Nonschool Skill-Development." *Journal of Child Psychology and Psychiatry* 30: 737–750.

Juby, Heather, and David P. Farrington. 2001. "Disentangling the Link between Disrupted Families and Delinquency." *British Journal of Criminology* 41: 22–40.

Kagan, Jerome. 1989. "Temperamental Contributions to Social Behavior." *American Psychologist* 44: 668–674.

Kandel, Elizabeth, Patricia Brennan, Sarnoff A. Mednick, and N. M. Michelson. 1989. "Minor Physical Anomalies and Recidivistic Adult Violent Criminal Behavior." *Acta Psychiatrica Scandinavica* 79: 103–107.

Kaplan, Robert M. 2000. "Two Pathways to Prevention." *American Psychologist* 55: 382–396.

Karoly, Lynn A., Peter W. Greenwood, Susan S. Everingham, Jill Houbé, M. Rebecca Kilburn, C. Peter Rydell, Matthew Sanders, and James Chiesa. 1998. *Investing in Our Children: What We Know and Don't Know about the Costs and Benefits of Early Childhood Interventions.* Santa Monica, Calif.: Rand.

Kasen, Stephanie, Jim Johnson, and Patricia Cohen. 1990. "The Impact of School Emotional Climate on Student Psychopathology." *Journal of Abnormal Child Psychology* 18: 165–177.

Kaukiainen, A., Kai Bjorkvist, Kirsti Lagerspetz, K. Osterman, Christine Salmivalli, S. Rothberg, and A. Ahlbom. 1999. "The Relationships between Social Intelligence, Empathy, and Three Types of Aggression." *Aggressive Behavior* 25: 81–89.

Kazdin, Alan E. 1997. "Parent Management Training: Evidence, Outcomes, and Issues." *Journal of the American Academy of Child and Adolescent Psychiatry* 36: 1349–1356.

Kazdin, Alan E., Helena C. Kraemer, Ronald C. Kessler, David J. Kupfer, and David R. Offord. 1997. "Contributions of Risk-Factor Research to Developmental Psychopathology." *Clinical Psychology Review* 17: 375–406.

Kellam, Sheppard G., Margaret E. Ensminger, and R. Jay Turner. 1977. "Family Structure and the Mental Health of Children." *Archives of General Psychiatry* 34: 1012–1022.

Kelley, Michelle L., Thomas G. Power, and Dawn D. Wimbush. 1992. "Determinants of Disciplinary Practices in Low-Income Black Mothers." *Child Development* 63: 573–582.

Kirp, David L. 2004. "Life Way after Head Start." *New York Times Magazine*, November 21, pp. 32, 34, 36, 38.

Kitzman, Harriet, David L. Olds, Charles R. Henderson, Carole Hanks, Robert Cole, Robert Tatelbaum, Kenneth M. McConnochie, Kimberly Sidora, Dennis W. Luckey, David Shaver, Kay Engelhardt, David James, and Kathryn Barnard. 1997. "Effect of Prenatal and Infancy Home Visitation by Nurses on Pregnancy Outcomes, Childhood Injuries, and Repeated Childbearing: A Randomized Controlled Trial." *Journal of the American Medical Association* 278: 644–652.

Kling, Jeffrey R., Jens Ludwig, and Lawrence F. Katz. 2005. "Neighborhood Effects on Crime for Female and Male Youth: Evidence from a Randomized Housing Voucher Experiment." *Quarterly Journal of Economics* 120: 87–130.

Klinteberg, Britt af, Tommy Andersson, David Magnusson, and Hakan Stattin. 1993. "Hyperactive Behavior in Childhood as Related to Subsequent Alcohol Problems and Violent Offending: A Longitudinal Study of Male Subjects." *Personality and Individual Differences* 15: 381–388.

Knapp, Martin. 1997. "Economic Evaluations and Interventions for Children and

Adolescents with Mental Health Problems." *Journal of Child Psychology and Psychiatry* 38: 3–25.

Kolbo, Jerome R., Eleanor H. Blakely, and David Engleman. 1996. "Children Who Witness Domestic Violence: A Review of Empirical Literature." *Journal of Interpersonal Violence* 11: 281–293.

Kolvin, Israel, Frederick J. W. Miller, Mary Fleeting, and Philip A. Kolvin. 1988a. "Risk/Protective Factors for Offending with Particular Reference to Deprivation." In *Studies of Psychosocial Risk: The Power of Longitudinal Data*, Michael Rutter, ed. Cambridge: Cambridge University Press.

Kolvin, Israel, Frederick J. W. Miller, Mary Fleeting, and Philip A. Kolvin. 1988b. "Social and Parenting Factors Affecting Criminal-Offense Rates: Findings from the Newcastle Thousand Family Study (1947–1980)." *British Journal of Psychiatry* 152: 80–90.

Kolvin, Israel, Frederick J. W. Miller, David M. Scott, S. R. M. Gatzanis, and Mary Fleeting. 1990. *Continuities of Deprivation? The Newcastle Thousand Family Study*. Aldershot, England: Avebury.

Kraemer, Helena C., Alan E. Kazdin, David R. Offord, Ronald C. Kessler, Peter S. Jensen, and David J. Kupfer. 1997. "Coming to Terms with the Terms of Risk." *Archives of General Psychiatry* 54: 337–343.

Krueger, Robert F., Terrie E. Moffitt, Avshalom Caspi, April Bleske, and Phil A. Silva. 1998. "Assortative Mating for Antisocial Behavior: Developmental and Methodological Implications." *Behavior Genetics* 28: 173–186.

Kumpfer, Karol L., and Rose Alvarado. 2003. "Family-Strengthening Approaches for the Prevention of Youth Problem Behaviors." *American Psychologist* 58: 457–465.

Lacourse, E., S. Cote, Daniel S. Nagin, Frank Vitaro, Mara Brendgen, and Richard E. Tremblay. 2002. "A Longitudinal-Experimental Approach to Testing Theories of Antisocial Behavior Development." *Development and Psychopathology* 14: 909–924.

Lally, J. Ronald, Peter L. Mangione, and Alice S. Honig. 1988. "The Syracuse University Family Development Research Program: Long-Range Impact of an Early Intervention with Low-Income Children and Their Families." In *Parent Education as Early Childhood Intervention: Emerging Directions in Theory, Research and Practice*, D. R. Powell, ed. Norwood, N.J.: Ablex.

Lang, S., Britt af Klinteberg, and Per-Olof Alm. 2002. "Adult Psychopathy and Violent Behavior in Males with Early Neglect and Abuse." *Acta Psychiatrica Scandinavica* 106: 93–100.

Larzelere, Robert E., and Gerald R. Patterson. 1990. "Parental Management: Mediator of the Effect of Socioeconomic Status on Early Delinquency." *Criminology* 28: 301–324.

Laub, John H., and Robert J. Sampson. 2003. *Shared Beginnings, Divergent Lives: Delinquent Boys to Age 70*. Cambridge, Mass.: Harvard University Press.

Lauritsen, Janet L. 1993. "Sibling Resemblance in Juvenile Delinquency: Findings from the National Youth Survey." *Criminology* 31: 387–409.

Layard, Richard, and Stephen Glaister, eds. 1994. *Cost-Benefit Analysis*. 2nd ed. New York: Cambridge University Press.

LeBlanc, Marc. 1996. "Changing Patterns in the Perpetration of Offenses over Time: Trajectories from Early Adolescence to the Early Thirties." *Studies on Crime and Crime Prevention* 5: 151–165.

Lewis, C., Elizabeth Newson, and John Newson. 1982. "Father Participation through Childhood and Its Relationship with Career Aspirations and Delinquency." In *Fathers: Psychological Perspectives*, N. Beail and J. McGuire, eds. London: Junction.

Lipsey, Mark W., and James H. Derzon. 1998. "Predictors of Violent or Serious Delinquency in Adolescence and Early Adulthood: A Synthesis of Longitudinal Research." In *Serious and Violent Juvenile Offenders: Risk Factors and Successful Interventions*, Rolf Loeber and David P. Farrington, eds. Thousand Oaks, Calif.: Sage.

Lipsey, Mark W., and David B. Wilson. 2001. *Practical Meta-analysis*. Thousand Oaks, Calif.: Sage.

Lipsitt, Paul D., Stephen L. Buka, and Lewis P. Lipsitt. 1990. "Early Intelligence Scores and Subsequent Delinquency: A Prospective Study." *American Journal of Family Therapy* 18: 197–208.

Littell, Julia H. 2005. "Lessons from a Systematic Review of Effects of Multisystemic Therapy." *Children and Youth Services Review* 27: 445–463.

Loeber, Rolf, and Thomas Dishion. 1983. "Early Predictors of Male Delinquency: A Review." *Psychological Bulletin* 94: 68–99.

Loeber, Rolf, David P. Farrington, Magda Stouthamer-Loeber, and Welmoet van Kammen. 1998a. *Antisocial Behavior and Mental Health Problems: Explanatory Factors in Childhood and Adolescence*. Mahwah, N.J.: Erlbaum.

Loeber, Rolf, David P. Farrington, Magda Stouthamer-Loeber, and Welmoet van Kammen. 1998b. "Multiple Risk Factors for Multi-problem Boys: Co-occurrence of Delinquency, Substance Use, Attention Deficit, Conduct

Problems, Physical Aggression, Covert Behavior, Depressed Mood and Shy/ Withdrawn Behavior." In *New Perspectives on Adolescent Risk Behavior*, Richard Jessor, ed. Cambridge: Cambridge University Press.

Loeber, Rolf, David P. Farrington, Magda Stouthamer-Loeber, Terrie E. Moffitt, Avshalom Caspi, Helene R. White, Evelyn Wei, and Jennifer M. Beyers. 2003. "The Development of Male Offending: Key Findings from 14 Years of the Pittsburgh Youth Study." In *Taking Stock of Delinquency: An Overview of Findings from Contemporary Longitudinal Studies*, Terence P. Thornberry and Marvin D. Krohn, eds. New York: Kluwer/Plenum.

Loeber, Rolf, Dustin Pardini, D. Lynn Homish, Evelyn Wei, Anne M. Crawford, David P. Farrington, Magda Stouthamer-Loeber, Judith Creemers, Stephen A. Koehler, and Richard Rosenfeld. 2005. "The Prediction of Violence and Homicide in Young Men." *Journal of Consulting and Clinical Psychology* 73: 1074–1088.

Loeber, Rolf, and Magda Stouthamer-Loeber. 1986. "Family Factors as Correlates and Predictors of Juvenile Conduct Problems and Delinquency." In *Crime and Justice*, vol. 7, Michael Tonry and Norval Morris, eds. Chicago: University of Chicago Press.

Long, Patricia, Rex Forehand, Michelle Wierson, and Allison Morgan. 1994. "Does Parent Training with Young Noncompliant Children Have Long-Term Effects?" *Behavior Research and Therapy* 32: 101–107.

Lösel, Friedrich, and Andreas Beelmann. 2003. "Effects of Child Skills Training in Preventing Antisocial Behavior: A Systematic Review." *Annals of the American Academy of Political and Social Science* 587: 84–109.

Lösel, Friedrich, and Andreas Beelmann. 2006. "Child Social Skills Training." In *Preventing Crime: What Works for Children, Offenders, Victims, and Places*, Brandon C. Welsh and David P. Farrington, eds. Dordrecht: Springer.

Lösel, Friedrich, and Peter Koferl. 1989. "Evaluation Research on Correctional Treatment in West Germany: A Meta-Analysis." In *Criminal Behavior and the Justice System: Psychological Perspectives*, Hermann Wegener, Friedrich Lösel, and Jochen Haisch, eds. New York: Springer-Verlag.

Luengo, M. A., J. M. Otero, M. T. Carrillo-de-la-Pena, and L. Miron. 1994. "Dimensions of Antisocial Behavior in Juvenile Delinquency: A Study of Personality Variables." *Psychology, Crime and Law* 1: 27–37.

Lynam, Donald. 1996. "Early Identification of Chronic Offenders: Who Is the Fledgling Psychopath?" *Psychological Bulletin* 120: 209–234.

Lynam, Donald, and Terrie E. Moffitt. 1995. "Delinquency and Impulsivity and IQ: A Reply to Block." *Journal of Abnormal Psychology* 104: 399–401.

Lynam, Donald, Terrie E. Moffitt, and Magda Stouthamer-Loeber. 1993. "Explaining the Relation between IQ and Delinquency: Class, Race, Test Motivation, School Failure or Self-Control?" *Journal of Abnormal Psychology* 102: 187–196.

Lytton, Hugh. 1990. "Child and Parent Effects in Boys' Conduct Disorder: A Reinterpretation." *Developmental Psychology* 26: 683–697.

Lytton, Hugh, and David M. Romney. 1991. "Parents' Differential Socialization of Boys and Girls: A Meta-analysis." *Psychological Bulletin* 109: 267–296.

MacKenzie, Doris Layton. 2000. "Evidence-Based Corrections: Identifying What Works." *Crime and Delinquency* 46: 457–471.

Magnusson, David, and Lars R. Bergman. 1988. "Individual and Variable-Based Approaches to Longitudinal Research on Early Risk Factors." In *Studies of Psychosocial Risk: The Power of Longitudinal Data*, Michael Rutter, ed. Cambridge: Cambridge University Press.

Mak, Anita S. 1991. "Psychosocial Control Characteristics of Delinquents and Nondelinquents." *Criminal Justice and Behavior* 18: 287–303.

Malinosky-Rummell, R., and D. J. Hansen. 1993. "Long-Term Consequences of Childhood Physical Abuse." *Psychological Bulletin* 114: 68–79.

Mason, W. Alex, Rick Kosterman, J. David Hawkins, Kevin P. Haggerty, and Richard L. Spoth. 2003. "Reducing Adolescents' Growth in Substance Use and Delinquency: Randomized Trial Effects of a Parent-Training Prevention Intervention." *Prevention Science* 4: 203–212.

Masse, Leonard N., and W. Steven Barnett. 2002. *A Benefit-Cost Analysis of the Abecedarian Early Childhood Intervention.* New Brunswick, N.J.: National Institute for Early Education Research.

Maxfield, Michael G., and Cathy S. Widom. 1996. "The Cycle of Violence Revisited 6 Years Later." *Archives of Pediatrics and Adolescent Medicine* 150: 390–395.

McCarton, Cecelia M., Jeann Brooks-Gunn, Ina F. Wallace, Charles R. Bauer, Forrest C. Bennett, Judy C. Bernbaum, R. Sue Broyles, Patrick H. Casey, Marie C. McCormick, David T. Scott, Jon Tyson, James Tonascia, and Curtis L. Meinert. 1997. "Results at Age 8 Years of Early Intervention for Low-Birth-Weight Premature Infants: The Infant Health and Development Program." *Journal of the American Medical Association* 277: 126–132.

McCord, Joan. 1977. "A Comparative Study of Two Generations of Native Americans." In *Theory in Criminology,* Robert F. Meier, ed. Beverly Hills, Calif.: Sage.

McCord, Joan. 1978. "A Thirty-Year Follow-up of Treatment Effects." *American Psychologist* 33: 284–289.

McCord, Joan. 1979. "Some Child-Rearing Antecedents of Criminal Behavior in Adult Men." *Journal of Personality and Social Psychology* 37: 1477–1486.

McCord, Joan. 1982. "A Longitudinal View of the Relationship between Paternal Absence and Crime." In *Abnormal Offenders, Delinquency, and the Criminal Justice System*, John Gunn and David P. Farrington, eds. Chichester, England: Wiley.

McCord, Joan. 1983. "A Forty-Year Perspective on Effects of Child Abuse and Neglect." *Child Abuse and Neglect* 7: 265–270.

McCord, Joan. 1991. "Family Relationships, Juvenile Delinquency, and Adult Criminality." *Criminology* 29: 397–417.

McCord, Joan. 1997. "On Discipline." *Psychological Inquiry* 8: 215–217.

McCord, Joan. 2002. "Counterproductive Juvenile Justice." *Australian and New Zealand Journal of Criminology* 35: 230–237.

McCord, Joan. 2003. "Cures That Harm: Unanticipated Outcomes of Crime Prevention Programs." *Annals of the American Academy of Political and Social Science* 587: 16–30.

McCord, Joan, and Margaret E. Ensminger. 1997. "Multiple Risks and Comorbidity in an African-American Population." *Criminal Behavior and Mental Health* 7: 339–352.

McCord, Joan, Richard E. Tremblay, Frank Vitaro, and Lyse Desmarais-Gervais. 1994. "Boys' Disruptive Behaviour, School Adjustment, and Delinquency: The Montreal Prevention Experiment." *International Journal of Behavioral Development* 17: 739–752.

McCord, Joan, Cathy Spatz Widom, and Nancy A. Crowell, eds. 2001. *Juvenile Crime, Juvenile Justice. Panel on Juvenile Crime: Prevention, Treatment, and Control.* Committee on Law and Justice and Board on Children, Youth, and Families, National Research Council and Institute of Medicine. Washington, D.C.: National Academy Press.

McCrae, Robert R., and Paul T. Costa. 1997. "Personality Trait Structure as a Human Universal." *American Psychologist* 52: 509–516.

McCrae, Robert R., and Paul T. Costa. 2003. *Personality in Adulthood: A Five-Factor Theory Perspective.* New York: Guilford Press.

McCrae, Robert R., Paul T. Costa, Fritz Ostendorf, Alois Angleitner, Martina Hrebickova, Maria D. Avia, Jesus Sanz, Maria L. Sanchez-Bernardos, M. Ersin Kusdil, Ruth Woodfield, Peter R. Saunders, and Peter B. Smith. 2000. "Nature over Nurture: Temperament, Personality, and Life Span Development." *Journal of Personality and Social Psychology* 78: 173–186.

Mednick, Birgitte R., Robert L. Baker, and Linn E. Carothers. 1990. "Patterns of Family Instability and Crime: The Association of Timing of the Family's Disruption with Subsequent Adolescent and Young Adult Criminality." *Journal of Youth and Adolescence* 19: 201–220.

Michel, Sonya. 1999. *Children's Interests/Mother's Rights: The Shaping of America's Child Care Policy.* New Haven, Conn.: Yale University Press.

Miczek, Klaus A., Joseph F. DeBold, Margaret Haney, Jennifer Tidey, Jeffrey Vivian, and Elise M. Weerts. 1994. "Alcohol, Drugs of Abuse, Aggression and Violence." In *Understanding and Preventing Violence*, vol. 3, *Social Influences*, Albert J. Reiss and Jeffrey A. Roth, eds. Washington, D.C.: National Academy Press.

Miller, Joshua D., Kate Flory, Donald R. Lynam, and Carl Leukefeld. 2003a. "A Test of the Four-Factor Model of Impulsivity-Related Traits." *Personality and Individual Differences* 34: 1403–1418.

Miller, Joshua D., and Donald R. Lynam. 2001. "Structural Models of Personality and Their Relation to Antisocial Behavior: A Meta-analytic Review." *Criminology* 39: 765–798.

Miller, Joshua D., Donald R. Lynam, and Carl Leukefeld. 2003b. "Examining Antisocial Behavior through the Lens of the Five Factor Model of Personality." *Aggressive Behavior* 29: 497–514.

Mills, Paulette E., Kevin N. Cole, Joseph R. Jenkins, and Philip S. Dale. 2002. "Early Exposure to Direct Instruction and Subsequent Juvenile Delinquency: A Prospective Examination." *Exceptional Children* 69: 85–96.

Moffitt, Terrie E. 1990. "The Neuropsychology of Juvenile Delinquency: A Critical Review." In *Crime and Justice*, vol. 12, Michael Tonry and Norval Morris, eds. Chicago: University of Chicago Press.

Moffitt, Terrie E. 1993. "Adolescence-Limited and Life-Course-Persistent Antisocial Behavior: A Developmental Taxonomy." *Psychological Review* 100: 674–701.

Moffitt, Terrie E., Avshalom Caspi, Michael Rutter, and Phil A. Silva. 2001. *Sex Differences in Antisocial Behavior.* Cambridge: Cambridge University Press.

Moffitt, Terrie E., and Bill Henry. 1991. "Neuropsychological Studies of Juvenile

Delinquency and Juvenile Violence." In *Neuropsychology of Aggression*, J. S. Milner, ed. Boston: Kluwer.

Moffitt, Terrie E., and Phil A. Silva. 1988a. "IQ and Delinquency: A Direct Test of the Differential Detection Hypothesis." *Journal of Abnormal Psychology* 87: 330–333.

Moffitt, Terrie E., and Phil A. Silva. 1988b. "Neuropsychological Deficit and Self-Reported Delinquency in an Unselected Birth Cohort." *Journal of the American Academy of Child and Adolescent Psychiatry* 27: 233–240.

Moore, Mark H. 1995. "Public Health and Criminal Justice Approaches to Prevention." In *Building a Safer Society: Strategic Approaches to Crime Prevention*, Michael Tonry and David P. Farrington, eds. Chicago: University of Chicago Press.

Morash, Merry, and Lila Rucker. 1989. "An Exploratory Study of the Connection of Mother's Age at Childbearing to Her Children's Delinquency in Four Data Sets." *Crime and Delinquency* 35: 45–93.

Morgan, Alex B., and Scott O. Lilienfeld. 2000. "A Meta-Analytic Review of the Relation between Antisocial Behavior and Neuropsychological Measures of Executive Function." *Clinical Psychology Review* 20: 113–136.

Mytton, Julie A., Carolyn DiGuiseppi, David A. Gough, Rod S. Taylor, and Stuart Logan. 2002. "School-Based Violence Prevention Programs: Systematic Review of Secondary Prevention Trials." *Archives of Pediatric and Adolescent Medicine* 156: 752–762.

Nagin, Daniel S., David P. Farrington, and Terrie E. Moffitt. 1995. "Life-Course Trajectories of Different Types of Offenders." *Criminology* 33: 111–139.

Nagin, Daniel S., Greg Pogarsky, and David P. Farrington. 1997. "Adolescent Mothers and the Criminal Behavior of Their Children." *Law and Society Review* 31: 137–162.

Najaka, Stacy S., Denise C. Gottfredson, and David B. Wilson. 2001. "A Meta-analytic Inquiry into the Relationship between Selected Risk Factors and Problem Behavior." *Prevention Science* 2: 257–271.

Nelson, S. E., and Thomas J. Dishion. 2004. "From Boys to Men: Predicting Adult Adaptation from Middle Childhood Sociometric Status." *Development and Psychopathology* 16: 441–459.

Newson, John, and Elizabeth Newson. 1989. *The Extent of Parental Physical Punishment in the UK*. London: Approach.

O'Donnell, Julie, J. David Hawkins, Richard F. Catalano, Robert D. Abbott, and L. Edward Day. 1995. "Preventing School Failure, Drug Use, and Delinquency among Low-Income Children: Long-Term Intervention in Elementary Schools." *American Journal of Orthopsychiatry* 65: 87–100.

Offord, David R., and Helena C. Kraemer. 2000. "Risk Factors and Prevention." *Evidence-Based Mental Health* 3: 70–71.

Olds, David L., John Eckenrode, Charles R. Henderson, Harriet Kitzman, Jane Powers, Robert Cole, Kimberly Sidora, Pamela Morris, Lisa M. Pettitt, and Dennis W. Luckey. 1997. "Long-Term Effects of Home Visitation on Maternal Life Course and Child Abuse and Neglect: Fifteen-Year Follow-up of a Randomized Trial." *Journal of the American Medical Association* 278: 637–643.

Olds, David L., Charles R. Henderson, Robert Chamberlin, and Robert Tatelbaum. 1986. "Preventing Child Abuse and Neglect: A Randomized Trial of Nurse Home Visitation." *Pediatrics* 78: 65–78.

Olds, David L., Charles R. Henderson, Robert Cole, John Eckenrode, Harriet Kitzman, Dennis W. Luckey, Lisa M. Pettitt, Kimberly Sidora, Pamela Morris, and Jane Powers. 1998. "Long-Term Effects of Nurse Home Visitation on Children's Criminal and Antisocial Behavior: 15-Year Follow-up of a Randomized Controlled Trial." *Journal of the American Medical Association* 280: 1238–1244.

Olds, David L., Charles R. Henderson, Charles Phelps, Harriet Kitzman, and Carole Hanks. 1993. "Effects of Prenatal and Infancy Nurse Home Visitation on Government Spending." *Medical Care* 31: 155–174.

Olds, David L., Harriet Kitzman, Robert Cole, JoAnn Robinson, Kimberly Sidora, Dennis W. Luckey, Charles R. Henderson, Carole Hanks, Jessica Bondy, and John Holmberg. 2004a. "Effects of Nurse Home-Visiting on Maternal Life Course and Child Development: Age 6 Follow-up Results of a Randomized Trial." *Pediatrics* 114: 1550–1559.

Olds, David L., JoAnn Robinson, Lisa M. Pettitt, Dennis W. Luckey, John Holmberg, Rosanna K. Ng, Kathy Isacks, Karen L. Sheff, and Charles R. Henderson. 2004b. "Effects of Home Visits by Paraprofessionals and by Nurses: Age 4 Follow-up Results of a Randomized Trial." *Pediatrics* 114: 1560–1568.

Oleson, James C. 2002. "The Worst of All: A Study of Offending in High IQ Populations." *Caribbean Journal of Criminology and Social Psychology* 7: 44–88.

Osborn, Stephen G. 1980. "Moving Home, Leaving London, and Delinquent Trends." *British Journal of Criminology* 20: 54–61.

Pagani, Linda, Richard E. Tremblay, Frank Vitaro, Margaret Kerr, and Pierre McDuff. 1998. "The Impact of Family Transition on the Development of Delinquency in Adolescent Boys: A 9-Year Longitudinal Study." *Journal of Child Psychology and Psychiatry* 39: 489–499.

Paternoster, Raymond. 1988. "Examining Three Wave Deterrence Models: A Question of Temporal Order and Specification." *Journal of Criminal Law and Criminology* 79: 135–179.

Patterson, Gerald R. 1995. "Coercion as a Basis for Early Age of Onset for Arrest." In *Coercion and Punishment in Long-Term Perspectives*, Joan McCord, ed. Cambridge: Cambridge University Press.

Patterson, Gerald. 1982. *Coercive Family Process.* Eugene, Ore.: Castalia.

Patterson, Gerald, Patricia Chamberlain, and John B. Reid. 1982. "A Comparative Evaluation of a Parent Training Program." *Behavior Therapy* 13: 638–650

Patterson, Gerald, John B. Reid, and Thomas J. Dishion. 1992. *Antisocial Boys.* Eugene, Ore.: Castalia.

Pepler, Debra J., Gillian King, Wendy M. Craig, Bill Byrd, and Linda Bream. 1995. "The Development and Evaluation of a Multisystem Social Skills Group Training Program for Aggressive Children." *Child and Youth Care Forum* 24: 297–313.

Perry, Cheryl L., Knut-Inge Klepp, and Cynthia Sillers. 1989. "Community-Wide Strategies for Cardiovascular Health: The Minnesota Heart Health Program Youth Program." *Health Education Research* 4: 87–101.

Petrosino, Anthony, Robert F. Boruch, Haluk Soydan, Lorna Duggan, and Julio Sanchez-Meca. 2001. "Meeting the Challenges of Evidence-Based Policy: The Campbell Collaboration." *Annals of the American Academy of Political and Social Science* 578: 14–34.

Piquero, Alex R., and Stephen L. Buka. 2002. "Linking Juvenile and Adult Patterns of Criminal Activity in the Providence Cohort of the National Collaborative Perinatal Project." *Journal of Criminal Justice* 30: 259–272.

Piquero, Alex R., David P. Farrington, and Alfred Blumstein. In press. *Key Issues in Criminal Career Research: New Analyses of the Cambridge Study in Delinquent Development.* Cambridge: Cambridge University Press.

Piquero, Alex R., and Norman A. White. 2003. "On the Relationship between Cognitive Abilities and Life-Course Persistent Offending among a Sample of African Americans: A Longitudinal Test of Moffitt's Hypothesis." *Journal of Criminal Justice* 31: 399–409.

Pogarsky, Greg, Alan J. Lizotte, and Terence P. Thornberry. 2003. "The Delinquency of Children Born to Young Mothers: Results from the Rochester Youth Development Study." *Criminology* 41: 1249–1286.

Pollard, John A., J. David Hawkins, and Michael W. Arthur. 1999. "Risk and Protection: Are Both Necesssary to Understand Diverse Behavioral Outcomes in Adolescence?" *Social Work Research* 23: 145–158.

Power, Michael J., M. R. Alderson, C. M. Phillipson, Elizabeth Shoenberg, and J. N. Morris. 1967. "Delinquent Schools?" *New Society* 10: 542–543.

Pratt, Travis C., Francis T. Cullen, Kristie R. Blevins, Leah Daigle, and James D. Unnever. 2002. "The Relationship of Attention Deficit Hyperactivity Disorder to Crime and Delinquency: A Meta-analysis." *International Journal of Police Science and Management* 4: 344–360.

Pulkkinen, Lea, and T. Pitkanen. 1993. "Continuities in Aggressive Behavior from Childhood to Adulthood." *Aggressive Behavior* 19: 249–263.

Raine, Adrian. 1993. *The Psychopathology of Crime: Criminal Behavior as a Clinical Disorder*. San Diego, Calif.: Academic Press.

Raine, Adrian, Patricia A. Brennan, and David P. Farrington. 1997. "Biosocial Bases of Violence: Conceptual and Theoretical Issues." In *Biosocial Bases of Violence*, Adrian Raine, Patricia A. Brennan, David P. Farrington, and Sarnoff A. Mednick, eds. New York: Plenum.

Raine, Adrian, Terrie M. Moffitt, Avshalom Caspi, Rolf Loeber, Magda Stouthamer-Loeber, and Don Lynam. 2005. "Neurocognitive Impairments in Boys on the Life-Course Persistent Antisocial Path." *Journal of Abnormal Psychology* 114: 38–49.

Raine, Adrian, Chandra Reynolds, Peter H. Venables, Sarnoff A. Mednick, and David P. Farrington. 1998. "Fearlessness, Stimulation-Seeking, and Large Body Size at Age Three Years as Early Predispositions to Childhood Aggression at Age Eleven Years." *Archives of General Psychiatry* 55: 745–751.

Raine, Adrian, Peter H. Venables, and Mark Williams. 1990. "Relationships between Central and Autonomic Measures of Arousal at Age 15 Years and Criminality at Age 24 Years." *Archives of General Psychiatry* 47: 1003–1007.

Rasanen, Pirkko, Helina Hakko, Matti Isohanni, Sheilagh Hodgins, Marjo-Riitta Jarvelin, and Jari Tiihonen. 1999. "Maternal Smoking during Pregnancy and Risk of Criminal Behavior among Adult Male Offspring in the Northern Finland 1966 Birth Cohort." *American Journal of Psychiatry* 156: 857–862.

Reiss, Albert J. 1986. "Why are Communities Important in Understanding Crime?" In *Communities and Crime*, Albert J. Reiss and Michael Tonry, eds. Chicago: University of Chicago Press.

Reiss, Albert J. 1988. "Co-Offending and Criminal Careers." In *Crime and Jus-*

tice: A Review of Research, vol. 10, Michael Tonry and Norval Morris, eds. Chicago: University of Chicago Press.

Reiss, Albert J., and David P. Farrington. 1991. "Advancing Knowledge about Co-offending: Results from a Prospective Longitudinal Survey of London Males." *Journal of Criminal Law and Criminology* 82: 360–395.

Reynolds, Arthur J., Judy A. Temple, and Suh-Ruu Ou. 2003. "School-Based Early Intervention and Child Well-Being in the Chicago Longitudinal Study." *Child Welfare* 82: 633–656.

Reynolds, Arthur J., Judy A. Temple, Dylan L. Robertson, and Emily A. Mann. 2001. "Long-Term Effects of an Early Childhood Intervention on Educational Achievement and Juvenile Arrest: A Fifteen-Year Follow-up of Low-Income Children in Public Schools." *Journal of the American Medical Association* 285: 2339–2346.

Richters, John. 1997. "The Hubble Hypothesis and the Developmentalist's Dilemma." *Development and Psychopathology* 9: 193–229.

Ripple, Carol H., and Edward Zigler. 2003. "Research, Policy, and the Federal Role in Prevention Initiatives for Children." *American Psychologist* 58: 482–490.

Roberts, Brent W., and Wendy F. del Vecchio. 2000. "The Rank-Order Consistency of Personality Traits from Childhood to Old Age: A Quantitative Review of Longitudinal Studies." *Psychological Bulletin* 126: 3–25.

Robins, Lee N. 1979. "Sturdy Childhood Predictors of Adult Outcomes: Replications from Longitudinal Studies." In *Stress and Mental Disorder*, J. E. Barrett, R. M. Rose, and Gerald L. Klerman, eds. New York: Raven Press.

Robins, Lee N. 1992. "The Role of Prevention Experiments in Discovering Causes of Children's Antisocial Behavior." In *Preventing Antisocial Behavior: Interventions from Birth through Adolescence*, Joan McCord and Richard E. Tremblay, eds. New York: Guilford Press.

Robinson, J. L., Jerome Kagan, J. S. Reznick, and R. Corley. 1992. "The Heritability of Inhibited and Uninhibited Behavior: A Twin Study." *Developmental Psychology* 28: 1030–1037.

Rosenbaum, Dennis P. 1988. "Community Crime Prevention: A Review and Synthesis of the Literature." *Justice Quarterly* 5: 323–395.

Ross, Robert R., and Rosslyn D. Ross, eds. 1995. *Thinking Straight: The Reasoning and Rehabilitation Program for Delinquency Prevention and Offender Rehabilitation*. Ottawa: Air Training and Publications.

Rothbaum, Fred, and John R. Weisz. 1994. "Parental Caregiving and Child Externalizing Behavior in Nonclinical Samples: A Meta-Analysis." *Psychological Bulletin* 116: 55–74.

Rowe, David C. 1994. *The Limits of Family Influence: Genes, Experience, and Behavior.* New York: Guilford Press.

Rowe, David C. 2002. *Biology and Crime.* Los Angeles: Roxbury.

Rowe, David C., and David P. Farrington. 1997. "The Familial Transmission of Criminal Convictions." *Criminology* 35: 177–201.

Rowe, David C., Alexander T. Vazsonyi, and Daniel J. Flannery. 1994. "No More Than Skin Deep: Ethnic and Racial Similarity in Developmental Process." *Psychological Review* 101: 396–413.

Rutter, Michael. 1981. "The City and the Child." *American Journal of Orthopsychiatry* 51: 610–625.

Rutter, Michael. 1983. "School Effects on Pupil Progress: Research Findings and Policy Implications." *Child Development* 54: 1–29.

Rutter, Michael. 1985. "Resilience in the Face of Adversity: Protective Factors and Resistance to Psychiatric Disorder." *British Journal of Psychiatry* 147: 598–611.

Rutter, Michael. 2003. "Crucial Paths from Risk Indicator to Causal Mechanism." In *Causes of Conduct Disorder and Juvenile Delinquency,* Benjamin B. Lahey, Terrie E. Moffitt, and Avshalom Caspi, eds. New York: Guilford Press.

Rutter, Michael, Barbara Maughan, Peter Mortimore, and Janet Ouston. 1979. *Fifteen Thousand Hours: Secondary Schools and Their Effects on Children.* London: Open Books.

Sampson, Robert J., and John H. Laub. 1993. *Crime in the Making: Pathways and Turning Points through Life.* Cambridge, Mass.: Harvard University Press.

Sampson, Robert J., Stephen W. Raudenbush, and Felton Earls. 1997. "Neighborhoods and Violent Crime: A Multilevel Study of Collective Efficacy." *Science* 277: 918–924.

Sansfaçon, Daniel, and Irvin Waller. 2001. "Recent Evolution of Governmental Crime Prevention Strategies and Implications for Evaluation and Economic Analysis." In *Costs and Benefits of Preventing Crime,* Brandon C. Welsh, David P. Farrington, and Lawrence W. Sherman, eds. Boulder, Colo.: Westview Press.

Sansfaçon, Daniel, and Brandon C. Welsh. 1999. *Crime Prevention Digest II: Comparative Analysis of Successful Community Safety.* Montreal: International Centre for the Prevention of Crime.

Sanson, Ann, Diana D. Smart, Margot Prior, and F. Oberklaid. 1993. "Precursors of Hyperactivity and Aggression." *Journal of the American Academy of Child and Adolescent Psychiatry* 32: 1207–1216.

Schinke, Steven P., Mario A. Orlandi, and Kristin C. Cole. 1992. "Boys and Girls Clubs in Public Housing Developments: Prevention Services for Youth at Risk." *Journal of Community Psychology*, OSAP special issue: 118–128.

Schutte, Nicola S., John M. Malouff, Lena E. Hall, Donald J. Haggerty, Joan T. Cooper, Charles J. Golden, and Liane Dornheim. 1998. "Development and Validation of a Measure of Emotional Intelligence." *Personality and Individual Differences* 25: 167–177.

Schwartz, C. E., Nancy Snidman, and Jerome Kagan. 1996. "Early Childhood Temperament as a Determinant of Externalizing Behavior in Adolescence." *Development and Psychopathology* 8: 527–537.

Schweinhart, Lawrence J., Helen V. Barnes, and David P. Weikart. 1993. *Significant Benefits: The High/Scope Perry Preschool Study through Age 27*. Ypsilanti, Mich.: High/Scope Press.

Schweinhart, Lawrence J., Jeanne Montie, Xiang Zongping, W. Steven Barnett, Clive R. Belfield, and Milagros Nores. 2005. *Lifetime Effects: The High/Scope Perry Preschool Study through Age 40*. Ypsilanti, Mich.: High/Scope Press.

Schweinhart, Lawrence J., and David P. Weikart. 1980. *Young Children Grow Up: The Effects of the Perry Preschool Program on Youths through Age 15*. Ypsilanti, Mich.: High/Scope Press.

Scott, Stephen, Quentin Spender, Moira Doolan, Brian Jacobs, and Helen Aspland. 2001. "Multicentre Controlled Trial of Parenting Groups for Child Antisocial Behaviour in Clinical Practice." *British Medical Journal* 323: 194–196.

Séguin, Jean, Robert O. Pihl, P. W. Harden, Richard E. Tremblay, and Bernice Boulerice. 1995. "Cognitive and Neuropsychological Characteristics of Physically Aggressive Boys." *Journal of Abnormal Psychology* 104: 614–624.

Serketich, Wendy J., and Jean E. Dumas. 1996. "The Effectiveness of Behavioral Parent Training to Modify Antisocial Behavior in Children: A Meta-analysis." *Behavior Therapy* 27: 171–186.

Shadish, William R., Thomas D. Cook, and Donald T. Campbell. 2002. *Experimental and Quasi-experimental Designs for Generalized Causal Inference*. Boston: Houghton Mifflin.

Shaw, Clifford R., and Henry D. McKay. 1969. *Juvenile Delinquency and Urban Areas*. Rev. ed. Chicago: University of Chicago Press.

Sherman, Lawrence W. 1997. "Communities and Crime Prevention." In *Prevent-*

ing Crime: What Works, What Doesn't, What's Promising, Lawrence W. Sherman, Denise C. Gottfredson, Doris L. MacKenzie, John E. Eck, Peter Reuter, and Shawn D. Bushway. Washington, D.C.: U.S. Department of Justice, National Institute of Justice.

Sherman, Lawrence W., David P. Farrington, Brandon C. Welsh, and Doris L. MacKenzie, eds. 2002. *Evidence-Based Crime Prevention.* New York: Routledge.

Shonkoff, Jack P., and Deborah A. Phillips, eds. 2000. *From Neurons to Neighborhoods: The Science of Early Childhood Development.* Committee on Integrating the Science of Early Childhood Development, National Research Council and Institute of Medicine. Washington, D.C.: National Academy Press.

Short, James F. 1969. "Introduction to the Revised Edition." In *Juvenile Delinquency and Urban Areas.* Rev. ed. Chicago: University of Chicago Press.

Simons, Ronald L., Leslie G. Simons, Callie H. Burt, Gene H. Brody, and Carolyn Cutrona. 2005. "Collective Efficacy, Authoritative Parenting, and Delinquency: A Longitudinal Test of a Model Integrating Community- and Family-Level Processes." *Criminology* 43: 989–1029.

Smith, Carolyn A., and David P. Farrington. 2004. "Continuities in Antisocial Behaviour and Parenting across Three Generations." *Journal of Child Psychology and Psychiatry* 45: 230–247.

Smith, Carolyn A., Marvin D. Krohn, Alan J. Lizotte, Cynthia P. McCluskey, Magda Stouthamer-Loeber, and Anne W. Weiher. 2000. "The Effect of Early Delinquency and Substance Use on Precocious Transitions to Adulthood among Adolescent Males." In *Families, Crime and Criminal Justice*, vol. 2, Greer L. Fox and Michael L. Benson, eds. Amsterdam: JAI Press.

Smith, Carolyn A., and Susan B. Stern. 1997. "Delinquency and Antisocial Behavior: A Review of Family Processes and Intervention Research." *Social Service Review* 71: 382–420.

Smith, Carolyn A., and Terence P. Thornberry. 1995. "The Relationship between Childhood Maltreatment and Adolescent Involvement in Delinquency." *Criminology* 33: 451–481.

Smith, Judith R., and Jeanne Brooks-Gunn. 1997. "Correlates and Consequences of Harsh Discipline for Young Children." *Archives of Pediatrics and Adolescent Medicine* 151: 777–786.

Stattin, Hakan, and Ingrid Klackenberg-Larsson. 1993. "Early Language and Intelligence Development and Their Relationship to Future Criminal Behavior." *Journal of Abnormal Psychology* 102: 369–378.

Stattin, Hakan, Anders Romelsjo, and Marlene Stenbacka. 1997. "Personal Resources as Modifiers of the Risk for Future Criminality: An Analysis of Protective Factors in Relation to Eighteen-Year-old Boys." *British Journal of Criminology* 37: 198–223.

Steinberg, Laurence, Susie D. Lamborn, Sanford M. Dornbusch, and Nancy Darling. 1992. "Impact of Parenting Practices on Adolescent Achievement: Authoritative Parenting, School Involvement, and Encouragement to Succeed." *Child Development* 63: 1266–1281.

Stern, Susan B., and Carolyn A. Smith. 1995. "Family Processes and Delinquency in an Ecological Context." *Social Service Review* 69: 705–731.

Stone, Wendy L., Debra Bendell, and Tiffany M. Field. 1988. "The Impact of Socioeconomic Status on Teenage Mothers and Children Who Received Early Intervention." *Journal of Applied Developmental Psychology* 9: 391–408.

Stouthamer-Loeber, Magda, Rolf Loeber, David P. Farrington, Quanwu Zhang, Welmoet van Kammen, and Eugene Maguin. 1993. "The Double Edge of Protective and Risk Factors for Delinquency: Inter-relations and Developmental Patterns." *Development and Psychopathology* 5: 683–701.

Stouthamer-Loeber, Magda, Rolf Loeber, Evelyn Wei, David P. Farrington, and Per-Olof H. Wikström. 2002. "Risk and Promotive Effects in the Explanation of Persistent Serious Delinquency in Boys." *Journal of Consulting and Clinical Psychology* 70: 111–123.

Sweden. Ministry of Justice. 1997. *Our Collective Responsibility: A National Programme for Crime Prevention.* Stockholm: Author.

Sweden. National Council for Crime Prevention. 2001. *Crime Prevention in Sweden.* Stockholm: Author.

Symons, Ronald L., Chyi-In Wu, Christine Johnson, and Rand D. Conger. 1995. "A Test of Various Perspectives on the Intergenerational Transmission of Domestic Violence." *Criminology* 33: 141–171.

Taylor, Terrance J., Paul C. Friday, Xin Ren, Elmar G.M. Weitekamp, and Hans-Jurgen Kerner. 2004. "Risk and Protective Factors Related to Offending: Results from a Chinese Cohort Study." *Australian and New Zealand Journal of Criminology* 37: 13–31.

Thornberry, Terence P., and Margaret Farnworth. 1982. "Social Correlates of Criminal Involvement: Further Evidence on the Relationship between Social Status and Criminal Behavior." *American Sociological Review* 47: 505–518.

Thornberry, Terence P., David Huizinga, and Rolf Loeber. 1995. "The Prevention of Serious Delinquency and Violence: Implications from the Program of Research on the Causes and Correlates of Delinquency." In *Sourcebook on Serious, Violent and Chronic Juvenile Offenders*, James C. Howell, Barry Krisberg, J. David Hawkins and John J. Wilson, eds. Thousand Oaks, Calif.: Sage.

Thornberry, Terence P., Timothy O. Ireland, and Carolyn A. Smith. 2001. "The Importance of Timing: The Varying Impact of Childhood and Adolescent Maltreatment on Multiple Problem Outcomes." *Development and Psychopathology* 13: 957–979.

Thornberry, Terence P., Marvin D. Krohn, Alan J. Lizotte, Carolyn A. Smith, and Kimberly Tobin. 2003. *Gangs and Delinquency in Developmental Perspective*. New York: Cambridge University Press.

Thornberry, Terence P., Alan J. Lizotte, Marvin D. Krohn, Margaret Farnworth, and Soon J. Jang. 1994. "Delinquent Peers, Beliefs and Delinquent Behavior: A Longitudinal Test of Interactional Theory." *Criminology* 32: 47–83.

Thornberry, Terence P., Alan J. Lizotte, Marvin D. Krohn, Carolyn A. Smith, and Pamela K. Porter. 2003. "Causes and Consequences of Delinquency: Findings from the Rochester Youth Development Study." In *Taking Stock of Delinquency: An Overview of Findings from Contemporary Longitudinal Studies*, Terence P. Thornberry and Marvin D. Krohn, eds. New York: Kluwer/Plenum.

Tobler, Nancy S. 1986. "Meta-analysis of 143 Drug Treatment Programs: Quantitative Outcome Results of Program Participants Compared to a Control or Comparison Group." *Journal of Drug Issues* 16: 537–567.

Tobler, Nancy S., Terri Lessard, Diana Marshall, Peter Ochshorn, and Michael Roona. 1999. "Effectiveness of School-Based Drug Prevention Programs for Marijuana Use." *School Psychology International* 20: 105–137.

Tolan, Patrick H., Deborah Gorman-Smith, and David B. Henry. 2003. "The Developmental Ecology of Urban Males' Youth Violence." *Developmental Psychology* 39: 274–291.

Tonry, Michael, and David P. Farrington. 1995. "Strategic Approaches to Crime Prevention." In *Building a Safer Society: Strategic Approaches to Crime Prevention*, Michael Tonry and David P. Farrington, eds. Chicago: University of Chicago Press.

Tracy, Paul E., and Kimberley Kempf-Leonard. 1996. *Continuity and Discontinuity in Criminal Careers*. New York: Plenum.

Tremblay, Richard E., and Wendy M. Craig, W.M. 1995. "Developmental Crime

Prevention." In *Building a Safer Society: Strategic Approaches to Crime Prevention*, Michael Tonry and David P. Farrington, eds. Chicago: University of Chicago Press.

Tremblay, Richard E., Louise C. Mâsse, Linda Pagani, and Frank Vitaro. 1996. "From Childhood Physical Aggression to Adolescent Maladjustment: The Montreal Prevention Experiment." In *Preventing Childhood Disorders, Substance Use, and Delinquency*, Ray D. Peters and Robert J. McMahon, eds. Thousand Oaks, Calif.: Sage.

Tremblay, Richard E., Linda Pagani-Kurtz, Louise C. Mâsse, Frank Vitaro, and Robert O. Pihl. 1995. "A Bimodal Preventive Intervention for Disruptive Kindergarten Boys: Its Impact through Mid-adolescence." *Journal of Consulting and Clinical Psychology* 63: 560–568.

Tremblay, Richard E., Frank Vitaro, Lucie Bertrand, Marc LeBlanc, Hélène Beauchesne, Hélène Boileau, and Lucille David. 1992. "Parent and Child Training to Prevent Early Onset of Delinquency: The Montréal Longitudinal-Experimental Study." In *Preventing Antisocial Behavior: Interventions from Birth through Adolescence*, Joan McCord and Richard E. Tremblay, eds. New York: Guilford Press.

Tremblay, Richard E., Frank Vitaro, Daniel S. Nagin, Laurent Pagani, and J. R. Séguin. 2003. "The Montreal Longitudinal and Experimental Study: Rediscovering the Power of Descriptions." In *Taking Stock of Delinquency: An Overview of Findings from Contemporary Longitudinal Studies*, Terence P. Thornberry and Marvin D. Krohn, eds. New York: Kluwer/Plenum.

United Nations. 2002. "Guidelines for the Prevention of Crime." Economic and Social Council resolution 2002/13, annex, adopted July 24, 2002. Vienna: Author.

U.S. Department of Health and Human Services. 2001. *Youth Violence: A Report of the Surgeon General*. Rockville, Md.: Author.

Utting, David, ed. 1999. *A Guide to Promising Approaches*. London: Communities That Care.

Vitaro, Frank, Mara Brendgen, and Richard E. Tremblay. 2001. "Preventive Intervention: Assessing Its Effects on the Trajectories of Delinquency and Testing for Mediational Processes." *Applied Developmental Science* 5: 201–213.

Wadsworth, Michael E. J. 1976. "Delinquency, Pulse Rates, and Early Emotional Deprivation." *British Journal of Criminology* 15: 245–256.

Wadsworth, Michael E. J. 1979. *Roots of Delinquency: Infancy, Adolescence, and Crime.* London: Martin Robertson.

Wadsworth, Michael E. J. 1991. *The Imprint of Time.* Oxford: Clarendon Press.

Waller, Irvin, and Daniel Sansfaçon. 2000. *Investing Wisely in Crime Prevention: International Experiences.* Washington, D.C.: U.S. Department of Justice, Bureau of Justice Assistance.

Waller, Irvin, and Brandon C. Welsh. 1999. "International Trends in Crime Prevention: Cost-Effective Ways to Reduce Victimization." In *Global Report on Crime and Justice*, Graeme Newman, ed. New York: Oxford University Press.

Waller, Irvin, Brandon C. Welsh, and Daniel Sansfaçon. 1997. *Crime Prevention Digest 1997: Successes, Benefits and Directions from Seven Countries.* Montreal: International Centre for the Prevention of Crime.

Walsh, Anthony, T. A. Petee, and J. A. Beyer. 1987. "Intellectual Imbalance and Delinquency: Comparing High Verbal and High Performance IQ Delinquents." *Criminal Justice and Behavior* 14: 370–379.

Wandersman, Abraham, and Paul Florin. 2003. "Community Interventions and Effective Prevention." *American Psychologist* 58: 441–448.

Wasserman, Gail A., and Laurie S. Miller. 1998. "The Prevention of Serious and Violent Juvenile Offending." In *Serious and Violent Juvenile Offenders: Risk Factors and Successful Interventions*, Rolf Loeber and David P. Farrington, eds. Thousand Oaks, Calif.: Sage.

Webster-Stratton, Carolyn, and Ted Taylor. 2001. "Nipping Early Risk Factors in the Bud: Preventing Substance Abuse, Delinquency, and Violence in Adolescence through Interventions Targeted at Young Children (Zero to Eight Years)." *Prevention Science* 2: 165–192.

Wei, Evelyn, Alison Hipwell, Dustin Pardini, Jennifer M. Beyers, and Rolf Loeber. 2006. "Block Observations of Neighborhood Physical Disorder Are Associated with Neighborhood Crime, Firearm Injuries and Deaths, and Teen Births." *Journal of Epidemiology and Community Health* 59: 904–908.

Weimer, David L., and Lee S. Friedman. 1979. "Efficiency Considerations in Criminal Rehabilitation Research: Costs and Consequences." In *The Rehabilitation of Criminal Offenders: Problems and Prospects*, Lee Sechrest, Susan O. White, and Elizabeth D. Brown, eds. Washington, D.C.: National Academy of Sciences.

Weinrott, Mark R., Richard R. Jones, and James R. Howard. 1982. "Cost-Effectiveness of Teaching Family Programs for Delinquents: Results of a National Evaluation." *Evaluation Review* 6: 173–201.

Weisburd, David, Shawn Bushway, Cynthia Lum, and Sue-Ming Yang. 2004. "Trajectories of Crime at Places: A Longitudinal Study of Street Segments in the City of Seattle." *Criminology* 42: 283–321.

Wells, L. Edward, and Joseph H. Rankin. 1991. "Families and Delinquency: A Meta-analysis of the Impact of Broken Homes." *Social Problems* 38: 71–93.

Welsh, Brandon C. 2003. "Community-Based Approaches to Preventing Delinquency and Crime: Promising Results and Future Directions." *Japanese Journal of Sociological Criminology* 28: 7–24.

Welsh, Brandon C., and David P. Farrington. 2001. "Toward an Evidence-Based Approach to Preventing Crime." *Annals of the American Academy of Political and Social Science* 578: 158–173.

Welsh, Brandon C., and David P. Farrington. 2004. "Effective Programmes to Prevent Delinquency." In *Forensic Psychology: Concepts, Debates and Practice*, Joanna R. Adler, ed. Cullompton, Devon, England: Willan.

Welsh, Brandon C., and David P. Farrington. 2006. "Evidence-Based Crime Prevention." In *Preventing Crime: What Works for Children, Offenders, Victims, and Places*, Brandon C. Welsh and David P. Farrington, eds. Dordrecht: Springer.

Welsh, Brandon C., David P. Farrington, and Lawrence W. Sherman, eds. 2001. *Costs and Benefits of Preventing Crime*. Boulder, Colo.: Westview Press.

Welsh, Brandon C., and Akemi Hoshi. 2002. "Communities and Crime Prevention." In *Evidence-Based Crime Prevention*, Lawrence W. Sherman, David P. Farrington, Brandon C. Welsh, Doris L. MacKenzie, eds. New York: Routledge.

Werner, Emmy E., and Ruth S. Smith. 1982. *Vulnerable but Invincible: A Longitudinal Study of Resilient Children and Youth*. New York: McGraw-Hill.

Werner, Emmy E., and Ruth S. Smith. 2001. *Journeys from Childhood to Midlife*. Ithaca, N.Y.: Cornell University Press.

West, Donald J. 1969. *Present Conduct and Future Delinquency*. London: Heinemann.

West, Donald J., and David P. Farrington. 1973. *Who Becomes Delinquent?* London: Heinemann.

West, Donald J., and David P. Farrington. 1977. *The Delinquent Way of Life*. London: Heinemann.

White, Jennifer L., Terrie E. Moffitt, Avshalom Caspi, Dawn J. Bartusch, Douglas J. Needles, and Magda Stouthamer-Loeber. 1994. "Measuring Impulsivity and Examining Its Relationship to Delinquency." *Journal of Abnormal Psychology* 103: 192–205.

Whiteside, Stephen P., and Donald R. Lynam. 2001. "The Five Factor Model and Impulsivity: Using a Structural Model of Personality to Understand Impulsivity." *Personality and Individual Differences* 30: 669–689.

Widom, Cathy S. 1989. "The Cycle of Violence." *Science* 244: 160–166.

Widom, Cathy S. 1994. "Childhood Victimization and Adolescent Problem Behaviors." In *Adolescent Problem Behaviors*, Robert D. Katterlinus and Michael E. Lamb, eds. Hillsdale, N.J.: Erlbaum.

Widom, Cathy S., and M. Ashley Ames. 1994. "Criminal Consequences of Childhood Sexual Victimization." *Child Abuse and Neglect* 18: 303–318.

Widom, Cathy S., and Helene R. White. 1997. "Problem Behaviors in Abused and Neglected Children Grown Up: Prevalence and Co-occurrence of Substance Use, Crime and Violence." *Criminal Behavior and Mental Health* 7: 287–310.

Wikström, Per-Olof H. 1985. *Everyday Violence in Contemporary Sweden*. Stockholm: National Council for Crime Prevention.

Wikström, Per-Olof H. 1990. "Age and Crime in a Stockholm Cohort." *Journal of Quantitative Criminology* 6: 61–84.

Wikström, Per-Olof H. 1998. "Communities and Crime." In *The Handbook of Crime and Punishment*, Michael Tonry, ed. New York: Oxford University Press.

Wikström, Per-Olof H. In press. "Doing without Knowing: Common Pitfalls in Crime Prevention." In *Imagination for Crime Prevention: Essays in Honor of Ken Pease*. Crime Prevention Studies, Graham Farrell, Kate Bowers, Shane Johnson, and M. Townsley, eds. Monsey, N.Y.: Criminal Justice Press.

Wikström, Per-Olof H., Ronald V. Clarke, and Joan McCord, eds. 1995. *Integrating Crime Prevention Strategies: Propensity and Opportunity*. Stockholm: National Council for Crime Prevention.

Wikström, Per-Olof, and Rolf Loeber. 2000. "Do Disadvantaged Neighborhoods Cause Well-Adjusted Children to Become Adolescent Delinquents? A Study of Male Juvenile Serious Offending, Individual Risk and Protective Factors, and Neighborhood Context." *Criminology* 38: 1109–1142.

Wikström, Per-Olof H., and Marie Torstensson. 1999. "Local Crime Prevention and Its National Support: Organisation and Direction." *European Journal on Criminal Policy and Research* 7: 459–481.

Wilson, David B. 2001. "Meta-Analytic Methods for Criminology." *Annals of the American Academy of Political and Social Science* 578: 71–89.

Wilson, David B., Denise C. Gottfredson, and Stacy S. Najaka. 2001. "School-Based Prevention of Problem Behaviors: A Meta-analysis." *Journal of Quantitative Criminology* 17: 247–272.

Wilson, James Q., and Richard J. Herrnstein. 1985. *Crime and Human Nature.* New York: Simon and Schuster.

Wilson, John J., and James C. Howell. 1993. *A Comprehensive Strategy for Serious, Violent, and Chronic Juvenile Offenders.* Washington, D.C.: U.S. Department of Justice, Office of Juvenile Justice and Delinquency Prevention.

Wilson, Sandra Jo, and Mark W. Lipsey. 2005. "The Effectiveness of School-Based Violence Prevention Programs for Reducing Disruptive and Aggressive Behavior." Unpublished revised report for the National Institute of Justice School Violence Prevention Research Planning Meeting, May. Washington, D.C.: National Institute of Justice, U.S. Department of Justice.

Wolfgang, Marvin E., Terence P. Thornberry, and Robert M. Figlio. 1987. *From Boy to Man, from Delinquency to Crime.* Chicago: University of Chicago Press.

Woolfenden, Susan R., K. Williams, and J. Peat. 2002a. "Family and Parenting Interventions in Children and Adolescents with Conduct Disorder and Delinquency Aged 10–17." In the Cochrane Library, iss. 4. Oxford: Update Software.

Woolfenden, Susan R., K. Williams, and J. Peat. 2002b. "Family and Parenting Interventions for Conduct Disorder and Delinquency: A Meta-analysis of Randomized Controlled Trials." *Archives of Disease in Childhood* 86: 251–256.

Zimring, Franklin E. 1981. "Kids, Groups and Crime: Some Implications of a Well-Known Secret." *Journal of Criminal Law and Criminology* 72: 867–885.

Zuckerman, Marvin. 1989. "Personality in the Third Dimension: A Psychobiological Approach." *Personality and Individual Differences* 10: 391–418.

INDEX

temperament, 46–47
See also delinquency; parenting
Children at Risk program, 146
Christchurch (N.Z.) Health and
  Development Study, 22, 30, 68, 69,
  80
Clarke, Ronald, 54
classroom management, 148–49, 161
Cloward, Richard, 77
cognitive behavioral methods, 150–51,
  161
cognitive deficits, 42
cognitive empathy, 47, 48
cognitive script model, 53–54
Cohen, Albert, 41, 77
Cohen, Patricia, 74, 84
Coie, John, 82
Cole, Kristin, 151
collective efficacy, 85
Colorado, 121, 168
Columbia County (N.Y.) Study, 29, 62
Communities That Care program, 171–
  73
community-based prevention, 94, 137,
  142–45, 151–56, 161
community influences, 84–88
conduct disorder, 60, 74
Conduct Problems Prevention Research
  Group, 118
Conger, Rand, 71
conscientiousness, 45
construct validity, 9, 10–11, 13
Copenhagen Perinatal project, 49
Copenhagen Project Metropolitan, 35,
  40, 79
Cornish, Derek, 54
cortical arousal, 44, 51
Costa, Paul, 45
cost-benefit analyses, 95, 101–2, 130
cost-effectiveness analyses, 101–2
counterfactual inference, 10
Craig, Wendy, 93–94

crime
  and age, 80
  community-based prevention, 142,
    154–55, 161
  definition of, 37
  in families, 57–60
  and personality, 43
  prevention, 163–73
  property, 155–56
  rates, 6, 84, 85, 86, 87, 88
  rational choice theory, 54
  school, 137
  violent, 40, 49, 55, 72, 124
  See also delinquency; early
    prevention; offending; prevention
criminal justice prevention, 94
criminal offending. *See* offending
criminal potential, 37–38
Culross, Patti, 123
Currie, Janet, 109, 117
Curtis, Nicola, 135

Danish Birth Cohort Studies, 33
daycare services, 122, 125–26, 130–32,
  134–36, 160
delayed gratification, 50, 52, 77
delinquency
  community-based prevention, 137,
    142–45, 151–56, 161
  community influences, 84–88
  definition of, 7
  family-based prevention programs,
    121–36
  family influences, 55–75, 159
  and impulsiveness, 49
  individual prevention programs, 105–
    19
  and intelligence, 39, 41
  peer-based prevention programs, 137–
    39, 145–47, 153–54, 156, 160
  peer influences, 80–84, 159
  risk factors, 20, 146, 155, 159–60

Florin, Paul, 155
Forehand, Rex, 74
Friedman, Lee, 102
functional family therapy, 135, 136

gangs, 81
Garces, Eliana, 117
Ge, Xiaojia, 71
gender, 73, 151
genetics, 59–60, 65, 67
Glueck Longitudinal Study, 31–32, 59
Gomby, Deanna, 123, 124
Gordon, Rachel, 81
Gorman-Smith, Deborah, 88
Gottesman, Irving, 67
Gottfredson, Denise, 19, 87, 139, 143, 147, 149
Gottfredson, Gary, 87
Gottfredson, Michael, 52
grades, 149–50, 161
Greenwood, Peter, 5, 111, 130, 134, 169–70
Grekin, Emily, 71
Grossman, Jean, 152
Grove, William, 60
"Guidelines for the Prevention of Crime," 161

Haapasalo, Jaana, 62
Hahn, Andrew, 147
Hare, Robert, 45
Harrell, Adele, 146
Hart, Stephen, 45
Harwood, John, 22
Hawaii, 121
Hawkins, David, 95, 148–49, 153, 171
Head Start, 108, 109, 111, 117
Health and Human Services Department (U.S.), 169–70
heart disease, 95
Heaven, Patrick, 45
Henry, Bill, 67, 69
Henry, David, 88

Herrnstein, Richard, 51–52
HIA. *See* hyperactivity-impulsivity-attention deficit
Hirschi, Travis, 52
Hispanics, 71
Hogh, Erik, 40
home visiting programs, 121, 122–25, 128–30, 134, 160, 168
Honig, Alice, 130
Horwood, John, 68, 69, 80
Hoshi, Akemi, 143, 144
Houston Parent-Child Development Center, 135
Huesmann, Rowell, 53–54, 58
Huizinga, David, 79, 87
hyperactivity, 49, 105
hyperactivity-impulsivity-attention deficit (HIA), 49–50

impulsiveness, 38, 41, 45, 48–52, 54, 105, 109, 159
impulsive unsocialized sensation seeking, 44
indicated programs, 93, 140
individual prevention, 105–19, 134
inner-city areas, 84, 86–87, 88
instructional management, 148–49, 161
intelligence, 38–43, 51, 54, 159
intensive efficacy interventions, 108
internal validity, 9, 10, 12
interventions, 96–97, 100, 108, 161
Iowa Strengthening Families Program, 133
IQ (intelligence quotient), 39, 41, 42
Ireland, Timothy, 73

Jaffee, Sara, 71
Johnson, Byron, 98
Johnson, Dale, 135
Johnson, Jim, 84
Jolliffe, Darrick, 47, 48
Jonassen, Clifford, 85
Jones, Marshall, 115

Montreal Two-Samples Longitudinal
Studies, 32
Morash, Merry, 70
mother love, 67
Moving to Opportunity program, 155
multidimensional treatment foster care,
135–36
multifinality, 21
multisystematic therapy, 135
Mytton, Julie, 140

Najaka, Stacy, 19, 139, 147
National Collaborative Perinatal
Project, 29, 39
national prevention strategy, 5–6, 161–73
National Survey of Health and
Development (U.K.), 35, 68, 78
National Youth Survey (U.S.), 29, 79,
80, 86
Nelson, Sarah, 82
neuropsychological deficits, 42, 50–51
neuroticism, 44, 45
Neuroticism-Extraversion-Openness
Personality Inventory, 45
Newcastle (England) Thousand Family
Study, 31, 67, 73
Newson, John and Elizabeth, 62
New York State Longitudinal Study, 29,
46, 74, 84
nonrandomized experiment, 12
Northern Finland Birth Cohort Study,
34, 71

odds ratio statistic, 18
O'Donnell, Julie, 149
offending
community-based prevention, 137,
142–45, 151–56, 161
definition of, 7
environmental influences, 86
family-based prevention programs,
121–36

family factors, 55–75, 159
individual factors, 37–54, 159
individual prevention programs, 105–
19
and marriage, 20
peer-based prevention programs, 137,
138–39, 145–47, 153–54, 156, 160
prospective longitudinal surveys, 25–
36
risk factors, 17–19, 25, 28, 38–54, 95,
96, 159–60
school-based prevention programs,
137, 139–42, 147–51, 153, 156, 161
school influences, 82–84
situational influences, 19, 38
and unemployment, 20, 79, 96
See also delinquency; predictors, of
offending; prevention
Offord, Dan, 17, 115
Ohlin, Lloyd, 77
Olds, David, 128, 168
openness, 45
Orebro (Sweden) Project, 32, 49
Oregon Social Learning Center, 114
Oregon Youth Study, 33, 69, 72, 79, 82
Orlandi, Mario, 151
Osborn, Stephen, 86

Pagani, Linda, 68
Panel on Juvenile Crime, 138
parental supervision, 17–18, 20, 24, 55,
56, 59, 62, 121, 159
parenting, 55–75, 159
child abuse and neglect, 65–67, 72, 123,
124
child-rearing methods, 61–65, 70, 74,
79–80, 121, 127
conflicted, 67–70
at early age, 70–71
education, 122–26, 128–32, 134–36, 160
home visiting programs, 121, 122–25,
128–30, 134, 160, 168